Placemaking

Placemaking

THE ART AND PRACTICE OF BUILDING COMMUNITIES

Lynda H. Schneekloth and Robert G. Shibley

School of Architecture and Planning
State University of New York at Buffalo
and
The Caucus Partnership
Buffalo, New York

JOHN WILEY & SONS, INC.
New York   Chichester   Brisbane   Toronto   Singapore

Library of Congress Cataloging in Publication Data:
Schneekloth, Lynda H.
    Placemaking the art and practice of building communities / by
Lynda H. Schneekloth and Robert G. Shibley.
       p.   cm.
    Includes bibliographical references and index.
    ISBN 0-471-11026-4 (alk. paper)
    1. City planning—United States—Case studies. 2. Community
development, Urban—United States—Case studies. 3. Architects and
community—United States—Case studies.   I. Shibley, Robert G.
II. Title.
HT167.S27 1995
307.1'2'0973—dc20   94-33124

Printed in the United States of America

10 9 8 7 6 5 4 3 2 1

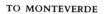
TO MONTEVERDE

CONTENTS

PREFACE

Placemaking has emerged from our work as academic practitioners engaged in a sustained inquiry about the activity of making and maintaining places. Our ideas about placemaking, which we share here in four stories of practice, are embedded in the concept *place* and grow out of a critical practice of making places. The theoretical and academic insights we offer emerged from the practice rather than being laid on it. We write with multiple perspectives and intentions and gather insights from many sources: academic, professional, and intensely personal.

In the initiation of a practice that now spans over twenty years, we had a vague idea about a focus on the interdependent relationship of acts of environmental and organizational change. We set out to learn by doing in the most immediate and place-based way we could, suspending questions about the nature of knowledge and theory in favor of exploring the capacity of place and people-in-place relationships to construct knowledge and theory. We are fortunate to be able to engage in professional practice while teaching in university-based professional schools of architecture and planning that are also concerned with landscape architecture, interior design, and facilities management. From this academic and professional standpoint, we have been able to engage in placemaking by drawing on the perspectives and critiques of the different worldviews.

Working as participant observers in our own practice, we wrote articles and book chapters about the critical capacities we observed in placemaking, acknowledging that the reflections were not in the mainstream of academic theory, nor were they necessarily consistent with the dictates of any single discipline or professional practice. We wrote about the implications of assuming human competence in any intervention as a starting point in discussions about both what to do and how best to do it. We struggled to understand the necessity and power of a collaborative practice that included a wide range of legitimate and "illegitimate" insights depending on one's standpoint. The processes of our placemaking work and of our academic reflection were messy, driven largely by what impressed, excited, saddened, fulfilled, or otherwise provoked us.

At times we have been asked by our colleagues to explain our peculiar form of intervention and ways of working which have emerged in collaboration with our different clients. What did we do, how did we do it, and how did we know it was any good? Many of our early writings were attempts to frame responses to these questions. This book continues that conversation by demonstrating our placemaking practices as they emerged (and are emerging) in several different contexts. As such, it invites people to critique and, when appropriate, *situate* insights from our placemaking stories into the context of their own standpoints, practices, academic intentions, and places.

We are indebted to contemporary postmodern theory in literature, philosophy, education, and feminist studies. This literature at its base posits the uncertainty of meaning inherent in any discussion. It reinforces for us the necessity of abandoning the security of any professional perspective and of creating a space in every intervention to affirm specific meanings, always leaving room for further critique and confirmation as the context shifts. In this literature, neither science nor art nor professional procedure has the moral authority to tell us what to do; each is simply one of several collaborators in the process of doing. The way of thinking embodied in the postmodern perspective has provided a critical lens through which we have viewed our practice, and we use this theoretical standpoint to place our practice in an emerging intellectual tradition.

But this perspective is by no means the only voice in the book. The structure of the text is four stories enfolded within an introduction and epilogue, layered with endnotes. While the stories tend to emphasize what is unique about the individual voices and places, the introduction, epilogue, and endnotes seek the common ground of theory and practice which may be found within all of them. The four narratives of our practice are chosen from over 200 commissions. Each story's "voice" is somewhat different because each project created its own dialogic space within which we as professionals and the people-in-place constructed meaning, included and excluded participants, and engaged placemaking in ways grounded in unique places and circumstances. In Chapter 2 we describe a largely university-based intervention in the development of a new church in a depressed neighborhood. In Chapters 3 and 4 we relate our experiences consulting as private practitioners with a large international corporation and again in a citywide neighborhood development project. In the last story (Chapter 5), we present work with a not-for-profit foundation in developing and implementing an urban place awards program.

A critical practice that uses place as the point of departure leaves the safe ground of professional standards that tell us what to do and where to begin. This gives us the opportunity to explore the relative importance of architecture, interior design, facilities management, landscape architecture, engineering, and a host of other contributors to placemaking as they become situated and related. Placemaking is not about who is in control; rather it is about the critical capacity of the placemaking process itself to confirm and interrogate the place-becoming.

Robert G. Shibley
Lynda H. Schneekloth

ACKNOWLEDGMENTS

The authors are grateful to many people and places for their contribution to this book. Foremost, we want to thank the people with whom we share our daily lives: Rachel, Nathen, Sarah, Loren, Jeremy, Jeff, and JoJo, who have taught us the importance of housework and what it means to create and maintain relationships in a dialogic space.

Without the collaboration of our coworkers in placemaking, our clients, critics, and other professionals, we would not have come to know about the power of placemaking. We are grateful to them for asking us to work with them, and for challenging us to be accountable and vulnerable to them as human beings. We thank them not only for working with us, but also for subsequently reading our account of the work and joining us in reflecting on the practice.

We also gratefully acknowledge the support of grants from the National Endowment for the Arts, which at various times supported our intellectual inquiry, and thank the School of Architecture and Planning at the State University of New York at Buffalo for creating a stimulating environment in which to work and for a sabbatical that was very helpful in framing the text of this book. We also owe a debt of gratitude to our colleagues, who have maintained a space for critical reflection and dialogue at conferences where we could explore ideas and offer our thoughts on critical practice: the yearly meetings of the Environmental Design Research Association; the "Design Practice for the 90's" project of the American Institute of Architects; the 1993 Ascona Conference on "Priorities for Research on the Built Environment" sponsored by the Swedish Research Council and by *Architecture and Behaviour;* the 1990 conference on "Critical Perspectives on Building Evaluation" by the *Centre Scientific et Technique du Batiment;* and the 1986 conferences at the University of Colorado on "Research and Practice in Design and Planning" and at Eastern Michigan University on "Organizations, Design, and the Future," both sponsored by the National Science Foundation.

We give a special thank you to colleagues and friends who over the years have taken the time to read and comment on our work: Mike Brill, Janet Carter, David Chapin, Michel Conan, Claire Cooper-Marcus, Dana Cuff, John Daish, John Forester, Karen Franck, Jim Franklin, John Gray, Maggie Grieve, Larry Hirschhorn, Bradshaw Hovey, Min Kantrowitz, Ellen Bruce Keable, Jean LaMarche, Dennis Lee, Jana and Carrie Loughry, Steve Margulis, Bonnie Ott, David Perry, Janina Philipson, Jan Reizenstein-Carpman, Susan Seagert, Ernest Sternberg, Joe Stuckey, John and Sue Trostle, Polly Welch, Ed Wilson, and others too many to mention. A special thank you goes to David Herzberg and, particularly, Rachel Schneekloth, for their careful reading and unerring editing of many evolving manuscripts.

Placemaking

1

INTRODUCTION: THE TASKS OF PLACEMAKING PRACTICE

Placemaking is the way all of us as human beings transform the places in which we find ourselves into places in which we live. It includes building and tearing buildings down, cultivating the land and planting gardens, cleaning the kitchen and rearranging the office, making neighborhoods and mowing lawns, taking over buildings and understanding cities. It is a fundamental human activity that is sometimes almost invisible and sometimes dramatic. Placemaking consists both of daily acts of renovating, maintaining, and representing the places that sustain us, and of special, celebratory one-time events such as designing a new church building or moving into a new facility. It can be done with the support of others or can be an act of defiance in the face of power.

As long as humans have dwelled[1] on earth, we have found ways to make our places meaningful. The making of places—our homes, our neighborhoods, our places of work and play—not only changes and maintains the physical world of living; it also is a way we make our communities and connect with other people.[2] In other words, placemaking is not just about the relationship of people *to* their places; it also creates relationships *among* people in places.

Over the course of the last century we have been losing our ability to make our places locations for dwelling. Our culture denigrates the simple, mundane, daily acts of maintaining the world, activities such as keeping the house clean, dealing with our wastes, rearranging the furniture, or maintaining our streets. Furthermore, the actions of planning, building, and renovating our places are considered technical, rational acts rather than essential, poetic ones. We have created a world in which most people do not engage in this work but assign planning, design, construction, and place management to specialists.

Professional placemakers—architects, planners, building tradespeople, facility managers, interior designers, engineers, and landscape architects—share a practice concerned with the making of places as a full-time vocation. As professional practitioners of placemaking, the work that we do in helping to make the world is critical to the functioning of our culture and we take pride and joy in it. And yet, the allocation of such work to a small body of professionals is fundamentally *disabling* to others.[3] In most industrialized countries, placemaking has been assigned to and appropriated by design-related professionals and academics who claim expert status regarding the knowledge of making places. Such appropriation ultimately disempowers others because it denies the potential for people to take control over events and circumstances that *take place* in their lives.

In this book we present the idea that the appropriation of placemaking activities by professionals denies a fundamental human expression, while we recognize that professional placemakers have something important to offer. The apparent contradiction dissolves when one explores placemaking as a universal activity that can occur with and without the assistance of professionals. Our intention is to explore the practice of placemaking to learn more about what professional placemakers and people in places can do to remind us how to dwell.

To demonstrate what we mean by placemaking and the role of professionals in the enterprise, we describe three experiences working with people in making their places: planning for a new church building, doing neighborhood development in a small city, and working with facility managers in a large banking institute. And to illustrate that the power of such stories is not unique to these three places, we examine an urban place awards program that involved hundreds of places. These four stories,[4] some of which had their beginning more than a decade ago, have been selected from our own practice, The Caucus Partnership.[5] They represent a diversity of places, people, and tasks and speak to a continued engagement in placemaking by the people who invited us to work with them over the years. These accounts are offered to affirm that daily and often mundane acts of placemaking can be significant acts of empowerment.

The Stories

The Power of Stories: The First Baptist Church

The members of the First Baptist Church of Roanoke, Va., founded in 1883, had been talking about a new church building for over forty years. This new church was a story about themselves, about their growth, their future, and their vision. It came time to make this story come true, but because it was an old and powerful story, it was difficult to know how to begin.

Over a two-year period, the members of the congregation struggled with questions about their mission, their community, what buildings were, and how they could be used. We assisted them in structuring events in which these questions could be explored, and helped them create a pattern book of over 590 ideas about what they wanted their new church building to be.

In our relationship with the church, we viewed our primary responsibilities to be discovering with them their hopes, giving voice and form to their visions, and facilitating their placemaking competence. Their story was a narrative of hope. It had the possibility of infusing the congregation with power in the making of the new church; it also had the power to fragment the people by confronting their vision with the real church-becoming.[6] This is the story of their courage and our participation in a new building and a new story about their lives as the First Baptist Church.

Organizational Development through Design: The International Banking Institute

"We have to introduce a whole line of new furniture to support office automation, and we don't want everybody yelling at us like they did when we changed the phone system. Can you help us?"

This was the plea. The Facilities Section of a large banking institute knew that they had the professional competence and expertise to do a good job, but they also knew that this was not enough. Changes in ways of working and in places of working alter the relationships between people and their places—and people in this office were not pleased to have anyone "doing changes to them."

This story focuses on the relationship between environmental change and organizational dynamics, between technical competence and an organization's ability to learn about itself and its place. Whether it is designing and testing new furniture, programming and managing moves for organizational units such as a library, or problem solving and resolving conflicts between interdepartmental units—all of these activities are opportunities to address environmental and organizational issues and the relationships between them. Making and maintaining places in institutions are special circumstances in which the practice of organizational development can be integrated with the work of environmental intervention. The type of intervention most common in facility management and interior design is a form of "public housework." A discussion of this work at the Institute demonstrates that the act of caring for and about workplaces and their people is a critical practice in placemaking and in developing organizations.

The Practice of Democracy: The Roanoke Neighborhood Partnership

The Roanoke Neighborhood Partnership in Roanoke, Va., was created in 1980 to forge a new relationship between neighborhoods, city government, nonprofit agencies, and the private sector. It is a community planning vehicle based on a simple belief: everyone cares about the preservation and enhancement of their own neighborhood and is willing to take action on behalf of their home, community, and city if the structure to do so is understood and accessible.

The Partnership process as it developed raised questions about the way the city was going about its daily business. It enabled a renegotiation of the distribution of power and changed the reward system in City Hall. The courage and trust of the city officials and neighborhood people to enter into this partnership demonstrate the power of the democratic process when it is given sufficient space to work. The citywide project of placemaking reveals how places and people change through the daily acts of living in particular neighborhoods, and how professionals can assist in the process. This story further demonstrates how the practice of placemaking can be a forum for the exercise of democracy.

Redefining Excellence in the Urban Environment: The Rudy Bruner Award Program

What makes places excellent? How do we know and who gets to decide? These are the fundamental questions being asked by sponsors of the Rudy Bruner Award (RBA) program. In our professional role as advisors to this program, we continued to problematize the issue of excellence, that is, to raise questions about its assumed meaning. We sought to vest the discussion about excellence in a group of people as broad as those who are affected by urban places. The RBA program confronts implicit professional myths of *excellence through an intensive evaluation process that directly involves the people who make and take care of excellent places.*

The stories of RBA projects and places reveal the origins of excellence to be grounded in what is often perceived locally as a crisis, and the corresponding personal and political courage and commitment of many people. The RBA stories about the maintenance and reclamation of excellent places reveals an aspiration of social health for the whole community and the creative ability to transform problems into collective and empowering projects.

Included in the places studied by the RBA program are such well-known projects as the Pike Place Market in Seattle, Wash., and the St. Francis Square Housing Cooperative in San Francisco, Calif. Projects also include very modest and little-known places such as the Casa Rita Shelter for Homeless Women and Children in the South Bronx, N.Y., and the Fairmont Health Center in North Philadelphia, Pa. A discussion of the projects evaluated for the award reveals the value of intellectual work in constructing and sharing stories about the complex and layered processes of collaborative placemaking. The storytelling itself becomes a form of placemaking that empowers others to consider the possibilities of place.

The Practice of Placemaking

Each of these stories follows people as they collectively create, transform, maintain, and renovate the places in which they live. We collaborated with them in these placemaking processes and so offer these stories as a demonstration of *professional practice* that focuses on enabling and facilitating others in the various acts of placemaking even while offering expertise in such discrete acts as planning, design, scientific inquiry, representation, construction, destruction, and maintenance.[7]

The goal of enabling has several implications for the broadly defined professional practice. In the activity of placemaking, an enabling practice focuses on *place* and the people-in-place as the basic unit—the frame through which any intervention occurs. The practice attends thoughtfully to the people who inhabit and are affected by the particular place and who therefore need to be an integral part of the processes of change. People know many things about the places in which they live, although this knowledge is often unstructured, informal, and hesitant. It is not the kind of knowledge normally given voice in professional arenas and could therefore be called a form of subjugated knowledge.[8] A critical practice of placemaking attempts to give legitimacy to all forms of knowledge. As such, it does not privilege any single interpretation or professional perspective over the dynamics of the whole place.

An enabling practice also attends to *relationships* as a goal of placemaking—the relationships between people and between people and their place. In order to facilitate relationships, critical placemaking stresses the importance of creating a dialogue wherein groups of people can affirm, interrogate, and construct the knowledge they need to make and maintain their own places. The professional placemaker has much to contribute to this dialogue but is only one of many voices. Furthermore, before professional knowledge about design, planning, engineering, and so on, can be understood, it must be *situated* and *transformed* in relationship to the people in places.

Placemaking as revealed in the four stories embodies a set of tasks performed to support the aims of practice. The first task is to create an open space[9] for dialogue about place and placemaking through developing a relationship with the place constituencies. This act of making a *dialogic space* is probably the most important activity of professional placemakers and others who wish to work on places, because it is within this set-aside time that the dialogue of placemaking occurs and decisions are made.

The second task is the dialectical work of confirmation and interrogation, which occur in the dialogic space.[10] *Confirmation* is the activity that looks at the context of work with an appreciative attitude in order to understand what is, and what has been, taking place. It involves focusing on the concrete experience of place as it has been made and experienced over time by the various inhabitants. Equally important is the *interrogation* of that context, which consists of asking questions and problematizing the work through disciplined and critical perspectives. The work of interrogation is not the commonsense notion of criticizing, that is, denigration and finding fault; it rather seeks the gaps, disruptions, and incongruities differentiating the material world and the worldviews of participants, and brings these into the dialogue.[11]

The third task of the professional placemaker is facilitating the *framing of action*. The ongoing, iterative, and dialectical acts of confirmation and interrogation reveal the opportunities and constraints for action. These processes direct attention selectively to some aspects of the work that emerge as critical to the project at hand, including decisions about what and who to include and exclude in the placemaking project.

As will be demonstrated in the stories, we are continually engaged in these tasks in our professional roles as placemakers. We structure a dialogic space within which we and others carry on sustained conversations about making places. Although we rarely talk about "confirmation, interrogation, and action framing," we collectively confirm, critically interrogate, and constantly frame action in the shifting world of placemaking.

In the following section we untangle and present the tasks of placemaking as we have come to understand them in our professional practice. The tasks are not discrete, sequential, or oppositional functions; they occur simultaneously and iteratively throughout any professional intervention. The knowledges and insights that emerge through the dialogue are often filled with excitement, tensions, and conflicts that are negotiated, affirmed, and interrogated. This conversation frames the possibilities for a course of action in *this* specific place with *these* particular people.

Dialogic Space: A Place for Conversation

Generating a dialogic space depends on the willingness of all parties to engage in a sustained conversation about the way they want to live and work. In each of the four stories in this book, individuals and groups of people agreed to opening and maintaining this space. Their commitment and ours created the opportunity to bring their experiences of place and our professional knowledges to a common ground so that together we were able to "reappropriate the world."[12] In this space, we explored many interpretations of place, actions, and fictions about the place-becoming.

The dialogic space is the context in which hopes, fears, ideas, and frustrations about a place and the people who live there are discussed. Through the process of sharing within this space, new insights and knowledge about what is and what could be are constructed. Knowledges[13] brought from the outside, such as the professional knowledge of an architect, interior designer, teacher, or office manager, are offered within the discussion and transformed as part of the developing collective world that will eventually frame any placemaking action.

Such a setting and its openness to many points of view will inevitably engender conflict and disagreements, not only about what should be done but even about what is. Friedmann argues:

Dialogue includes the possibility and indeed the likelihood of conflict. Outside the domain of dialogue, such conflict is destructive: we seek victory over the other. But within a relation of dialogue, conflict—insofar as it leads to discoveries and transformations of the self—will only strengthen the relation. In agreement, we confirm each other in our shared experiences; but in disagreement, we affirm each other in our difference.[14]

A commitment to a relationship among all participants and to the space for dialogue creates a continuing story in which conflict is accommodated. As long as participants remain committed to each other and the dialogic space, the relationship works. It is only when someone withdraws from the circle and refuses dialogue that the relationship and the potential power of placemaking fails.

In the stories we have selected to tell, all the players have continued, for over a decade and into the present, to keep open this space for ongoing conversation about their place. This is not always the case. There have been times in our professional experience when the dialogic space has collapsed and when ethical and personal compromises have had to be made in order to complete the technical work. Yet we find these situations to be exceptions rather than the rule. What we continuously encounter are courageous people willing to work together to make their places better for themselves and for those with whom they have relationships.

Our approach to professional placemaking can be conceptualized as the insertion of a thoughtfully conceived dialogic space into existing full lives.[15] It is based on a worldview that assigns legitimacy to every person's experience of living, to the potential competence and compassion of human action, and to the fundamental importance of place as an actor in living well.

The Dialectic of Confirmation and Interrogation

Each act of intervention in the world is unique even when framed by the same practice, based on similar theories, and using similar methodologies. The practice of placemaking is about "everything," and it is always about different things. There is often no easy way to bound the sphere of intervention or the starting or stopping of it.[16] Each place occurs only once. To act responsibly in that historical moment requires knowledge of that time/place/cultural reality; wisdom to recognize that one never has sufficient information or insight on which to base a "rational" decision; and courage to proceed anyway.[17]

As professional placemakers, we intervene in a layered and complex world. This work demands that we come to understand a new place, develop relationships with the people with whom we are working, and understand their experience and interpretation of that world. It requires us to uncover aspects of that world of which they and we may not be aware, or may not be interested in sharing. This is the work of confirmation and interrogation. We offer here some thoughts on each of the tasks separately but recognize that they are always at work simultaneously.

CONFIRMATION

To act both with and for others requires an understanding of the complex nature of social and environmental relationships, both formal and informal. Placemaking requires knowing who the decisionmakers are, what their rewards are, and how projects are implemented. Ethical action also requires knowing who has no access to power or influence but will be affected by an action nonetheless. This will only occur if the experts and those "in charge" listen to and empower formerly unheard and subjugated knowledges in framing an intervention. This listening recognizes that all knowledges and insights, including those of professional placemakers, are particular interpretations of the world.

Social change, environmental change and management, and competent research in the practice of placemaking occur when there is a congruence between the various goals of the place dwellers and other people affected by this place, and the goals of the interventionists. This does not happen by chance; it must be nurtured, as must all human relations. Part of the professional's role is to embed the work, research, and action in the framework of the people who must live in, manage, and maintain the environment in question. This is a complex task of translation.[18] It is rooted in understanding and fully "appreciating" the context of each professional intervention.[19]

In our stories, the confirmation of the everyday experience of people occurs through careful observation and through much talking and listening in workshops, meetings, and interviews that carefully record participant perceptions and values. These records are open and public, often displayed on large sheets of newsprint, in newsletters, in the press, or through other forms of communication. Such records confirm interpretations of everyday experience and are part of the media with which we all work as we engage the placemaking tasks.

To suggest that people's worldviews and experiences be affirmed may sound suspiciously like a process of cooptation, a "feel-
good" experience where everybody gets their say and then the
professionals get to work. This is not our intention, nor is it the
process of confirmation as we are describing it within the critical
practice of placemaking. The knowledge and experience offered
within the dialogic space is neither ignored nor removed from that
space to be disembodied and returned in a way unrecognizable to
the person who offered it. To affirm the experience and knowledge
of place and to work with that knowledge requires that the processes of translation, transformation, and knowledge construction
—that is, professional practice—occur in the *public* space of dialogue. At the very least, any work done by professionals outside of
the dialogic space is brought forward again and tested within the
collective dialogue.

If the space for dialogue is sufficiently open to allow honest
comments about the perceptions of place and people in their places,
then the process of confirmation is an act of placing trust in each
others' intentions. To appreciate people and their place affirms their
experience of the world and recognizes that their lives and their
place have meaning to them. In a critical practice, the work of
confirmation acknowledges that this place and the people who live
in it have existed prior to a professional intervention and will continue long after that presence. It accepts and understands their interpretation of their lives and place as their truth and affirms that their
knowledge and experience is critical to the processes of environmental change and management.

INTERROGATION

To appreciate a place and people does not, however, imply an
uncritical stance toward it. The practice of placemaking is inherently about transformations, changes, modifications, and preservation—all acts of intervention. In order to make judgments about
any form of intervention one must understand and confirm what it
is and simultaneously ask how it might be changed in accordance
with negotiated goals. To do both of these things, the interventionists must present as clear an understanding of the situation as is
possible, revealing what they have discovered in dialogue with others and through their own experience.

The task of interrogation involves a process of inquiry designed
to uncover the basic values and assumptions forming human institutions and actions. We have found the work of Habermas very

useful in developing our ideas about the dialectic of confirmation and interrogation. He has developed a theory of knowledge, that is, about the way people "know" what they know, that uses the concept of *critical theory*.[20] Critical theories, unlike theories in science which are about the establishment of "objective" knowledge, are squarely located in the domain of human action, focused on intentions for and activities in the world. To conduct critical theory is to aim for empirically adequate descriptions of places *and* to be concerned about the values and interpretations of those constructed descriptions. Critical theory is not "out there" to be applied somewhere else, but is rather the way humans actively construct knowledge and theories about *this* place right now.

Conducting critical theory in placemaking is a practice of asking questions about each intervention focused on different aspects of any event, place, or proposal. In each situation, questions are framed on three layers: the first seeks to understand empirically what is; the second tries to understand why this particular condition exists; and the third attempts to uncover the underlying structure and to critically explore the implications of this condition. The conduct of critical theory is embedded in the belief that human life and sociopolitical structures are complex, and that we are required to engage in sustained intellectual and interpersonal work to see and understand them well.

Thus the *empirical* layer describes *what* and *how* things are and usually uses the method of science to make judgments. The questions posed seek to objectify reality, and the language used is often framed within a scientific-technological discourse. Data on a neighborhood's income distribution or infant mortality rates, for example, often have an empirical foundation. This form of knowledge is what we usually mean when we describe what we experience as "real," and what we mean when we say, "be realistic." Even though empirical observations are based on a description of what is, they nevertheless open the possibility of asking "what if" and proceeding through various scenarios. The empirical discourse also demands that we acknowledge what is lacking as well as what is present. If we need computer-compatible furniture based on new technological changes and we do not have it, then the lack is empirically real.

But the question arises, how did *this* get to be "real" or "realistic" instead of some other way of being? What makes this "legitimate knowledge"? The second layer of critical theory, which can be referred to as the *hermeneutic,* seeks to understand *why* the particular cluster of activities and/or meanings is considered real. The methods of history and philosophy are frequently used to uncover why a certain condition exists. It is also useful to explore various perspectives on the same situations and ask why these different interpretations exist. For example, there are many reasons given for the fact that the single-family detached home is the dominant form of American housing, from homeowner preference to the history of federal housing programs and tax structures. It is only through the gathering of different interpretations and justifications—including an investigation into what options were discarded, when, and why —that any sense of why this condition exists is possible.

The third layer, the *critical,* asks a series of questions that explore the underlying value structure. If this is reality, we ask, and these are the reasons we think it came to be this way, where is the power, who metaphorically "wins," and what are the implications for this and not some other way of doing things? For example, if the chain of command in an organization dictates that only some people get to make suggestions on how to change the workplace, questions at the critical level ask who benefits and who is disempowered. Critical theory would direct us to inquire how political and/or organizational arrangements maintain power structures that might mean, for example, that some people get paid more than other people, or that some neighborhoods have street trees and others do not. The act of engaging in critical theory, then, because it comes from understanding the humanly constructed basis of what we often call "reality," contains the possibility of change.[21]

The context of every situation in which we take action, professionally and personally, is framed by legitimated and subjugated knowledges that are mingled and interdependent.[22] It is only through an inquiry into the various knowledges that we can construct an understanding of the world that addresses the questions of what a condition is, how it exists, why it came to be that way, and what it means. The uncovering and possible integration of these different layers of knowledge assures that instrumental action, which rests in the empirical discourse, will be informed by the hermeneutic insight, that is, the whys of any condition. Wherever we find ourselves, we can critique and deconstruct the structure of institutions and organizations to test the adequacy of their aims and form to the project of both community and individual emancipation.[23]

Critical theory offers insight into the socially constructed reality of a place, which has been reified through history and is maintained by the social and physical structures of its institutions. The purpose of engaging in critical theory is to deconstruct, and thereby reveal, socially constructed worldviews. Because the practice of placemaking is contained in particular socially constructed realities, all actions either maintain existing worldviews or challenge them.[24] By asking questions about the history and societal purposes of any place (such as an institution, city, or neighborhood), the views of the multiple members, and the power relationships, one gains insights into how the environment is used to support, maintain, and/or subvert the agreed–on purposes of the social form. Such an inquiry is required for competent and informed practice.

However, engaging in critical theory is not a magic answer, nor is confirmation and interrogation adequate grounding for human action, which is embedded in political and social contexts. Yet the process of confirmation and interrogation is the foundation of a collaborative dialogue that affirms meanings and activities and, at the same time, problematizes those activities and meanings from a perspective that reveals their structure and inequalities. Decisions for action that rely on these understandings are thus recognized as noninnocent political and ethical positions.

Framing Action: Processes of Inclusion and Exclusion

Every time we decide to do something, we are simultaneously deciding not to do something else, whether we are aware of it or not. Placemaking is no different. It requires that we decide what we are going to do by naming the players, the boundaries of action, and the rules for action. Placemaking thus includes and excludes people in every intervention. Those involved select and exclude aims and boundaries for any project; privilege ways of working at the expense of alternative methods; and produce knowledge, products, and processes as a result of specific ways of working with specific people. Through the activity of inclusion and exclusion, those who engage in the tasks of placemaking determine who owns the work of practice: products, knowledges, and processes.

All professional placemaking activities are interventions in that professionals step into a context and then leave again. In a sense, the professionals are asked to participate in the lives of other people, and this knowledge embodies the imperative to work collaboratively.[25] Collaboration does not, however, suggest that the role of the professional in placemaking is only that of facilitator and never contributor. This attitude would deny the knowledges and experiences that the professional brings to each act of making. Such an attitude is insulting not only to professionals and their knowledges; it is also patronizing to the people with whom the professionals works. Yet neither is the "expert" form of knowledge to be privileged above the knowledges of others. The professional can engage in a dialogue with others in which all knowledges are valued, shared, and used in the process of decision making.

WHO CAN PLAY?

Placemaking, whether it is design, construction, or research, is best done collectively within its own social and political context. To be effective, people involved in social and environmental change must be involved in the process of generating knowledge about that change, in posing issues to be researched, in implementing plans, and in evaluating results. This does not preclude the involvement of professionals or knowledge from outside the context, but it does suggest that insights and knowledge from the outside must become situated within the social and political conditions.

Thus, one of the most difficult technical and ethical decisions is the decision of who will be involved. The inclusion and exclusion of peoples and knowledges frame all action by limiting what can be known and who is empowered to make decisions. Democratic theory provides insight into the question of who can play. As Dewey said: "The outstanding problem of the Public is discovery and identification of itself."[26] The determination of the boundary of "the Public" is one of the most critical acts in the discussion of placemaking action.

As currently constructed, much of our democratic action is based on the idea of a *personal interest requirement:* If a person or group has a direct and personal interest in any act, they should be included in the discussion and subsequent actions. As an ethical and logical guide for inclusion and exclusion, the personal-interest requirement appears just. And yet this very requirement has been used as a major form of exclusion in the practice of democracy in the United States through the power of some to decide who has a personal interest and therefore who is directly and personally affected. Significant domains of action are placed outside the public interest, domains such as private property, contract rights, and so on. The separation of what is considered public and what is considered private within cultures is always a contested terrain.

Furthermore, even within public discourses, the personal interest requirement can be used as a tool of exclusion. For example, the process of zoning allows for persons within a zone to be heard in debates about zoning changes; those outside are not granted the same status. This seemingly fair requirement has been used as a bastion of racial segregation and is still used, very effectively, as a mechanism for socioeconomic and, increasingly, gender demarcations.[27]

The deconstruction of the personal interest requirement and the concept of public and private spheres through the use of critical theory further exemplify the complexity of the acts of inclusion and exclusion and the power of such action. Practically, all decisions cannot, and should not, be made by everyone. But ethically, the process of exclusion serves specific interests, always at the expense of others. The task of selecting who can play, therefore, frames the discourse and privileges perspectives and knowledges. There are no rules or simple guides for selecting who plays, only values and beliefs. However, the tasks of confirmation through an appreciation of the context, and interrogation through the conduct of critical theory, offer insights into the implication of those selected to be included and excluded.

WHAT ARE THE BOUNDARIES FOR ACTION?

Another domain of inclusion and exclusion in the practice of placemaking is the selection of the boundaries of any action, focusing attention on what is part of the dialogue and what stands outside this particular intervention. Each act of intervention may address many universal and theoretical issues, such as the issue of public and private spheres discussed above. Yet when one is confronted with an actual act of placemaking in a specific place, the questions are always concrete; planners and other professionals can be seen as "selective organizers of attention to real possibilities of action."[28] The task of selectively focusing attention to include and exclude issues and boundaries for action can be engaged to silence opposition or to empower people.

For example, when working in community development, the decision of what issues are permissible for discussion sets the context within which action can be taken. To present the neighborhood with alternatives for rehabilitating the physical infrastructure of their community without confronting segregation by race or class permits positive action in an aspect of community life; however, this boundary denies discourse on one of the basic structural conditions that permitted the infrastructure to deteriorate in the first place. To rehabilitate only the physical structure does not create the conditions for change that would eventually give a community the ability to manage and maintain its infrastructure so as to avoid serious deterioration in the future. But if in the dialogic space there is the possibility for an expanded discussion, even if the discussion is outside the scope of professional services, then a space has been opened for future inquiry by the community.

As practitioners, we know that not every act of placemaking can address all issues of the human condition; often we must accept boundaries for action that do not allow for significant social or physical change. Yet we recognize that each inclusion and exclusion is a noninnocent decision that has significant political and ethical ramifications. We must have the courage to know what we are not doing as well as what we are able to do.

WHAT ARE THE RULES FOR ACTION?

The rules for action, or methods for intervention, embody the same kinds of questions as selecting who can participate and outlining the boundaries of discussion. How should we proceed? What are the implications of one way of working as opposed to another? What happens if we choose not to act?

There are many methods and ways of working available to professional practitioners developed in the domain of the social sciences, science, art, and architecture. These can be helpful in specific contexts of placemaking, and, we argue, they should be used with rigor when engaged. But the selection of methods of work and approaches to framing and solving problems is not a technical activity but an ethical one. Any method, strategy, or procedure can be used for many purposes. For example, small-group methods developed in the applied behavioral sciences can empower many voices and ensure that formerly subjugated knowledges are revealed; they can also be used in different circumstances to diffuse and deny collective action. Furthermore, the application of any method must be questioned if that method has been overlayed on the context rather than emerging from the specific situation. If a method is opaque to the people in places, then its use is a form of methodological tyranny.[29]

The approach to critical practice we are describing employs state-of-the-art research and methods, practitioner expertise, and the structure of everyday life as foils for one another. The result of the ongoing interrogation opens a dialogue about the underlying agreements and perceptions of conflicts among participants in the process. If the dialogic space is working, then as the work progresses to decisions about action, all voices can see themselves in the approach, have a higher level of commitment to the decisions, and often be more willing to live with and care for the resultant conditions.

Every approach to work and method employed in the professional practice of placemaking is rooted in beliefs and ideologies, and these meanings are communicated in placemaking processes. Freire writes:

> [M]ethodological failings can always be traced to ideological errors. . . . If one is to adopt a *method* which fosters dialogue and reciprocity, one must first be *ideologically* committed to equality, to the abolition of privilege, and to non-elitist forms of leadership wherein special qualifications may be exercised, but are not perpetuated.[30]

The problem of irresponsible action is not usually a problem of method but of attitude and intention. The selection of ways of working and the ways in which methods are employed are always rooted in basic assumptions about human beings and the ultimate aims of a placemaking practice.

The Beloved Place

We all live in places. Sometimes we love and care for our places, sometimes we hate our places; often we have no "right" to change our places, and not infrequently we leave them, physically or imaginally. Much of U.S. history has been about leaving—about heading out for the frontier, whether that frontier is the Wild West, the suburbs, a new city, or space, "the final frontier." The idea of being somewhere else has occupied our cultural imagination for a long time.[31] And this desire to "light out for the territory" and leave the confines of our current communities has had significant impact on our places and our dwelling. If we always want to be someplace else, how will we ever take the time to love, nurture, and maintain the places we are?

The world does not exist simply for our consumption. If we pay attention, we will see that it presents itself to us in so many ways as an active presence in our lives—as colors, smells, openings, faces, all enclosing, exposing, or protecting us. Our places offer themselves to us in a special relationship, and as a form of reciprocity our recognition is expected. Berry writes that "[w]e speak of 'paying attention' because of a correct perception that attention is *owed*—that without our attention and our attending, our subjects, including ourselves, are endangered."[32]

Without our attention, our *places* are endangered. And when our places are endangered, as revealed in the current ruins of our inner cities, our poisoned rivers, our inhospitable offices, and our dilapidated houses, we are at risk. To decide to be someplace as members of a community demands that we become active placemakers again, that we participate with others in our communities in thoughtful, careful, responsible action. At times, this may indeed require the decision to leave some places, abandoning them as uninhabitable, at least in the short term. But more often it means staying where we are with the people of our communities and attending to our places through placemaking activities.[33]

What we need to enable us to live well, to dwell, is to trust in the possibility of a beloved place and our own significant part in the making of such places. This does not mean that we will not have to struggle constantly against forces that work toward the disintegration of places and communities. It does mean that we trust the world of community life that has always opposed, corrected, and forgiven in order to dwell.

Placemaking as described in this book is about everything, because the making and sustaining of place is about living—about places, meanings, knowledges, and actions. Those of us who engage professionally in placemaking with and next to others are involved in the practice of creating beloved places through the maintenance and renewal of relationships among all participants and their world.

The tasks of placemaking—opening the dialogic space, confirming and interrogating contexts, and framing action—are inherently political and moral acts. There is no formula or method that can simplify the tasks or free any of us from the ethical implications of taking action. We make mistakes, have errors in judgment. And we often find ourselves in situations in which we know through critical interrogation that our work will not be as liberating as it could be. But with the promise of forgiveness embedded in communities of people working together in special spaces for dialogue about places, we proceed in our collective, very human work of placemaking.[34]

2

THE POWER OF STORIES: THE FIRST BAPTIST CHURCH

The First Baptist Church of Roanoke, Va. had been talking about building a new church for at least forty years.[1] The new church building was a part of their story about themselves, about their growth, future, and vision. The story had survived the Depression, World War II, racial integration and flight to the suburbs, and urban renewal. When the Reverend Kenneth Wright accepted the position as pastor at the First Baptist Church in the early 1970s, he understood the power of the narrative for the people, and began working to transform the story into a new church building.

The existing church building was built in 1898 in the railroad town of Roanoke. This particular area of Roanoke had been settled by former slaves and was an established black community called Gainsboro. The First Baptist Church was an important participant in the life of this vibrant center of culture and community, especially in the 1930s, 1940s, and 1950s. The church building, a landmark on Gilmer Avenue, is visible from downtown Roanoke and reminds the city of the community across the tracks.

But the building was no longer meeting the needs of the congregation. It was almost 100 years old and in need of serious repair. The sanctuary was two storeys above street level, and many of the 800 members were elderly and had difficulty managing the steps. There was little space for a Sunday program, and the day care run by the church was located in inadequate facilities. Furthermore,

Figure 2.1 The First Baptist Church, Roanoke, Va. (Photo courtesy of the First Baptist Church)

there was insufficient space to hold meetings, especially social gatherings that required food preparation. These were all serious limitations of the existing facility.

The church that existed was a symbol of the past, a container of the history of the lives of the members and their parents. And although they were proud of their heritage and history, many knew it was time to rethink "the church" in light of all of the changes that had occurred to them as a congregation and as a community. Much of the rethinking was embedded in the idea of a new church facility, and the vision of the new church was a project of hope about who they and their children might be.

The story of the new church was an old story shared among the members of their congregation. But the process of making a real church building was just starting, and it was not clear how to

Figure 2.2 Historic Gainsboro (circa 1900) with the steeple of the First Baptist Church visible in the center. (Photo courtesy of the Roanoke Valley History Museum, Roanoke, Va.)

begin. When Reverend Wright requested support and assistance from us in the fall of 1976, he knew that the making of the new building had to become as familiar as the story itself.[2] As he said: "We want to build a new church. And if we want our new church to *belong* to the people of the church, they have to be involved."

In discussions with Reverend Wright, we explored what he perceived to be the issues and why he felt we might be of assistance to the congregation in their project. To begin with, the church as a congregation had not engaged in a building project for almost 100 years, and many members had only a vague idea of how to develop and carry through their ideas for a new facility. Furthermore, members had individual notions of what they thought the church building would be but no collective vision. Reverend Wright feared that the making of the new church facility could be a source of conflict rather than unity.

Through these discussions with the pastor and a few other members of the congregation, we tried to find a way to support the environmental change that would be coming to the congregation over the next few years. In this context, it was decided that our most useful role was as program facilitators and educators. We would work with the congregation, in as participatory a manner as

Figure 2.3 First Baptist Church in 1980.

possible, to give voice to their visions[3] and to prepare them to work with an architect when the time came to engage one.

As professionals we were excited about the possibilities of working with Reverend Wright and the First Baptist Church. Here was a group of people actively seeking, in our language, to construct the history of their place and themselves—to make their beloved place. The new church project was the vehicle of affirmation of the congregation; it was an occasion for them to reflect on their life as a church, to confirm and interrogate the nature of their congregation, and to decide what and how to be.

Furthermore, the new church project had important urban implications for the city of Roanoke. The congregation had made the decision to stay in their present location in Gainsboro, a designated "urban renewal area," rather than moving to the suburbs as many other churches had done. Reverend Wright and the elders had already begun talks with the Roanoke Housing Authority for the acquisition of land. The intervention into the fabric of a seriously distressed community was a statement of hope about the future of their church and its home. The way this new building came into existence in the neighborhood was a critical factor in its interpretation by the community-at-large.

The Practice of Work

We worked with the congregation as program facilitators and educators. Our intention was to find a way to give voice to their stories, hopes, and fears for their church, and to find a way to insert our knowledge about the process of making places into the conversation. The interplay of these voices and knowledges would frame for them an architectural program that would describe the goals for building and its performance criteria.

As we began meeting with people from the church, we made no assumptions about how we were going to engage the congregation in this effort other than the aspiration of dialogue as a primary way of working. The methods we eventually used evolved from the questions and problems that emerged during our discussions.

Reverend Wright and the elders emphasized from the beginning that this effort was to involve as many members of the congregation as possible. The First Baptist Church had an experiential basis for a participatory effort. The autonomous nature of churches associated with the Progressive National Baptist Convention encourages active involvement of members, and this way of working was the norm for the Gainsboro congregation. Each year, more than 100 of the 800 members were installed as officers in some internal organizations. Many members knew intimately, and were committed to, various functions of their church. Reverend Wright requested that the knowledge and experience of his members, as well as their years of living in Gainsboro, be incorporated into the programming and design effort.

We wanted a Coordinating Committee of eight to ten people to work closely with us in designing a process for involving the congregation in the planning and programming effort. We asked Reverend Wright to recommend people he thought would make a commitment to the effort, would be excited about participating, and had contact with different domains within the church. Eight people from the congregation agreed to serve on this committee with Reverend Wright, and almost everyone stayed with us throughout the two-year process. This Coordinating Committee was asked to lead the church in its deliberation about the new church building.[4]

Those of us who were invited to work with the congregation did not present ourselves as "the experts" who could tell them what they should do to make this new building. We entered with the assumption that they knew much about what their church is and what they wanted their new church to be. Our work was to enable them to frame their ideas in a form that would make their new church a reality, contributing our knowledge and skills about design and how to get things done.

The Coordinating Committee began meeting regularly in the fall of 1977. The decisions we made about the Committee's way of working had implications that both empowered and limited our work. One of the first questions was who was to be the chair of this newly formed Coordinating Committee. The committee, of course, deferred to Reverend Wright, who declined. He was clear about the extent of his other responsibilities and, furthermore, he felt it inappropriate for him to be the chair. After much discussion and resistance on the part of individual members to accepting this responsibility, we suggested that they begin without a permanent chair and ask a different person to chair each meeting. Although this process was unfamiliar to them, they were willing to try. The rotating chair proved to be very satisfactory to the committee and worked over the next two years; it gave each person an opportunity to experience the leadership role. This decision did, however, make Reverend Wright central. When we had to communicate between meetings, he was the person contacted, and therefore he knew most intimately what was occurring. If a permanent chair had been elected, this primary responsibility might have been removed from his office and transferred to another person.

Other practices of work made this rotating chair possible. We used large newsprint sheets taped on the wall to serve as a public agenda and a space for taking notes. This open and visible form focused our work and helped everyone know precisely where we were on our agenda and how much longer the meeting was likely to last. By writing notes on the newsprint, it was public which issues were resolved and which deferred to a future meeting. The large sheets remained on the wall until the next meeting. Furthermore, before the adjournment of any meeting, we brainstormed the next agenda, set priorities, posted the next meeting's agenda, and decided on time and place. The collective work of the group in these leadership functions facilitated the existence of the rotating chair. Between meetings it was the responsibility of the Coordinating Committee members to communicate the committee work with other people in the congregation; we wrote up the notes from the newsprint sheets for a notebook kept at the church.

During the initial sessions, when we were getting to know each other and establishing some work habits, we began to frame questions about the purpose of their work and the reasons for building the new church. Our focus in these interactions was to learn and to facilitate their exploration of the meaning of this new facility by problematizing their assumptions.[5] We framed questions that confirmed their experience of living in this church and community, and interrogated their experiences to seek connections and contradictions in the conversation. We asked them to consider what they needed to understand and know as they started thinking about the physical aspects of the church.

The committee struggled to define a purpose to guide their deliberations about the new building. As part of the ongoing dialogue, they developed an aim that was sufficiently general to guide the work but specific enough to engage other members of the congregation. The goal statement created by the Coordinating Committee was to design a process that would engage the congregation in creating a new building for the First Baptist Church that was uniquely suited to its members and the Gainsboro community.

"What is the Mission of Our Church?"

Having set a goal for their work as a group, the Coordinating Committee felt it important to quickly involve other members of the congregation in the deliberations of what a church "uniquely suited" to its members might be. We were able to offer them an array of ideas of how they might engage the rest of the congregation, from some kind of survey instrument to a very large group meeting using small working groups. The committee members were insightful about their community and felt that the survey would be inappropriate for the aural culture of their church but that the members would willingly spend an afternoon working together on the question of what their church was about. Furthermore, and very importantly, an event such as this would clearly mark a beginning; it would be a community celebration that the dream of a new church building was going to come true.

In creating a framework in which members could share their ideas, the Coordinating Committee hoped to engender commitment to the process they were beginning. They intuitively knew this endeavor would only succeed if most of the members of the First Baptist Church were ready to work to make the new building happen; this meant a commitment in time, energy, and money.[6]

On March 12, 1978, we had our first large gathering to plan for the church, "A Beginning for the New Church Building," commonly referred to as the "Mission Workshop." The day began when Reverend Wright spoke of the upcoming workshop and the beginning of planning for the new church building in the morning worship service. He reminded the congregation about the significance of this work. "We are going to the Mountain. . . . I have

Figure 2.4 Woman speaking at the Mission Workshop.

been there, I know. And you have been there, *you know!*" The afternoon workshop was introduced by Mr. Wheaton from the Coordinating Committee. He echoed Reverend Wright's morning message with an affirmation that because they lived their daily lives with the First Baptist Church, they already know about what this church might be—they had been to the mountain! It was time to share their individual experience and knowledge with others in the forum of this workshop.

After sharing a meal in the church basement, nearly 200 members of the congregation and fifteen Virginia Tech faculty and students worked for three hours in small-group brainstorming sessions. Everyone was seated at a table with approximately ten other people. Each group had a process facilitator, either a student or faculty member from Virginia Tech, or one of the Coordinating Committee members who had been through a training process on small-group facilitation.[7] The committee had selected this method of work, small facilitated groups, because they wanted each person to have time to speak about the issues.

We used the techniques of brainstorming, discussion, and rank ordering of items around three key questions. The issues to be discussed and the wording of the questions had been framed by the Coordinating Committee after much discussion about what they wanted to know from the membership and what the congregation should understand about making a new building.[8]

The three questions were:

Mission: In what ways can our mission of saving souls be best accomplished for the members of our church and for the community in which it lives?

Activities: What kinds of activities, in addition to worshipping in the sanctuary, should we plan for?

Keep/Change: What are those things that are important and should not be changed? What do we want to have changed, or added, in the new building, inside and outside?

All afternoon the church basement was filled with the serious work of the congregation, struggling together to affirm their mission as a church and to decide how best to accomplish this mission. The participants left reminded of the shared sense of who they were as a church and with a sense of the differences of opinions held by various members. Furthermore, the event convinced many that their new church building was really going to happen, and that they had personally contributed to the making.

We, as consultants to the church, had the task of making order of the piles of information contained on the newsprint sheets. We did a content analysis of the work of the eighteen tables, generating categories for the specific comments. As we did this, we knew it was important to maintain the quality and character of the comments so that the intent would not be lost in the analysis. Furthermore, this information had to be returned quickly to the Coordinating Committee so that the results of their work could be made public to the members of the congregation who had not attended. After a discussion with the Coordinating Committee, it was decided that we would prepare a brief summary to be presented by the pastor on Sunday after service within two weeks of the workshop. The Coordinating Committee also decided to create and maintain a "New Building Corner" in the basement where information about the ongoing process could be displayed for anyone interested.

The result of the 200-person meeting was a rich narrative of the church and the congregation—an affirmation of who they were and what their mission was. It was also substantial critique of what was currently working and what needed serious modification and/or attention in their programs and facilities. The nature of this public conversation, which was both confirmatory and interrogatory, gave a direction to the work of the Coordinating Committee. The summary reported back to the church was organized around the generating themes of Mission, Activities, and Keep/Change.

MISSION

The response to the query about the mission was an affirmation of the Christian ministry of the First Baptist Church to its members —the struggle for unity and togetherness. There was a recognition that this was the aim of their fellowship, and that they desired to do it better.

There was also a shared desire to minister to the community. The First Baptist Church was committed to staying in Gainsboro, not just physically but as an active participant in the spiritual and social life of the community. Some members of the Coordinating Committee had felt less secure that the general congregation actually shared this goal, and so the Mission Workshop had been a confirmation and an endorsement of their goal statement. It also gave us confidence that the Committee selected to work with us was a legitimate voice for the congregation, and that their aspiration to develop a process of participation for the larger body to explore how a new church building could support an internal and community ministry was within grasp.

Like the Coordinating Committee, the congregation members who participated in the Mission Workshop were concerned that the old church building was actually hampering their mission. They felt that if they could provide more physical support to their own members and the community, they could more fully engage their Christian ministry.

ACTIVITIES

The question about activities discussed during the Mission Workshop was framed to explore how the work of the church might be better done with a new church facility. The activities question generated endless lists of what the congregation would like to provide for in their new church building. Most of these activities reflected the work of the church that could be improved and/or expanded "if only things were better." The activities lists and descriptions the congregation developed were organized into six functional areas:

1. Education facilities and program
2. Activity support and recreation facilities
3. Music program
4. Sanctuary and worship facilities
5. Supportive functions and facilities
6. Administrative and organizational facilities

This information was presented back to the congregation in a format that connected their desired activity and its space requirements. This list of functions became the skeleton of a program for the new building because it identified the relationship between needs and spaces. These six areas were later used to organize the Building Committees, which developed criteria for individual programs and spaces.

KEEP/CHANGE

The responses to the third question were a good indicator of the strength of commitment to certain aspects of the church life and identified potential conflicts among members. Many of the things they requested to keep, such as "Reverend Wright," and "the hand of fellowship," had no physical implications. But they did identify

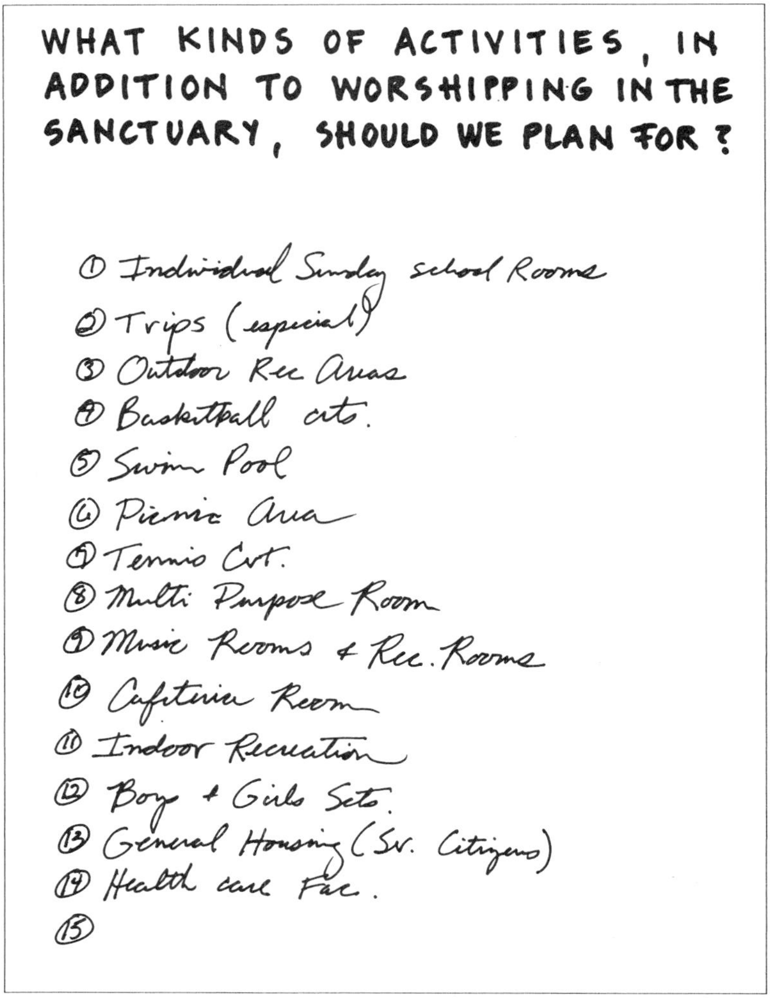

WHAT KINDS OF ACTIVITIES, IN ADDITION TO WORSHIPPING IN THE SANCTUARY, SHOULD WE PLAN FOR?

① Individual Sunday school Rooms
② Trips (especial)
③ Outdoor Rec Areas
④ Basketball cts.
⑤ Swim Pool
⑥ Picnic Area
⑦ Tennis Crt.
⑧ Multi Purpose Room
⑨ Music Rooms + Rec. Rooms
⑩ Cafeteria Room
⑪ Indoor Recreation
⑫ Boys + Girls Sets.
⑬ General Housing (Sr. Citizens)
⑭ Health care Fac.
⑮

Figure 2.5 Sample Sheet from the Mission Workshop.

other things, such as the existing windows of the church and the statue behind the baptistery, as very meaningful to them. They wanted to find a way to incorporate these pieces of the old church into the new one. The items listed under "change" signified those things about which they were most critical—change the second-floor sanctuary, get rid of all of the steps, get rid of the small and almost unusable spaces in the basement that currently served as the fellowship hall. This session gave strength and definition to many issues listed in the first two rounds, and also identified an area of conflict. There was a serious disagreement about the organ. Many wanted to keep the old pipe organ; others wanted to replace it with a new electric organ. This issue remained with the congregation as a source of tension throughout the entire process.

The Mission Workshop set a precedent for future work on the new church project. The Coordinating Committee was enthusiastic about the possibilities of actively involving many members in the planning process to get everyone's best ideas and to develop commitment to the new church. This event confirmed for all of us that the story of the new church was a shared vision and that the congregation was ready to work to expand that vision into a physical place.

"Where Do We Live?"

The commitment to stay in Gainsboro was, as are all decisions, founded on diverse motivations. There were personal, historical, political, and economic reasons for this decision. A major impetus to stay was the opportunity to work with the Housing Authority to purchase land at a reduced rate. In and of itself, however, this would not have been a sufficient reason for them to stay adjacent to downtown in a seriously depressed area. There was also the church's and individual members' intimate connections to this particular neighborhood and a long-standing political commitment to working with other black people collectively for the betterment of their lives.

Gainsboro was the place where many of the congregation had grown up; they had rich memories of their lives and of those of their parents in Gainsboro when it was a thriving community. But many members had moved away from Gainsboro in the 1960s and 1970s as a result of increased suburbanization and integration. The vibrant community of their past became a shell of what it had been. Many now knew the area only as visitors when attending church functions.

The population left in the Gainsboro area was mostly elderly and black and lived primarily on social security and pensions. Many of these people owned their own homes; indeed, in 1979, 78% of the homes were owner-occupied, 16.4% were rented, and about 5.6% were vacant.[9] Most of the housing stock was between forty and fifty years old, and much in need of repair. Many of the people living in the area did not have the resources, financial or otherwise, to keep up with the maintenance.

The appearance of the community had changed as radically as

Figure 2.6 Traditional housing pattern in the Gainsboro neighborhood. (Photo by Sharon Booker)

the population. The Gainsboro neighborhood of Roanoke had been selected as an urban renewal site; in accordance with early federal policy, blocks of the old urban residential houses that lined the hills along the streets had been demolished and the hills themselves bulldozed into flat planes. When we began to work with them, fewer than twenty-five ranch-style houses had replaced the almost eight city blocks of urban housing removed during the demolition process. These few new houses were radically different from the front-porch, street-oriented, dense urban housing; they were suburban ranch houses on small suburban lots on curvilinear streets. Both the street fabric and the house form had been radically altered.

These new houses were very much like the suburban houses in which many of the congregation now lived outside of the city. Many liked these houses because they found them to be more modern, cleaner, and more efficient. They had fond memories of street life and porches, but they knew that behind much of the outward vitality was poverty and poorly constructed and maintained houses. Life was better for them in their new homes and neighborhoods, yet they believed that life should be better for those who remained in Gainsboro. The congregation's decision to keep the church in the area was grounded in the conviction that their presence would support the efforts of those who stayed by choice or because they had no options.

(a)

(b)

Figure 2.7 "Urban renewal" in Gainsboro (a) demolished and leveled many city blocks and (b) replaced traditional houses with ranch-style housing.

Many discussions of the Coordinating Committee revolved around the question of the Gainsboro community. It was felt that many members of the congregation did not know their community well. The older members had memories of good times in a strong neighborhood; the younger and newer members saw only the depressed physical presence of Gainsboro. The question "Where do we live?" was felt to be important in light of the investment in the neighborhood that they were about to make. Furthermore, the voice of the congregation in the Mission Workshop had stressed that it wanted to increase its ministry to the community. How was this to be done if many in the congregation were unfamiliar with the community? And how was the congregation to present itself physically in the community by the making of a new church building? What kinds of facilities would both support their internal programs and meet some of the needs of the neighborhood?

These questions led to the decision to hold an event in which the congregation would be invited to "visit" their neighborhood and to which neighborhood people would be invited. The decision to hold such an event opened a long and thoughtful discussion about how best to accomplish the goal of reinserting many of the congregation into the neighborhood. They decided to name this event "Close Encounters of the Fun Kind."

Part of the idea of "Close Encounters" was to get people to walk through the neighborhood in small groups and to talk about what they remembered, what they were seeing, and what they might imagine. This process would give both the members who still lived there and those who had lived there an opportunity to share their experiences and memories with younger and newer people. It would permit everyone to have better insight into the actual conditions of both the "urban renewal" area and the older sections of the community. It was hoped that Close Encounters would facilitate a critical attitude for differentiating between what was unique and special about Gainsboro and should be carefully preserved, and what needed transformation for the sake of those who lived there.

There are many different ways to have people walk through a neighborhood and various strategies to accomplish the general goals of experience and critique. We offered our professional experience as part of this discussion, and together we decided on a format for the event. The day would be divided into three parts: a community picnic celebration, a loosely organized walk through the neighborhood, and a time for reflection and discussion among the people who went on the walk. The members of the Coordinating Committee assumed primary responsibility for organizing the community picnic, and we worked to structure the walk and reflection time.

To facilitate the walk and discussion, we suggested using a method developed by Halprin and Burns called "scoring."[10] Each participant is given an environmental script for a walk that includes things to look at, places to explore, and a series of questions designed to engage these places and things. An environmental script is similar to a score for a piece of music or dance that guides the players or dancers through their movements, serving the same function as a script for a play. It helps focus attention on specific features in the environment. The Coordinating Committee thought that scoring would be a good way to have the participants experience the neighborhood because it would give them a reason to walk around the adjacent blocks and, it was hoped, to see them in more detail. Long-term residents of Gainsboro assisted us in preparing the scores by walking through the neighborhood with us and pointing out things they thought were important. The Coordinating Committee named the scores "Space Walks."

We divided the surrounding neighborhood into twelve zones and prepared a score for each area that included questions about historical, environmental, or social aspects that could be revealed in the physical environment or in conversation among the participants. We prepared large maps of the twelve zones to be used in the discussion session after the walk and to make a public record of the comments people had written on their individual scripts.

Close Encounters of the Fun Kind was set for June 3, 1978, and invitations were extended to members of the congregation and community to come and spend a few hours eating, going on "Space Walks," and talking about Gainsboro and the First Baptist Church. Unfortunately, that morning was gloomy and rainy, and we were disappointed to have fewer people than we had planned for.[11] However, about fifty hardy members of the church and people from the community came to participate in Close Encounters, along with the Coordinating Committee and faculty and students from Virginia Tech. Each Space Walk was led by a Coordinating Committee member and an architecture student. Groups were purposefully mixed—young and old, community and church. Groups of five to seven went to one of the geographic areas, using the scores to assist their conversation about the neighborhood walk, some filling in comments on their sheets. When the groups returned, they worked around a table on the large map, talking about their impressions and recording their experiences with magic markers. At the end of the session, each group shared what it had learned with others.

One group talked about the 1913 opening of the Odd Fellows Building, where Mr. Reamy, one of the members of the Coordinating Committee, had played the trumpet as a young boy. Many good times had been had in the building. Another group walked up the steep hill to the Catholic church, where they could see the new urban renewal houses embedded in the older residential fabric. One

SPACE WALK
Second Street #4

1.   Neighborhood Resources

Walk to the library. Go inside and sit down. The library is an excellent source of information and pleasure for everyone in the community. What other things are there in Gainsboro that give the same kinds of opportunities?

Housing Authority Bldg   Hunton YMCA
Church Buildings
SVCDF Building

What other sources of learning and pleasure would you like to see in Gainsboro? (For example, neighborhood museum, a place for crafts, etc.)

Claytor House - Neigh. Museum   Gym - Rec. Center
Theater Workshop Center   Sr. Citizens Home
                                Swimming Pool

2.   YMCA Building

Walk across the street to the YMCA. Look at the cornerstone. What was this building built for? Grand United Order of Odd Fellows 1921

Can you think of other buildings in Gainsboro that have changed uses? List several: Abandoned building - was a drugstore
                    was a funeral
Reda Place -   home   Claytor Clinic - part of it is used for jobs training
Hughes Funeral Home - now a
cleaning est. + residence   Lawson Building - Community Service Group

Think of some of the ways the old First Baptist Church building could be used when the new building is complete.

Education Center; Bus Office; Lodge; Community Center
for Group meetings; History + Culture Center; Family
Restaurant

Do you think that a community needs the recreational services that YMCAs usually provide? yes   Name some other services that you would like to have here.

Gym, Swimming Pool

Figure 2.8 One of the Space Walk scripts.

3. Porches

Walk up to the top of the hill on Patton. As you go down the street, note the number of porches and how people use them. Names some of the ways:

Sitting, (Casual), Storage, Grow Plants,

TAP Community Center - Finney House

Read papers, visit with neighbors

Are the porches all alike? In what ways?

No. Sizes vary. Some are in very poor condition.

Some are very neat and attractive

4. Buildings as Symbols

Stop at the intersection of Patton and 2nd Street. Look around at all the places and things that have symbolic meanings. What do you think when you see the following?

Star The Star City of the South

FNEB Money - prosperity

Poff Building Federal Power and Authority

St. Andrews Catholic Influence and History / Monuments

First Baptist Church My Christian Roots which gives me great pride

Other Vacant lots - signs of decay

5. The New Site -- IMAGINE!

Walk up Patton until you can look back and see the Hotel Roanoke and the N&W Buildings. The new church site is right in front of the N&W Building. If the new church building is to be a symbol, what would you like it to say?

That it is a beacon in the community for worship,

help for the less fortunate; warmth and fellowship

6. Houses in Good Repair

As you walk back on 2nd Street and Gilmer, mark on your map which houses are in good shape and might be saved.

Go back to the church, and find your table in the Fellowship Hall!

Thanks

Figure 2.9 Geneva Hale, Coordinating Committee member, leading a group through the Gainsboro neighborhood during Close Encounters of the Fun Kind.

seventy-six-year-old woman remarked that it was better that they leveled the hills because old people (herself not included) found it hard to walk up the hills.

Comments were made about the incongruity between the newer and older houses: "I didn't realize that mixing good houses with bad ones makes an area feel like it is going downhill." They talked about the different pattern of life in the ranch-style houses (they

Figure 2.10 One of the maps of Gainsboro annotated by Space Walk participants.

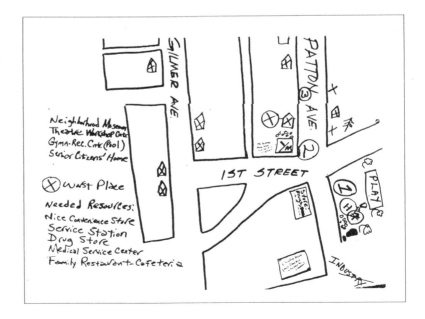

Figure 2.11 "I didn't realize that mixing good houses with bad ones makes an area feel like it's going downhill" (participant's comment).

were easier to keep clean; they were more private because your life wasn't on the porch; you didn't have to worry that people might see if your porch wasn't clean) versus the older residential houses (they were more friendly, and there was more "neighboring"; it was fun to see what was happening in the neighborhood).

Another group spent considerable time talking about the limestone walls that lined the older streets in the neighborhood and were a symbol of Gainsboro. The idea of "wall" was thoroughly explored on the walk and later in conversation. People talked about how strong the walls felt; there was a sense that they were thick enough to really hold back the earth. The walls felt good to touch as you walked by, and very importantly, they were the right height to stop and rest on when you were tired.

Each of the groups found intriguing aspects of their area that they wanted to share with others, such as the walls and tiles, the life of the porch, the symbols of various buildings, the important educative role of the Gainsboro Library, the personal history of many of the members in the area, and the advantages and disadvantages of the urban renewal houses. The notes and comments made on the maps and on the individual score sheets served as the generators of the group discussions.

The intention of reintroducing the Gainsboro neighborhood to the First Baptist Church and the First Baptist Church to Gainsboro was realized in the discussions. The annotated maps that were made during the group sessions, along with photographs of the neighborhood, were posted in the New Building Corner for other members to see. This poster form of communication was especially important because many of the congregation had not participated in Close Encounters.

At the first congregational event, the Mission Workshop, the congregation had stated its strong support for its mission to serve the community of Gainsboro. Yet this mission remained distant and abstract to many church members because they did not live in the area and were frankly unfamiliar with the place. The Coordinating Committee arrived at the decision to have the Close Encounters event because its members had come to understand the relationship between actually knowing and experiencing the community, on the one hand, and coming to understand what it might mean for the First Baptist Church to be more of a contributing member of the neighborhood, on the other. This was a moment of insight. As one member of the committee put it: "I now understand

Figure 2.12 Limestone walls in Gainsboro. (Photos by Sharon Booker)

why we did this. At first I just didn't see any connection between our new building and walking around the neighborhood." For the people who participated—Coordinating Committee members, church members, and neighborhood residents—this event suggested a renewed relationship based on a confirmation and interrogation of their previous experiences and perceptions of the place.

"What is a Church Building?"

As the Coordinating Committee continued meeting in the fall of 1978, they turned their focus to the question of what kind of church they wanted. As we explored with them the images of what this new church was to be—as we problematized this issue with them— questions emerged. One committee member was particularly troubled by the lack of comparison with other facilities. He brought up questions about the possibility of expecting too much for what they could afford, or conversely, not asking for the kinds of facility support they needed in order to meet their mission and offer their programs. How could they learn more about church building programs and church facilities and evaluate how well these two supported each other?

This began a discussion within the Committee of how to expand awareness and experience of other church facilities within the culture of their own church. Many of their members had never been in any church building other than the First Baptist Church; most had spent much of their lives as members of this congregation. There was even a sense that some members might feel it would somehow be "wrong" to go to another church, especially a non-Baptist church. Yet, in the discussions about what the new church building might be, the Coordinating Committee members recognized that their images were limited and probably unrealistic. Because many members of the congregation would feel uncomfortable going to a different church on Sunday morning, it was important to think about how any kind of visitation might occur. There were many things to discuss. What kinds of churches should be seen? New ones only, or different old ones too? Baptist churches only, or other denominations? How far away could we go? Who should go? How could it be made to "feel OK" to attend a different service? How would other congregations respond to a group of outsiders visiting? How could we make judgments about whether certain aspects of the design of other churches were appropriate for our own church? How do we focus on the physical aspects anyway? And should this visit happen on Sunday, when the churches were being used, or some other time? These issues occupied the meetings.

What emerged was another event, which the Coordinating Committee named "Visitation." Members would visit other churches on a designated Sunday morning and return to the First Baptist Church for lunch and about two hours of discussion in the afternoon. This was an invited event; members of the congregation were personally invited to attend a specific church in a group of four or five on a Sunday morning in November. Each group would meet at the First Baptist Church and travel together to the church they were visiting. It was decided that a variety of different churches would offer the best experience—new, old; Baptist, other denominations; urban, suburban.

In order to make the Visitation easier, we called churches throughout the city and discussed the visit with them. Twelve churches throughout the Roanoke area warmly welcomed the visitors; the various congregations were pleased to show off their facilities. Some of the churches had just recently completed building programs and thought this visit was an excellent way for the First Baptist Church to learn about opportunities and problems before getting involved in its own building program. This response was great reinforcement for the Coordinating Committee.

In preparation for this event, we designed different scores for each of the ten roles of the church developed by the Coordinating Committee, such as ushers, deacons, First Aid Committee, choir, youth group, administration, kitchen, Sunday school, and so on. The Coordinating Committee thought these particular roles were important and wanted to be certain that the congregation understood the physical requirements for each of these domains of church life. The Committee helped us prepare the scores for each of these roles so they would focus attention on the contribution the physical environment made to the experience of the churches and give a common ground for discussion upon return. As before, these scores were not used as data for us, but rather as a prompt to the church members in their visitation and evaluations.

In their invitations, people were asked to represent one of the ten functions of the church. Representatives responsible for different roles attended a church together, but each was asked to look closely at the aspect of their concern. People who attended the same church had lunch together afterwards in the First Baptist Church basement to share their impressions of the visit and to validate and/or question each other's perceptions. After lunch, we organized small group sessions by role; that is, all the choir people sat together, all the deacons, all youth leaders, and so forth. Each was asked to share with their group his or her experience of the visited church. We then brainstormed lists of likes and dislikes that could serve as the basis for the development of their own church program.

These discussions were important in transforming perceptions into images that had physical implications. For example, one visitor kept emphasizing the feeling that the church he had visited was "very friendly." As we explored friendliness with him, the group came to understand that the friendliness was enhanced by the design of the narthex. There was a space for people to mingle before and after the service outside of the sanctuary. This arrangement preserved the holiness of the sanctuary but also encouraged friendly interactions before and after services, and also permitted the pastor to greet members and visitors freely in a comfortable environment. This was lacking in the First Baptist Church's building because of the 1898 configuration of the stairs and front door: After shaking

VISITATION WORKSHOP - First Baptist Church
November 26, 1978

Choir Members

Try to get to the service at least 15 minutes early to see where the choir prepares and if they practice before service.

1.   Is there a special choir practice room? _____   Where is it located? _____
     _____

     Describe the room_____

     _____.

2.   Where does the choir dress for service?_____

     _____.

     Is there enough room to store robes? _____ Is there sufficient room to dress? __

     _____ Is there a safe place to keep personal belongings during service? _____

3.   Where is the choir located in the sanctuary? _____

     _____

     Does the choir face the altar, the congregation, the minister?_____

     Watch how the choir enters and exists the choir area. Does the position of the choir

     seating make this easy? _____ Do you like this arrangement for the

     choir? Why or why not? _____

     _____

     _____

     If someone had to leave the choir area during service or needed to be taken out, how

     would this happen? _____

     _____

4.   What kind of musical instruments were used during the service? _____

     _____ Did they have an electric or pipe organ? _____

     What advantages and disadvantages do you see with their choice?_____

     _____

5.   Did the choir use electrical amplification? ____ If so, did it add to or detract from the

     service?_____

     _____

Figure 2.13 Script for Choir Member participants in the Visitation Workshop.

Reverend Wright's hand, each parishioner was immediately on the street.

Those concerned with the Sunday school program had lengthy discussions about the advantages and disadvantages of using separate classrooms versus one large open space with internal dividers. Before the Visitation, most church members involved in the Sunday school thought that separate classrooms were what they wanted, because that way each group could have lessons without being distracted by other age groups. After visiting churches that had separated classrooms rather than one large room, it was clear that much of the space was underutilized during the week. Now they were less sure that separate classrooms was the best idea because they had a new understanding of the relationship between the Sunday School space and other aspects of the church program. The decision about the type of space for educational programs would have to be resolved.

A display in the New Building Corner showed the results of the Visitation Workshop and discussion; it included the names and addresses of the churches visited, the participants, and large newsprint sheets listing likes and dislikes. Also, to keep the entire congregation current with the planning process, a summary was given by Reverend Wright during the next Sunday worship.

"How Do We Want Our New Church To Be?"

After the Visitation event, the Coordinating Committee felt the time had come to begin the process of selecting an architect. We discussed the option of having the Coordinating Committee serve as the group in charge of selecting an architect. The committee felt it was important that some of them be involved but were clear that this was also an opportunity to bring other people into the process, including more of the trustees and deacons. And so the Architectural Selection Committee was formed. We had discussions with the group about the kinds of credentials they might seek from an architectural firm and what kinds of questions might be most useful during an interview. The newly formed committee was concerned not only with professional experience, but also with how the architects involved the clients in their work, what kind of communication skills they had, and what they believed in. It was important that the person entering the process appreciate and use the work that had been done so far and know how to interact with the members of the congregation. The Selection Committee prepared a time schedule for themselves and hoped to have the architect contract signed by summer 1979 (it was actually completed in early 1980), the same time it was hoped that the land negotiations would be completed with the Housing Authority. We worked with the church as support to the Architectural Selection Committee but did not in any way involve ourselves in the selection process itself.

The creation of the Architectural Selection Committee put pressure on the Coordinating Committee to develop and record a physical image and program for their new church building. The Coordinating Committee felt they had been very successful in involving many members of the congregation in thinking and talking about the new church building through the three events of the previous year: the Mission Workshop, Close Encounters of the Fun Kind, and Visitation. Now it was time to prepare an architectural program. The Coordinating Committee was troubled by the task's complexity, importance, and constraints. We talked with them on how to gather the insights and understandings of the congregation, preserving the richness and voices of the members, into a form that could be communicated to an architect. Many Coordinating Committee members felt that talking about design was beyond their competence and certainly outside the experience of the congregation. They felt this was the realm of experts.

We interrogated this perception and suggested that there were ways for all people to record their insights about places. In this particular instance, we suggested the use of *pattern language* as the vehicle for recording the insights. To explain pattern language, we jointly developed some *patterns*.[12]

Each pattern had to name the *idea,* explain *what* the problem was that the idea was to address, and explain *how* the problem might be resolved. We started with some perceived problems with the current church building—what wasn't working—to use as issues about which to develop a pattern. The Coordinating Committee discussed the problem of the service being interrupted by crying children but expressed concern that the parents ought to be able to participate in the service and not be denied simply because their children were unhappy. How might this be resolved? Were there other "disturbances" during the service that might be similar? Yes, latecomers often entered before they knew where they could sit, and moved around the church looking for seats. Was there some way to handle these types of "disturbances"? The Coordinating Committee suggested that what was needed was a place where one could see and hear the service but be physically outside of the sanctuary. This discussion led to the following pattern, which they called, "A Window into the Sanctuary":

Idea: A Window into the Sanctuary

What: Crying infants and latecomers often disturb the service for those in the sanctuary.

How: Place a glass wall between the foyer and the sanctuary so that parents with infants can see the service without disturbing others and so that latecomers can stand and wait until they see an available seat. Include a speaker system so the service can be heard as well as seen.

As we developed a few patterns together, the hesitation they had had about their ability to make design suggestions disappeared. This pattern process was accessible and easy to work with. The Coordinating Committee became convinced that it was possible for the congregation to develop patterns and design guides for their new church building. The structure of pattern language was appropriate to the task we had collectively set for ourselves because the structure was sufficiently flexible to take information, particular or general, in whatever form it came; it was easy to understand and use; it accommodated many kinds of languages and experiences; and it encouraged richness of description. Furthermore, developed in such a way, the program would reflect the images held by many individuals, which could then be publicly discussed and refined. And probably as important as any other aspect of the language was the ability of pattern language to initially accommodate conflicts and contradictions. These would later have to be resolved, but in the beginning, all ideas could be brought onto the table for discussion.

In other words, using the structure of pattern language and writing discrete patterns gave a framework to begin a building program. It was understood that the new church created through the pattern language process would then be transformed within the constraints of budget, time, energy, and design possibilities. This is precisely the way the patterns were used in the following year—as the basis for dialogue between the church and architect.

Once the Coordinating Committee felt comfortable with patterns as a way to capture ideas about the church, the conversation addressed such questions as who should be involved at this stage, how much involvement it would take to gather the ideas, and when this should be. The committee felt that this activity was different in kind from the beginning Mission Workshop and the educational activities of Close Encounters and Visitation. This was going to require a more sustained commitment by some members to actually evaluate what was needed, and to write patterns about the main ideas. It would also require the expertise of members familiar with different aspects of the church. This activity was closer to the commonly understood idea of what a new building program might be.

With all of these concerns in mind, they decided to invite members to become participants in Building Committees, which were organized around various functions of the church. The Coordinating Committee developed a proposed scope of work for each of the committees to focus the discussion. They asked individuals to chair each of the functional Building Committees—Worship/Sanctuary, Music/Choir, Educational Programs, Ushers, Site and Entrance, Support Facilities, Kitchen/Eating, Recreational, Nursery, and Administrative/Organizational. These chairs then participated in selecting people to serve on their committees.

The goal for the series of three meetings, held once a week for three weeks, was to clarify and record the design ideas for specific areas of the church in a format that could be given to the architect. The four-step process was to:

1. Brainstorm all of the ideas important to the area of concern.
2. Write patterns (idea, what, how) for each.
3. Discuss the relationships between the patterns, writing new ones as necessary, or combining if appropriate.
4. Prepare rough sketches, images, and plans to convey the committee's concept to the other Building Committees.

As each Building Committee worked, it developed sets of patterns about its area of concern and addressed the specific relationship of the ideas to each other. From these discussions, it developed an image of what the place should look like and how it should function. These ideas were recorded in the patterns and a few sketches. For example, the Kitchen Committee, made up of members who had prepared many suppers during the years and some who worked in the food industry, generated thirty patterns for the cooking and dining areas, ranging from the relationship between the dining room and the kitchen, to the type of appliances and the location of the exhaust fan. The Kitchen Committee made a diagram of the organization of the space to be sure that the architect really understood what they hoped for.

Figure 2.14 Building Committees meet to develop patterns for their area of concern.

The patterns generated ranged from the most global issues, such as the role of the church in the community, to details such as the type of covering on the floors. Also reflected in their patterns were some concerns about the original church building which they hoped to fix in the new building, as demonstrated by the pattern "Access for All." There were over 500 patterns and a few rough

Idea:	Window for Disposing of Dirty Dishes
What:	Whenever there is a large group of people eating, there will always be a large amount of dirty dishes.
How:	Create a window into the kitchen that doesn't interfere with the serving lines, so that people can return their dirty dishes to one place. Also try to locate the window near the dishwasher so that the dishes can be easily loaded.

Idea:	Restroom near the Kitchen
What:	It takes time to prepare meals for groups of people, and those working in the kitchen often have to use the restroom during their work.
How:	Locate a restroom near the kitchen to make it easy for people to use when they are working in the kitchen.

(a)

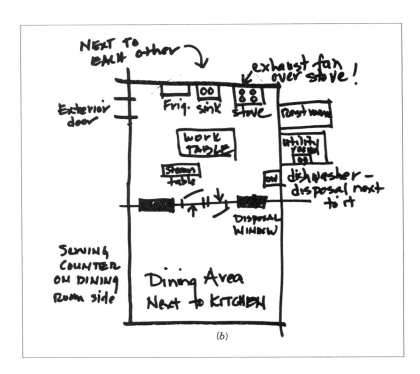

(b)

Figure 2.15 Kitchen Committee report: (a) selected patterns, (b) diagram.

sketches generated by the Building Committees and Coordinating Committee about what they wanted their church to be.

The Coordinating Committee worked to coordinate the different pattern sets and to prepare the global patterns based on their reflections and the work of the earlier events. This set of patterns was concerned with overall ideas about the church and the relationships between the specific patterns developed by the Building Committees. As consultants, we served as facilitators and recorders for the Building Committees. Between sessions, we took the patterns they had developed during their meetings and transformed them into a common form that could be discussed and reviewed by other committees the following week.

We compiled the patterns and all of the information generated through the workshops and produced *The First Baptist Church Pattern Book,* a document of the process and patterns organized according to the six functional areas generated during the Mission Workshop. The Pattern Book was reviewed by the Coordinating Committee and the chairs of the individual Building Committees and was later presented to the architect selected for the project. The patterns covered *global* criteria such as the expenditure of resources, the use of the site, and parking; *building-specific* patterns, which addressed the relationship between various functions, the sanctuary, and the nature of the entry; and *detail* patterns, which included such issues as what kind of lighting to have in the kitchen, what materials to use, how to create space for hanging robes, where to put wet umbrellas, and so on.

From Pattern Book to New Church Building

Once the Pattern Book had been completed and reviewed in early 1980, Reverend Wright and the Coordinating Committee felt it was time to begin a more traditional building process. By now their preparatory goals had been addressed; they all felt more confident in working with an architect and in being clear about what they wanted. Many voices had been heard; many people's ideas and hopes had been expressed.

The previous two-year process in which we worked with the church had demystified the design and building process. It had developed a language to speak about design issues and the confidence to use that language to influence design. As one of the Coordinating Committee members said, "I came not knowing anything and finished well informed. When I talk with the architect, I can communicate. I'm not being left in the dark."

Idea:	## The Church is the People
What:	The church is a body of people whose mission is to spread the good news of Christ. Its energies should therefore concentrate on people, not material possessions.
How:	While the church facilities should enhance and support the activities of the people, they should be at a small enough scale and easy enough to maintain so as not to strain the resources of the people.

Idea:	## Foot Tapping
What:	Some sounds are important during the worship services, especially foot tapping while the choir and congregation sing.
How:	Surfaces under the church pews should be designed to reflect the sound of tapping feet. Do not put carpet under the pews.

Idea:	## Access for All
What:	Not all people are blessed with youthful, healthy bodies and should not be excluded from church activities because of physical barriers, such as long flights of stairs, steep inclines, and slippery surfaces.
How:	Eliminate barriers and provide access to all major parts of the church buildings. This can be accomplished by ramps, elevators, and handrails.

Figure 2.16 Three of 593 patterns for the new First Baptist Church.

People of the congregation who had participated in the various stages of the project understood what they wanted their building to be; they were familiar with the details of the program because they had participated in making it. And they were committed to making a new church, as was evident through the time volunteered and the increase in contributions to the building fund.

The Architectural Selection Committee had begun to interview firms. The original Coordinating Committee, after long discussion, decided to disband. Most members felt they had accomplished the goal they had set for themselves: to design a process to

engage the congregation in creating a new church building. Together with the Architectural Selection Committee, they suggested
the formation of a new, single Building Committee to work with
the architect in preparing a traditional building program and over-
seeing the building construction. A few of the members from each
committee would serve on this new committee.[13]

Our original goal, to serve as facilitators and educators, was very
much vested in the Coordinating Committee. Like that committee,
we felt our original goals had been met. After the creation of the
Building Committee, we became interested observers. Although
we continued to visit the church and responded to requests from
Reverend Wright and former members of the Coordinating Committee, we explicitly stepped aside as the architects began their
work with the congregation.

The commitment to the now familiar participatory process was
evident in the ongoing design work. The contract the church negotiated with the architect contained two provisions that were indica-
tive of the learning process of the previous two years and of the
congregation's commitment to their own work: (1) The architect
must use the materials already developed by the congregation in an
explicit way; and (2) the architect must continue working with the
committees who wrote the patterns during the design development
process.

By early 1980 the First Baptist Church had selected an architect
to work with them, and had completed negotiations with the
Roanoke Housing Authority for land. One year later, ground was
broken for the new church. The Pattern Book was used by the
architect to structure the program and to make difficult and often
painful decisions about priorities in relation to the budget available.
The congregation's commitment to their ideas about their church
was reflected in many aspects of the program. The final design was
remarkably similar to the sketches drawn by members of the Building Committees. Furthermore, it was significant that members felt
so strongly about the collaborative work of their committees in
writing patterns and diagramming adjacencies that when faced with
a budget overrun, they were unwilling to change the key relationships and basic design. Instead, they chose to eliminate an element
introduced by the architect that contributed significantly to the
"image" of church but that was not their idea.

On June 20, 1982, the First Baptist Church of Roanoke, Va.
dedicated its new church building in a procession that started at the
original church building, marched across the streets of Gainsboro,

*Figure 2.17
Groundbreaking ceremony.
(Photo courtesy of the
First Baptist Church)*

*Figure 2.18 Diagram of
church sanctuary by
Building Committee
members.*

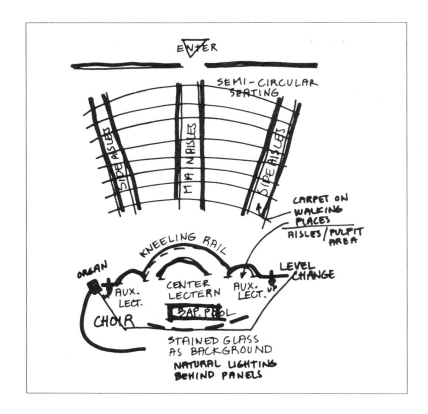

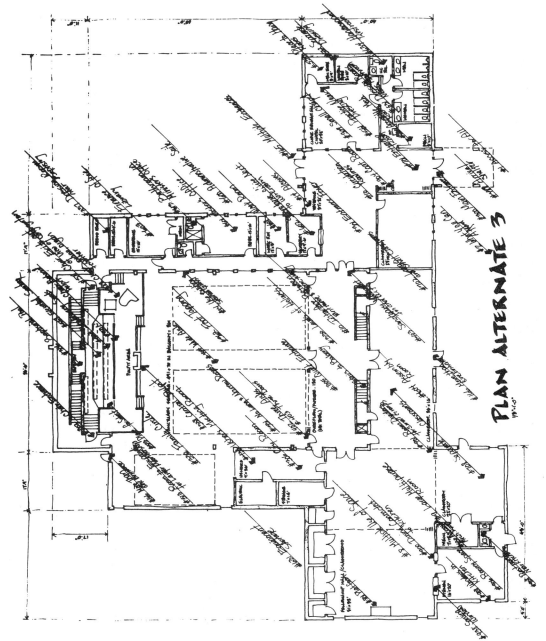

Figure 2.19 Floor plan of new church building annotated with patterns written by the Building Committees.

and entered the new building. This celebratory service was another beginning: the beginning of a relationship with a new, yet known, place that would need time and attention in order to be understood and cared for properly. But the congregation was well equipped to engage in this relationship. Many members knew intimately why the church was designed and built the way it was; they had participated in the decisions that located the first aid room adjacent to the choir area; they had suggested the arrival shelter and the location of the umbrella stand; they appreciated the windows that had been removed from the old church building and brought to the new, and so forth.

The First Baptist Church has a new chapter in its story—the creation of this building as a part of their life together. The making of the church was an affirmation of the very mission of the church and an explicit determination of how the congregation chose to share its life with its members and the Gainsboro community.

Reflections

Facilitating Competence

All professional consultation is intervention; all intervention is educational. There is no such thing as a neutral intervention or neutral education. In the most basic sense, our work as professionals is an act of influence: We dare to enter into the lives of other human beings and change them, and, in this process, to restructure their reality and our own. The attitude of our intervention determines whether the educational process will be liberating and educational for all, professional placemakers included, or destructive, essentially an act of cultural invasion.

In the First Baptist Church intervention, we were asked to engage the congregation as educators. This provided us with an enormous opportunity to make the discourse of education explicit in our work and in our critical thinking about professional practice. But this "naming" should not suggest that only this particular project is about education and others are about design, or programming, or evaluation. All are educational, some more explicitly than others, and in our field, all environmental interventions are about design.

The wisdom in the way Reverend Wright presented the problem revealed the competence of this congregation. We were asked to

Figure 2.20 The new First Baptist Church, Roanoke, Va. (Photo courtesy of the First Baptist Church)

assist them in thinking about a new church, what it might be, and how it might become. At this point we were not asked to design a church for them but to engage with them in thinking about the church. The existence of the powerful "story of the new church building" created a bond among members of the congregation, and its narrative and repetition were an energy source for them. This story had a life of its own; to make a new church would challenge the story by forcing a form. A physical, material form could transform the vision into a new source of energy. It also could tear apart the bond that the story, in its power, was holding together. Reverend Wright recognized that care would be required to transform the story into a physical reality. The congregation was committed originally to the story, not to a physical new church building. There was an enormous amount of working and thinking to be done.

Our role in this process was to discover the generative themes that formed their thinking about what a church was: to confirm their image, vision, and reality and at the same time to question it, add to it, and together re-create a shared theme. We were there to facilitate their competence and to uncover with them the themes that gave them a sense of place, especially the themes that limited them. We explored the language and thoughts they used to interpret, construct, and act on reality. As facilitators and educators, we *re-presented* their thinking to them in a way that permitted them to establish new relationships to these themes, by confirming and/or interrogating their reality.[14]

Our primary way of working was to problematize what they perceived to be true and obvious. As we entered into a dialogue about "how to plan for a new church building," we began to ask questions about their perceptions of their world and the ways they felt limited by them. The intent of this questioning was not to direct their thinking to some end; the concept of *right answers* is incomprehensible in this form of work. Our purpose was only to question their assumptions and ideas sufficiently so that they could examine them, confirm them, or transform them. The effort of our dialogue was not to dismiss their worldviews or ours, but to collectively construct knowledge about what a new church might be for the First Baptist congregation.

Ways of Working: Reconceptualizing "Methods"

Our intervention with the First Baptist Church over the two-year period was not planned in advance, nor did we set a time frame for when the work would be completed. We did, however, have a way of proceeding that started with the creation of what we call a dialogic space. Within this special space and time, we continually engaged in the tasks of confirmation, interrogation, and action framing with the Coordinating Committee and with many other members of the congregation.

Themes for examination arose in conversation with the Coordinating Committee, and the actions we took were responses to their recognition that these ideas were important to the making of a new church. The structuring of the major events—the Mission Workshop, Close Encounters, and the Visitation—were designed to problematize the themes for the larger congregation. We used many different methods in the conduct of this work, but we always attempted to approach the dialogic space without any determination of what was to happen other than conversation itself.

This approach may appear contradictory in light of the First Baptist Church's request for assistance in planning, which may imply setting long-term goals and framing work in response to those goals. However, we trusted the thinking of the people of the church and the direction in which they would take the discourse, as long as we were faithful to our role in facilitating their inquiry. In retrospect, the direction of our collaborative inquiry did begin with the familiar setting of goals. But this activity came from the concerns they brought into the dialogic space and was framed in their language and their questions about what they (the Coordinating Committee in particular) should be doing, and how they might expand their understanding of the purposes for the new building itself.

The first workshop, the Mission Workshop, grew out of a desire to expand the discussion about goals to include the larger community of the church. Through our discussions, the Coordinating Committee began to realize that assumptions about the church's mission were not as simple and obvious as they had believed. And they recognized that there were few opportunities to affirm and/or challenge these assumptions. They never questioned the basic purpose of "saving souls"—they were a Christian church. But they knew that there many ways to save souls, and furthermore, that the church was a complex and important social network, and that this function might be explored. So the framing of the questions for discussion at the Mission Workshop reflected their faith in their primary mission, and their willingness to make vulnerable their convictions about how their mission might be accomplished and what other purposes the church might affirm, change, or adopt.

Once this series of questions was framed by the Coordinating Committee, we were able to suggest from our professional experience different methods for engaging the congregation. The selection of a workshop format, with such elements as small-group discussion tables, newsprint, and reporting back to the rest of the congregation, was determined by the purposes framed by the group. From our perspective, it was the best method we could use to encourage an intense engagement by a large group of people around issues about which they cared deeply. It was public, oral, participatory, and celebratory. This same method has been extremely useful in many different contexts, but it is never "applied," always uniquely situated. The workshop format is simply one way of working, and it does not tell participants what to do, but rather how to be.

The other questions around which we structured events were framed in a similar fashion by the Coordinating Committee: "Where do we live?" "What is a church building?" and "How do we want our new church to be?" For each of the questions the committee initially assumed that they knew and understood what the response might be. But in the process of dialogue and questioning, the initial responses became more problematic and the questions more intriguing. And always, the engagement of other members of the congregation in the inquiry served to both confirm and interrogate their reality. The series of inquiries in the events we designed with the Coordinating Committee were opportunities for the congregation to reframe the story of the new church building into a story about *making* a new church.

The use of scoring methods and pattern language were effective ways to re-present the congregation's language and thoughts to them and enabled them to actively inquire into their perceptions of place. The scoring was particularly useful in bringing other domains of knowledge into their thinking. The process of asking questions about specific person/environment activities facilitated the development of language and thoughts about the role the physical environment plays in social relations. Moreover, the members' questions and thinking did not remain within the privacy of each individual but were brought into conversations in which all of us could share insights and hear the thinking of others engaging the same questions. This was an opportunity to collectively create new knowledge that confirmed or challenged what we had known.

Pattern language was particularly effective as a vehicle to reveal and present the place images of the congregation. To ask someone to envision something that *will be* is to ask them to imagine, to plan, to design. The power of the human mind to see what might be is emancipatory. But to record, convey, and share these images without the skill in graphic representation that design professionals have developed are complex tasks. Pattern language, because it takes discrete decoded pieces of projected reality, facilitated the church members' discussions about what their new church might be. It could hold their concrete knowledge about their activities and the physical world that would be needed to support the life they desired to live.

The process of problematizing in a dialogic relationship required the participants to use all their faculties of thinking and doing. Although there was a serious analytical component to their exploration of their life and new church, by no means was the process of engagement analytical and abstract. The inquiry started with their concrete life experiences, their hopes, their images. The events were collaboratively designed to introduce experiences in which the congregation could appropriate new knowledges into their lives and thinking.

These events were educational in the fullest sense of that word, akin to the practice of "craft" where the mind, heart, and hands are used together. To construct knowledge is a consuming labor; it engages the intellect, feelings, attitudes, and values, and it involves action in the world. The inquiry occurred in the context of dialogue, which includes talking and doing. We structured activities together; we felt and validated and problematized each other's ideas and feelings; we worked together in an intellectual and physical sense, participating in each others lives and in the material world of the church. [15]

There are always tensions in a dialogic relationship in which problematizing occurs. The process of confirming and interrogating one's own worldview and the worldviews of others creates a tension that is only resolved in the trusting relationship. Confirmation at the expense of interrogation negates the possibility of new knowledge and understanding; interrogation at the expense of confirmation can destroy interpersonal relationships. As a professional placemaker engages in dialogic practice, the dialectic of confirmation and interrogation requires balance and a constant focus on evaluation. How do I bring up an issue that is clearly intended to be repressed? How do I give feedback when it is not requested? On what basis would I bring up a theme, an issue, that might threaten a relationship or even the dialogic space? How do I respond when my most cherished values are being challenged by others in the dialogue? The value of problematizing is that it never challenges a worldview by denying the person who holds that worldview; it simply, and often elegantly, re-presents that worldview in the form of a problem. The participants can select to engage or ignore the problematized version. Each of us selects our own level of engagement.

However, there are situations in which, as a consultant, you know that an issue not addressed now will have to be discussed, aired, and resolved later as the work proceeds. Your responsibility as a facilitator is complex: To confirm uncritically is to deny the potency of the unframed issue, but to interrogate might jeopardize the dialogic space. In our work with the First Baptist Church, there were instances when the tensions could have been resolved differently and our collective work might have proceeded differently.

For example, as early in the process as the Mission Workshop, the participants revealed conflicting ideas about the organ. Some wanted to move the existing pipe organ to the new church building, while others wanted to replace the old organ with a new, modern electric organ. These views represented radically different ideas about old and new, preservation and replacement, about economies, and certainly about music. We knew that this particular issue would not go away but had to be resolved before the new church was constructed. Although we introduced the question a few times to the Coordinating Committee, they did not want to engage it, probably because of the intensity of feelings of the various participants. We did not insist. Yet at one point, this issue caused the greatest tension and conflict within the congregation before the church was built—after we had left and the architect was working. We ask ourselves whether we should have continued to problematize the question of music in the church so that we could have worked with them to resolve the conflict. It was resolved, and the design and construction were completed with a new electric organ, but we wonder whether the resolution could have been done differently so that there were not such extremes of "winning" and "losing." This type of issue may sound mundane to those who are confronted with questions of purpose and mission, but it is precisely these concrete realities that often tear groups apart. The process of problematizing in a dialogic practice continually involves making judgments about the nature of the questions and relationships.

The Power of Stories

The First Baptist Church of Roanoke, Va. was joined together in part because of its origin story, its ongoing commitment to a place, and its story about a new church building. Stories are the adhesive that hold groups together; they are the narratives that remind us of who we have been and what we might become. Before we began working with the church, their story of the new church building had been a narrative of hope that tied them both to the Gainsboro community and to those in the community and congregation who had gone before. The story had served them well. It had provided a commitment to the future through some very difficult years for their membership, in which they had seen their community decline from a vibrant and centered place to a devastated shell of its former self.

To change a story of hope into a reality is delicate, but not impossible, work. In the life of a family there is always the tension between the story of the child-to-be (she or he will be a good parent; she or he will be a doctor), and the child as he or she is. The story can either give strength to or destroy the child-becoming as she or he grows. So the story of the church-to-be had the power to infuse the congregation with creative growth through making a story become real. But the power of the narrative of the imagined new church could also be fragmented by the real church-becoming if the new building did not become what was hoped for, or if the story, appearing to be one story, were really many stories with many conflicting themes. The act of the storytelling can displace the actual story unfolding.[16]

The story had to be re-presented to the congregation with care so that they could participate in the transformation of the story of the church-to-be into a story of the church-becoming. Reverend Wright knew this work was critical to the success of the new church building and to the well-being of his congregation. We struggled to make the structure of our intervention respectful of the knowing embedded in the story, the storytelling competence itself, and our roles as listeners and constructors. Myriad opportunities to revisit the story were created, and many people participated in re-forming the narrative. The new building has become a part of the story of the First Baptist Church.

3

ORGANIZATIONAL DEVELOPMENT THROUGH DESIGN: AN INTERNATIONAL BANKING INSTITUTE

The Setting

We have described the work of our firm as "consultants on environmental and organizational change" since 1974 under the assumption that environmental interventions are significant opportunities for organizational development. We also believe that organizational change often requires an examination of the environmental fit between new organizational programs and existing physical conditions. Yet until 1984 the problems presented to us by clients were usually framed in terms of our training as design and planning professionals. Any organizational development benefits to the clients were supplementary, that is, not central to our commission but "nice to have."[1] Then we received the call from the facilities management section of a large international finance institute (here referred to as the Institute[2]) in 1984.

The Phone Fiasco

The call was from a former student, who asked, "Do you remember when you used to talk about organizational development through design?" What followed was a description of how the Institute's Facilities Section, where this former student now worked, had recently completed a lengthy and very professional study on telecommunication needs and submitted its findings to the director of administration. It subsequently received approval for the complete conversion of the telecommunications systems in the Institute's ten-storey headquarters building. The Facilities Section had completed procurement and were installing the systems when real trouble started. Angry questions and memos and snide references to the phone system change "requiring a Ph.D. in phones to operate" all suggested that the users of this new phone system were furious. The system was complex; the people for whom it was implemented did not know how to use it, and they had not been consulted in its procurement. The change was seen as an outrageous imposition on their daily lives. As a result, the relationship between the Facilities Section and a large proportion of the employees of the Institute was severely strained.

Well, the caller explained, the problem would settle down after a while. Efforts to provide instruction on the system were already in place, and over time the employees would see the wisdom and usefulness of the procurement decision. Meanwhile, the Facilities Section continued to work in a low-trust environment while other, even more significant decisions were on the horizon. This lack of trust had generalized to an attribution of "thoughtless management," straining staff relations in often completely unrelated areas. The telecommunications decision, while correct technically, had helped to create an atmosphere of distrust and several organizational development problems. Wasn't there some way to go on with the new work that avoided angering constituents?

The Institute was preparing to automate the offices of over 2000 employees, beginning with virtually no personal computer equipment in place and anticipating full automation in five years. The Facilities Section had to establish the infrastructure for the new systems, including the office automation furniture, telephone and data communications, electrical power, and local area network system support. The caller was clear that the staff in the Facilities Section were able to make the correct technical decisions, but their discussions on how best to proceed led their supervisor to ask how they knew their approach would engage the Institute staff in a manner more acceptable than what had occurred during the telephone procurement. They needed to develop a way to proceed with office automation that would actually improve the relationship with the rest of the Institute staff. No one wanted to repeat what they called "the phone fiasco." In short, the caller requested help in using the technical decision process they were about to undertake to address the organizational development goal of restoring trust between her section, her superiors, and the majority of Institute employees.

The stories that follow are about an institution that has come to believe it can and should use its facilities as tools to rethink both the why and how of the work itself, that uses departmental moves as opportunities for inter- and intraunit team building, and that actively uses all levels of organization in the making and maintenance of its place. This Institute has created and engages the concept of a dialogic space, recognizing that the making and remaking of the workplace ultimately makes the institution, which makes the place, which makes the institution.

The process of each of a series of interventions in the Institute has been different, yet all the interventions share some common characteristics. All the processes seek to confirm staff perceptions and experiences while also interrogating and challenging them, framing actions relevant to everyday life in the workplace. This account describes our now ten-year history with the Institute and the way we collaboratively came to understand the nature of our work there as being fundamentally about the development of the organization. Included in the account is a description of the context of the Institute, some examples of our experiences, and reflection on those experiences as "self-correcting work" and "public housework."

The Institute

The Institute's office headquarters does not conform to conventional stereotypes. It has characteristics in common with public service institutions, corporate headquarters, universities, bank offices, governmental and regulatory offices, and embassy offices. Yet it is sufficiently different from these types to warrant a description that goes beyond an identification of organizational and functional types.[3]

The Institute serves the collective interests of its members around the world, with operating departments related to geographic areas of interest, each reporting to separate area directors. In turn, all directors report to a managing director, a position filled through periodic elections by members. The organization chart is flat at the top with the one general managing director and about twenty geographic area directors. However, there is a steep hierarchy within each directorate with clear chains of command, limited spans of control, and well–defined, task–specialized job categories. The full complement of bureaucratic procedures requires multiple signatures on even routine administrative actions and tough sanctions for leapfrogging the chain of command.

The Administration Department is the largest of the departments. It has primary responsibility for all administrative services regardless of geographic area of concern. Facilities, Procurement, Graphics, and Security sections are located within the Administrative Support Services Division of the Administration Department. This division is larger than most geographic area departments in staff size and budget. The Facilities Design Unit of the Facilities Section, our point of entry, is staffed to do routine internal office moves and reorganizations with in-house personnel, relying on contract support through professional service firms for large or more complex moves and building modifications.

The culture of the Institute is influenced by its global economic mission, international work force, and organizational structure. These factors combine to create the most often cited organizational metaphor that "the Institute is like a university without students." Indeed, the employment practices of the Institute offer something closely akin to university tenure, with ancillary "untenured" contract or vendor employees. The international makeup of the workforce significantly influences staff values. For example, there are widely varying perspectives on the role of women in the workforce, the proper exercise of authority, the importance of collaboration in management, the importance of technology to the future of the Institute, the importance of physical facilities in the conduct of work, and the employment of consultants. Even in relatively homogeneous organizations there is significant divergence on such topics, but the Institute staff is diverse in the extreme.

The Institute tends to take a long-term view. It has been in existence for approximately fifty years and sees itself in a position to continue into the foreseeable future. The essential nature of its functions tends to assure continued financial solvency through assessments made to member countries. The headquarters staff are concerned with the Institute's image as an important part of the world's economic and political scene and, at the same time, are interested in assuring each member that it is fiscally accountable and allocates resources wisely.

As a result, doing things "properly" is important to the Institute, and it tries to avoid being too showy. Its internal organization is concerned with the efficient management of its operations. Traditional cost/benefit analyses are often applied to procurement decisions and are considered carefully in the delivery of services to members. Because the output of the Institute is information, member services, and some regulatory functions, the cost/benefit analysis more often resembles the analysis one would do for a government agency than that needed to sustain profitability in a for-profit corporation. Like most governmental or corporate office environments, the Institute is trapped between austerity and the need to appear modern and efficient. It must be collegial yet extraordinarily accountable.

Contract Work with the Institute

An important aspect of our involvement with the Institute is that it has been incremental and progressive. What ultimately became known as the Office Automation program began with a modest project to acquire the user's perspective on such automation. This led to the formulation of a test-site project involving extensive evaluations of furniture and layout prototypes. The test-site work, in turn, led to a project on developing workspace standards and to design and installation procedures. In our continuous involvements we have tested and modified the results of the Office Automation program in incrementally more complex office moves.

Our methods of work on the Office Automation program and its related User's Perspective, Test Site, and Office Automation Workspace Standards projects have established a basis for supplementary commissions involving organizational development and conflict resolution work, life safety procedure documentation, computing support for facilities management operations, as well as staff training in interview, small-group dynamics, and research techniques. Each piece of work grew from its predecessors but without the assumption of further consulting by us. The nature of the commissions awarded to us continues to change based on the development of staff capabilities and Institute organizational changes, which are influenced by its growth and advances in technology.

Broad participation by the Institute staff in the Office Automation program led to our involvement in other kinds of problems within the organization. For example, the procurement process for the entire Institute was somewhat fragmented and not yet fully automated. The increasing need to coordinate computer acquisition with office automation hardware and software sharply illustrated the concern. Following our initial work on the User's Perspective project, we used a similar collaborative approach in conducting several problem-solving workshops on integrated procurement procedures. We were invited to participate in this effort because several staff suggested that the procurement work should proceed "like the work done in the User's Perspective project" in the Office Automation program. Previous work became a metaphor used by Institute staff for how to proceed with other problems that required more than routine coordination.

As we earned the trust of the Facilities Section and their clients at the Institute, they began to engage us in large-scale moves, such as the space programming and space planning for the Computing Services Department. The commission was primarily focused on improving the functional operations of the unit by consolidating functions that had been spread out over parts of seven floors in "leftover" space. The consolidation effort was not expected to fully accommodate the computing workforce in the kind of space viewed as consistent with the Institute's workplace standards; its more modest goal was the equitable distribution of crowded conditions in a manner that would be least disruptive of the delivery of services. Clearly, negotiations for the allocation of scarce available space would be strained, and some measure of care during the process of discussion would be essential to maintain close collaboration between units in the Computing Services Department. Facilities staff were aware of the necessity of working with computing staff to coordinate technical service delivery to other constituents. It would not serve them well to leave this department angry about the consolidation effort.

Our work was *technical* in the collaborative collection and analysis of information required for the interior design of the new offices. The work also involved *organizational development* as we managed the competition for scarce resources in a manner conducive to continued good work relations. Our dual focus on technical and organizational considerations was public and accountable, making the competition for scarce resources a legitimate topic of discussion. The units that were competing for resources in the consolidation defined the rules for the competition within a dialogic space where the maintenance of good relationships was an explicit goal.[4]

We have worked on other commissions over the years involving this same dual focus, which is required for good technical decisions and supportive work relations. For example, the life safety procedures and systems within the building were well known to a core group of building engineers who were approaching retirement. It was important to the management of the Institute to have these engineers record the knowledge they had gained over years of experience in order to pass it on to those that would replace them. As a result, we were asked to interview key individuals responsible for life safety procedures and to draft a manual of procedures based on what we learned. During the course of the interviews, however, it became clear that the manual project was offensive to the senior building engineers. They saw the process of creating standard procedures as a simplistic reduction of a complex set of judgments that had to be based on each particular situation. The attempt to reduce these judgments to simple "by rote" applications was seen as devaluing the contributions of seasoned professionals and, in their opinion, would lead to less competent building management.

We reported the criticisms by the engineers along with a basic understanding of life safety procedures as we had come to understand them. The interviews and discussion process affirmed the requirement for professional judgments to supplement the technical manual on the basics of life safety. Ultimately this discussion led to a redistribution of responsibilities, and experienced people were placed on teams with those just starting to assume responsibility for life safety. The resulting manual became a place for the continued recording of insights that were amenable to standardization, while the process of professional development for junior engineers was also assured. The senior engineers became valuable mentors who made willing contributions to the development of reasonable standardization.

A final type of commission we have enjoyed in our relation with the Institute is "training" Facilities staff in the skills of interviewing, survey research, group dynamics, and small-group research methods. These skills support the desire of the Facilities staff to deliver services as efficiently as possible, where efficiency is understood to require willing collaboration between operational units. The conduct of daily work in the Facilities Section depends on the facilitation of trust and collaboration between units within the Institute, and specifically between the Facilities Section and its constituents.

In all, there have been over thirty separate commissions during our ten years of work with the Institute. In reviewing these projects, several themes are surprisingly consistent across all of the work, themes previously described as confirmation, interrogation, and the framing of action.

Two of Many Stories

We have selected two stories from the placemaking work at the Institute: the Office Automation program and the Library Move project. Both stories illustrate how the simultaneous focus on confirmation and interrogation led us to place considerable emphasis on the facilitation of repair rather than on creating new conditions that "resist breakage" in facilities management.[5] In effect, we worked to create the conditions for continued maintenance and change over time, rather than making once-and-for-all fixes. Implicit in the idea of facilitating repair is a recognition that repairing is a confirming process that addresses the value of existing conditions even while it improves them.[6]

A variation on the repair idea addresses the multiple motives for work that include and transcend the narrow definition of increasing technical competence. At the Institute repair came to involve the need both to fix the problem at hand and to teach the organization how to work as teams, identifying and repairing future problems. There was always a background aspiration to use the present problem as an opportunity to learn.

The practice of simultaneously focusing on confirmation and interrogation helps us to be explicit about what to include and what to exclude in framing action. The practice at times even modifies what is initially perceived to be the problem. For example, part of the confirmation process involves the recurrent uncovering and displaying of conflict between an organization's or individual's actual behavior (*theory-in-use*) and the way they describe their intentions (*espoused theory*).[7] The simultaneous display of both kinds of information at the Institute tended to establish the conditions for self-interrogation by those involved in the projects. This interrogation further framed the boundaries of the problem.

Facilitating repair through the critical practice of confirmation and interrogation became part of the placemaking stories shared within the Institute. Each story helped in turn to establish the context for current work and, by contrast with current circumstances, also helped to interrogate how problems were presented, worked on, and resolved. Perhaps the most powerful pattern that has emerged from reviewing our contracts with the Institute is the power of the stories themselves to influence the creation of new stories. A good placemaking experience that becomes part of an institution's corporate culture can have a transformative influence on several other facets of work life. The story becomes a metaphor on how to work, on the nature of possible human relationships, and on the ability of the workforce to author their own stories.

The facilitation of repair and the aspiration to couple workplace development with organizational development establish a context within which one can view two of the Institute's many placemaking stories. The stories in turn reveal how acts of confirmation become acts of critical interrogation and how they establish the conditions for problem framing and action framing. In short, the stories reveal how the ideas of confirmation, interrogation, and action framing merge in practice.

The Office Automation Program

The sequence of events after the initial telephone call began with a small meeting with the staff of the Facilities Section.[8] The initial contract was only for us to attend this meeting and facilitate staff discussion. Staff listed all their aspirations for the Office Automation project and for the process it would employ. Given that list and the beginning of an understanding of the organizational structure of the Institute, we collaboratively developed a "proposed approach" to the project that would be reviewed by·project constituents. At this point our contract was extended to include facilitating the proposed approach developed during the first meetings. The goals and the process were seen as tentative and expected to change during the conduct of the work. The structure of the contract allowed us to bill time and expenses for our involvement rather than constraining us to a fixed fee, and it called for us to produce working papers for review by the constituents after each increment of work.

The next step in the program was to prepare and conduct a series of briefings on the best way to approach the administrative officers, a group representing administrative support functions for all of the geographic departments. These twenty-two administrative officers service operating departments in the Institute by handling their procurement requests, by working as liaisons to the Facilities Section and Computing Services Department, and by managing routine processing of personnel paperwork, training requests, new equipment, and so forth. They have the ear of the Institute's senior management and staff. These officers are also the people who complained the most vigorously about the telephone decisions. The administrative officers were an important group with which to start in the establishment of a new relationship between the Facilities Section and the Institute.

The administrative officer briefing began with the Facilities Section expressing honestly their desire to avoid repeating the dynamics of the telephone system procurement as the Institute moved forward with automating its offices. In essence, the Facilities Section and our team began by confirming what these officers perceived to be the experience of past work by owning the errors that had become legend and proposing to write a new story of collaboration. The briefing was presented as an invitation to the administrative officers to interrogate that experience and to influence how best to proceed with staff and management consultations. We indicated that we were primarily interested in developing a commitment to the actions necessary to make the Office Automation program successful in the eyes of those who would be affected by it. The briefing was approximately fifteen minutes long and left a full forty-five minutes for questions, discussion, and summation. The questions and issues raised, including suggestion for changes in the proposed approach, were recorded on large newsprint sheets and accounted for in a summation at the conclusion of the session.

The approach derived from the two rounds of collaboration, first with the Facilities Section and then with the administrative officers, called for a brief review of the literature on office automation in order to make a tentative list of performance criteria for new furniture. The process also employed the resident expertise of the in-house design staff at the Institute and the experience of our firm. From these sources, lists of criteria were drafted to serve as the starting point for a series of workshops drawing on a wide cross section of the Institute staff. The administrative officers decided to seek volunteers from representative user types for three half-day workshop sessions, which they also attended. In this fashion, the officers were affirming the value of their experience with the briefing-and-workshop approach. They liked the aspiration expressed by the Facilities Section for a fresh start and appreciated the openness of the discussion. They also felt that face-to-face discussions should occur with users in order to further the development of users' trust and ownership in the process. The discussions were seen as partially restoring some of the trust lost earlier by the Facilities Section and helped to fulfill the organizational development goal of the program.

The small-group workshops with users and administrative officers came to be called the User's Perspective project. Each of three workshops, with different constituencies, reviewed the tentative list of performance criteria for office automation furniture, discussed their relative merits, and modified the criteria. The work sessions concluded with participants rank ordering the revised performance criteria according to importance, proposing and discussing next steps, and expressing concerns on the direction of the project. Workshop results helped establish furniture users' priorities for more horizontal work surfaces than they currently enjoyed, for more storage space to accommodate computer manuals, and for more flexibility in layout so they could adapt to the demands of their newly emerging job descriptions and to the availability of hardware.

One other result of the workshops was the staff suggestion that the project proceed in small increments from performance specification to procurement so that about fifty of almost 2000 new office setups might be tested in use prior to the large-volume purchase. This suggestion resulted in what came to be called the Test Site project, which was one of the cornerstones of the Office Automation program. The work resulting from the Test Site project played a major role in workspace standards development, installation and inventory procedures development, a custom furniture design modification project, and wire management studies.

The clearly stated user priorities from the User's Perspective project, combined with a number of other factors, led the Facilities Section to propose experimenting with renovations of the existing line of furniture, in addition to new vendor and furniture line options. This "repair" of the existing furniture line appeared to accommodate the users' perspectives while also allowing the Institute to maintain a ten-year relationship with a furniture manufacturer they had come to know well and trust. The manufacturer was willing to retool to help with the office automation modifications related to work surfaces, layout flexibility, computer hardware accommodations, and ergonomics. If the test were viewed as successful by the test-site participants, office automation and conventional furniture would be "compatible," and there would be cost savings because the existing inventory could largely be reused.

It was important to test staff reactions to the idea of retooling the existing furniture line. Some staff and some of the leadership in the Facilities Section were afraid that most of the staff at the Institute would see the retooling as a kind of "secondhand store" approach to a complex problem and wanted to be sure working with the existing line of furniture was a viable alternative before initiating the Test Site project. As a result of the concern, the second phase of the User's Perspective project started with an open house for the entire Institute. Over 400 staff members gave feedback on the pro-

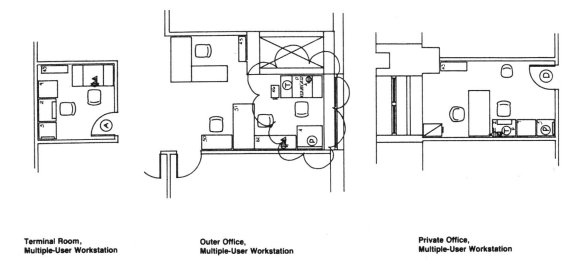

Terminal Room,
Multiple-User Workstation

Outer Office,
Multiple-User Workstation

Private Office,
Multiple-User Workstation

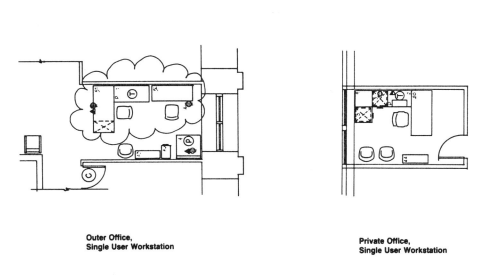

Outer Office,
Single User Workstation

Private Office,
Single User Workstation

Figure 3.1 Office Automation project: Types of test sites investigated during the furniture field tests.

posal to retool existing furniture at the event, which featured examples of the modified furniture on display as well as off-the-shelf office automation furniture for staff to see and compare. Facilities section staff were stationed throughout the exhibition area to explain some of the features of the options under consideration. The open house was followed by another workshop with administrative officers and those designated to receive test furniture installations. This workshop, designed to review the proposed Test Site project, also confirmed that staff perceived the idea of retooling existing furniture to be worthy of testing. The users, now "co-researchers," were invited to evaluate the entire test-site protocol, challenging and in some cases modifying the approach.[9] For example, the participants in the test site wanted to add an open log of their experiences to a structured set of essay-type questions they were to respond to at the end of each day. The log became a valuable tool for recording experiences with test furniture.

The process and results of the inquiry were designed to receive different insights and to take advantage of them. It was never too late to have an influence. Even now the Office Automation program is still making adjustments to office standards, furniture inventory, and procedures for installation. The process and the product of our work facilitated repair and commitment to the repair process. Almost a decade after the work started on office automation, the Institute supervisory staff has reported that what were once chronic complaints on the furniture line have virtually disappeared. The Institute continues to work with the same basic inventory of furniture items designed during the project, adding approximately $1 million of new furniture a year because of increases in Institute staff size and the need for inventory replacement. After the initial $7 million renovation and new furniture procurement process, the Institute is now fully automated and continues to experiment with new technology and workspace relationships.

The Library Move

It was to be the Library's fourth move in eleven years; its last move had been five years prior to the scheduled move date. It added insult to injury when the Library staff understood that they were not moving to another part of the building but were instead being moved out of the overcrowded Institute headquarters building and into leased space three blocks up the street. As one might guess, there was considerable anger about being told to move out, even while there was recognition that existing conditions were overcrowded. To a large extent the Library staff attributed their current unsatisfactory condition to the Facilities Section. Many staff were present for the earlier move, which they described as having been "done to them." Their expectations were that this move would be as bad, and they were not optimistic about the results.

The Library director was new, hired only six months prior to

TABLE 3.1
Office Automation project: Furniture modification chart based on test-site results.

DESCRIPTION	FIRST GENERATION

TABLES AND PRINTER STANDS

Terminal Table

The terminal table is fast becoming the basic piece of furniture. Two different tables were developed in the first generation (adjustable top and articulated keyboard). The first was found unsuccessful; modifications were made to the dimensions of the other. A new unit, the corner terminal table, is being evaluated along with a unit to be placed on top of an existing desk frame.

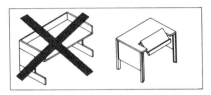

Printer Stands

There are many types of printers used: very small units and some large units which, when covered with an acoustical hood, need large surface space. Two printer stands were tested; the larger one was abandoned because it was too bulky and inaccessible. The smaller unit was modified to facilitate loading and to accept almost all of the large printers.

Corner Table

The corner table was designed to be used as a building block in the modular system to facilitate the design of L- or U-shaped configurations. It was modified to accommodate wire management and its measurements were adjusted to fit other units exactly.

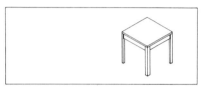

STORAGE UNITS

Storage Units

Desk storage units were developed to fit into existing desks or special frames. Even this additional storage did not meet the needs for more and varied storage; additional units were designed, and the basic terminal table was designed to receive one or more of these units.

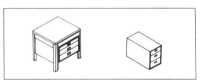

CPU Storage

The CPU storage unit was designed to house the central processing unit and to get it off the desk. It was abandoned because of heat build-up and difficulty in servicing the unit once installed. The work-surface problem is adjusted by designing the basic terminal table to accept the CPU along one of the inside walls and by the creation of overhead storage to remove other things from the work surface.

Vertical Storage

Storage is of primary concern for all test-site participants. The original five-tiered bookcase will continue to be used where there is sufficient space; however, most workstations require the vertical storage unit, which can be placed on top of an existing work surface to adequately provide storage within limited square-footage space allocations.

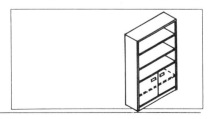

TABLE 3.1
(Continued)

SECOND GENERATION

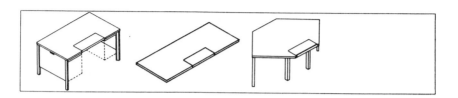

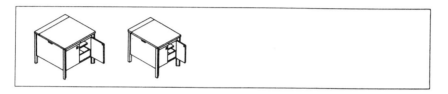

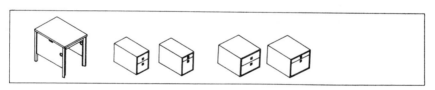

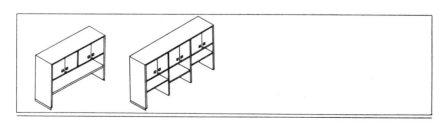

the initiation of move planning. He was explicit about his perception that the Library staff had some major organizational problems, and his superiors had given him the task of changing what they saw as a "contentious and fractious" staff. He specifically requested that the Facilities Section use the moving process to aid his overall effort to build more coherent work teams as the Library staff decided what the nature of their new home should be.

The Library director's request for staff involvement in the process was a confirmation of their knowledge and experience. Library patrons were also included in the programming, design review, and move planning; their current experience with Library operations was an important source of insight to the Library staff and Facilities Section. In addition, patron representatives communicated the changes in Library location and operation to the broader public of Library users.

The knowledge and experience of the Facilities Section team assigned to the Library move were also central to the project because they understood the building systems, interior design, and resource constraints, and they knew the history of the Library's moves. The teamwork between the Facilities staff, the Library staff, its patrons, and our consulting team provided four critical perspectives that had to be related in the final move.[10] All of these different kinds of knowledge were confirmed through explicit inclusion, and each served as a source of interrogation for the others. The process of creating this relationship involved a broad public exchange of information and accountable decision making.

Unlike the Office Automation program, the Library Move project began with a very pragmatic and clearly stated scope of services. We were asked to develop the new space program for the Library, develop activity zoning diagrams, participate in design and construction review meetings, and consult on the process and planning for the actual physical move. The development of the process by which we would contribute to the move, however, was not dictated but emerged from group interviews and workshops with all participants. The sessions were used to clarify emerging goals each participant had for the work, both to illustrate their basic compatibility and to identify sources of possible conflict.

By the conclusion of the initial interviews, the goals were summarized in two categories: (1) the technical competence of the physical design and the moving-in process; and (2) the further development of the Library as an organization. Physical design

TABLE 3.2
Furniture for the automated office: diagrams illustrating the inventory of furniture at the conclusion of the Test Site project.

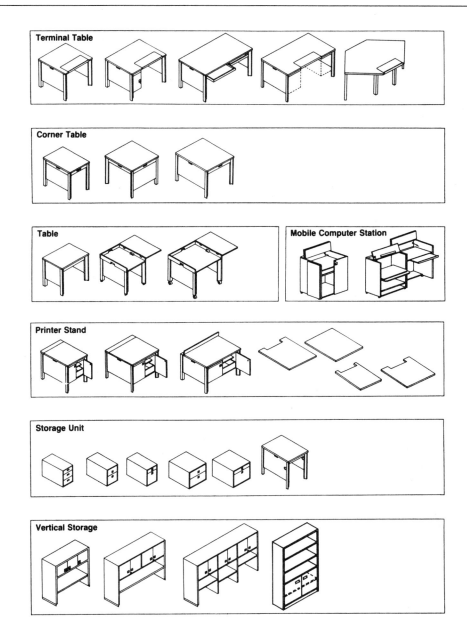

needed to address issues such as crowding, natural light, territorial distinctions, and the increasing demand for automation. Furthermore, the moving process itself needed to be "smooth" and result in a minimum of service disruption and downtime. Concerns for organizational development were addressed using the process of design and moving management to facilitate staff commitment, improve internal relations within the Library, and mitigate staff's and patrons' negative reactions to the move. Client relations, as part of the organizational development agenda, focused on sustaining and improving relations between the Library and the Facilities Section and between the Library and its patrons.

The full Library staff, patrons, the Facilities Section, and the consulting team were involved in a series of interviews, workshops, and briefing sessions throughout the project, all of which were designed to elicit goals and programming information and to clarify values. The agenda for these events included collecting key programming information, making trade-offs prompted by the envelope of the leased space, and identifying anticipated problems with the delivery of patron service during and after the move. Action strategies were brainstormed and tested on larger audiences as needs dictated. The collaborations were fluid and iterative and often involved changes in program, design, or move processes based on new insight.

For example, asking Library unit heads and their staffs to describe individual perceptions of the unit missions provided the groups with functional information, affirmed common ground, and led them to question relationships between units. They each had to tell a stranger who they were, why they were important to the operation of the Library, and what they thought they needed to improve their role. The process revealed contradictions in staff reports on who was responsible for what and on how work was performed. In displaying these different descriptions, the process clarified the organizational structure, unit responsibilities, and related work flow. The subsequent discussions with the units resulted in their rethinking and redesigning internal functions and priorities.

A meeting with selected representatives of frequent and not-so-frequent Library users was instrumental in clarifying patron perceptions of the Library's services and gave insights into how to communicate the effects of the change to all of the Library's patrons. The process in these meetings was very direct: We simply asked the representatives to describe what they saw the Library's

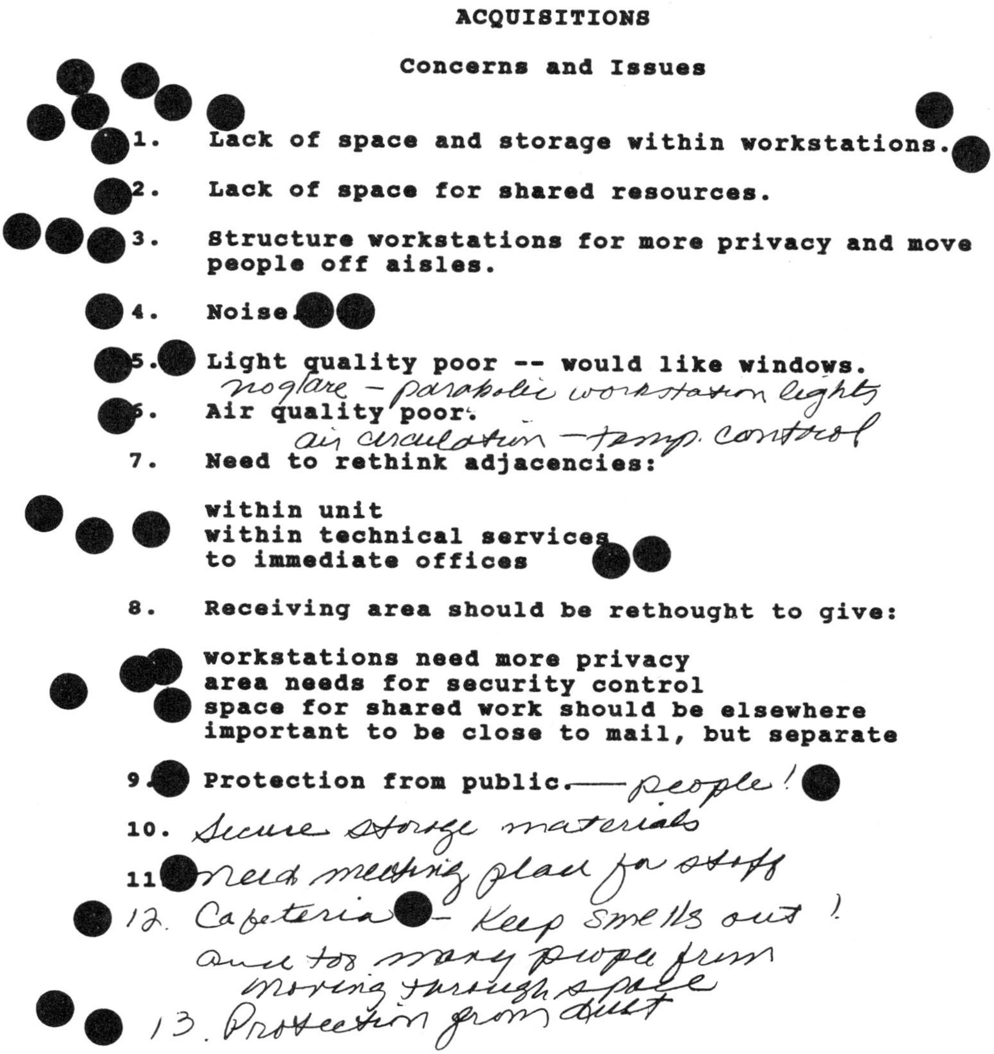

ACQUISITIONS

Concerns and Issues

1. Lack of space and storage within workstations.
2. Lack of space for shared resources.
3. Structure workstations for more privacy and move people off aisles.
4. Noise.
5. Light quality poor -- would like windows.
   noglare — parabolic workstation lights
6. Air quality poor.
   air circulation — temp. control
7. Need to rethink adjacencies:

   within unit
   within technical services
   to immediate offices

8. Receiving area should be rethought to give:

   workstations need more privacy
   area needs for security control
   space for shared work should be elsewhere
   important to be close to mail, but separate

9. Protection from public.— *people !*

10. *Secure storage materials*

11. *need meeting place for staff*

12. *Cafeteria* — *Keep smells out !*
    and too many people from moving through space

13. *Protection from dust*

Figure 3.2 Wall charts of tentative concerns and issues raised during initial interviews in the Library units were displayed in workshops with staff, discussed at length, amended, and then rank ordered in terms of relative importance indicated by using different color dots.

role in the Institute to be, how they engaged the Library, and what they saw its strengths and weaknesses to be. In addition, we informed the patrons about the planning for the move and recorded their concerns and suggestions regarding how to notify their colleagues about the details of the move schedule and the new location. These patron representatives became an informal advisory group that followed the project, offering comments relevant to patrons at several stages in program and design development.

In addition to our goal of organizational development within the Library and between the Library and its patrons, we also worked to build a better relationship between the Library and the Facilities Section project team. We had no wish to place ourselves between the Facilities Section and its client, and we therefore did not present ourselves as an umpire between competing forces but rather as one of a large number of players on the same team. Toward this end, a member of the Facilities Section participated in most of the interviewing done by the consulting team during the data collection phase of the project. Facilities staff also attended all the briefing sessions and helped to facilitate a workshop for the full Library staff. The teaming enabled the evolution of personal relationships between Library staff and Facilities staff, while it familiarized the Facilities Section with the full range of Library concerns. Yet this process commanded only a fraction of the time that would have been required of the Facilities staff had a consultant not been available to organize the interviews, identify key conflicts for resolution, and summarize the resulting framework for decision making in brief interview reports. Eventually, the interior designers on staff in the Facilities Section concluded the detailed individual interviews of Library staff, building on the group work that was a part of the planning process. These interviews ultimately resulted in the development of detailed workstation layouts with individual members of the Library staff.

Each document reporting findings or results of interviews, workshops, or evaluations of existing space conditions produced was widely distributed as a draft. Comments on the drafts were public and often involved hands-on markup sessions during which conflicts were identified and resolved in small-group work settings and reviewed for implications by the larger audience. Participants were asked to comment, so that data on "how things are" might be examined from the perspective of "how they should be." Descriptive information was presented in chart or briefing form along with tentative understanding of the implications of such information. As such, participants were invited to add value to descriptive data, preparing it for decision making.

The pivotal event in data collection and interpretation during the project was a workshop with the entire Library staff. The event put the staff to work in small groups to review the detailed information that had been collected on their organization, activities, work flow, issues, and priorities. Outlines and flow charts were enlarged to wall-chart size and annotated in this public review session.

During the workshop the charts and diagrams describing the work of each unit were revised and annotated by the Library personnel. They used this information and their own experience during a "mini–design charette" to collaboratively diagram their ideal library configuration. Each unit was given a stack of green cards with the name of a different staff member printed on each card. Additional green cards were also issued with the names of individual areas identified as necessary for their work, as well as the tools they used such as book carts, copy machines, binding machines, and so forth. The staff in individual Library units were asked to consider their own needs and to literally diagram their unit as they wanted to see it. They were then asked to locate related units on the diagram, illustrating which units they saw as central to their functions and which as more peripheral. The names of all the other

TABLE 3.3
Key design and moving process issues derived from interviews and workshops with library staff.

DESIGN ISSUES

1. Increase and organize *space within workstations.*
2. Provide *dedicated space for shared resources* between and within Library's units.
3. Address concerns for direct access to *natural light* and good *air quality.* Reduce *noise.*
4. Restructure *periodicals stacks.*
5. Address *systemwide concerns:* mail/messenger service, equipment distribution and constraints, security and life safety.
6. Establish satellite *reference center at headquarters building.*
7. *Redefine location and responsibilities* for travel, research papers, reserve periodicals, and other special collections.
8. Redesign *receiving area and mail room.*
9. Rationalize *part-time staff workstation allocations.*
10. Provide *coat, umbrella, and boot storage.*
11. Improve *wayfinding and boundary conditions* between patron and staff areas.
12. Provide flexibility and capacities for *wiring computing equipment.*
13. Limit access to *unsecured materials and terminals.*

MOVE PROCESS ISSUES

1. *Move the collection only once*; incorporate reorganizations into move planning.
2. Coordinate the movement of the *shelves and stack frames*; have stack frames ready at new location.
3. *Minimize staff downtime, reduction in services, and Library closing* during the move.

units and joint areas of the Library were listed on white cards. The unit staff discussed, negotiated, and finally "designed" their unit among themselves and suggested their desired relationship to the rest of the Library. After each unit team taped its cards on large newsprint sheets in such a way as to show agreed-on relationships, they made special annotations with markers indicating concerns for such issues as privacy, controlled access, and patron movement.

The charette results included diagrams, annotated flow charts, organizational charts, and brainstormed lists of conditions to keep or change that were all used on comparing visions of the future Library. Areas of conflict and agreement about the vision were clarified and openly discussed between units. Where conflict was evident, the logic of each position was diagrammed and discussed in the large–group setting. In virtually all cases, the group review of alternative diagrams and relationships led to an agreement about the principles that should be employed in the layout of the Library. These principles were written as patterns and employed in final design development in a manner that enabled staff to hold the design development accountable to their deliberations.

It was important to the Library staff to maintain this kind of accountability throughout the construction and moving process. As a result, the Library director assigned members of his staff to Facilities teams responsible for such issues as sign systems, stacks organization, moving sequence, and computer data connections. He also sent representatives to regularly scheduled construction and move coordination meetings. The representatives worked hard at keeping the staff of the units informed of issues and progress and helped with "rumor control." All of these interviews and workshops, and committee participation, gave the Library personnel an opportunity to practice both teamwork and interteam coordination outside their routine. The story of the way the move was occurring became a metaphor for thinking about other interunit coordination problems.

The actual Library move was accomplished with surprising grace over one weekend, and the staff settled into their new expanded facility with a modified organizational structure that both fit their new facility and their new understanding of work relationships. The dialogic space in which the entire process was planned and implemented was characterized by a climate of positive regard in which conflict and struggle as well as openness and confirmation made it possible for issues to be brought forward and resolved.

ACQUISITIONS

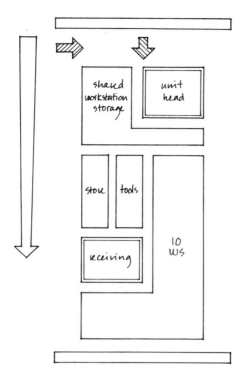

1. Ordering people must be adjacent to tools.
2. Wilson-Anderson should be in position to supervise receiving.
3. Casella's should be adjacent to Neider.
4. "Stor" area should be locked storage.
5. Workstations in receiving should be somehow indicated / separated within receiving area.

Figure 3.3 Diagram of the Acquisitions staff work area derived from their design workshop.

Reflections: Self-Correcting Work

The two stories we have told are simply two events in the on-going work of facilities management in this particular organization. The management and maintenance of a facility and its people are

TABLE 3.4
A typical pattern constructed by staff to help guide design development of the new library.

PATTERN: Territorial Markers and Boundaries

Units within the Library require clear definition for new staff, mail/messenger service, and (on occasion) patron traffic. All units within the Library should have their own place for mail, phone messages, and limited supply storage. Within the technical services, include a small table and chairs for required layout space that cannot be accommodated in the individual workspaces.

Therefore:

Use the unit mail, message, and supply storage area as unit identifiers. Locate the central point places in the units convenient to unit head offices to allow for casual contact. Consider the installation of artwork or other identifiers to mark these places. Within reasonable limits, be generous with the circulation space surrounding such a central point to encourage communication.

---

never-ending and repetitive jobs—very similar to housework, as we will discuss in the last section of this chapter. The Office Automation program and the Library Move project were marked as events within the flow of work, and certainly our intervention in these two projects had a beginning and an end. But for the people who work in facilities, they are simply parts of a much larger project.

The Facilities Section does not get to leave when a job is over; they remain to care for both the project and its inhabitants long after completion. Such dynamics influence the motivation for work and reinforce the desire to maintain positive working relationships with one's constituency over the long haul. It is part of the open dynamic that never completely finishes any task. The job is to retain enough confirmation to permit a perception of temporary closure while concurrently being open—to new personnel and to organizational and technological changes.

This condition—of needing to finish work and at the same time leaving the conditions open for other changes—requires an approach that focuses on the facilitation of repair and the possibility of self-correcting work processes. There is no way to "fix" anything once and for all; too many variables are shifting within the modern workplace to secure anything over the long term. Therefore self-correcting work seeks out, confirms, and protects what is perceived as good while concurrently correcting or improving what is problematic or in need of repair.[11]

In the next section we share some thoughts about our work within the context of an organization such as the Institute, including the approach we have adopted and the manner in which goals and methods are negotiated in order to frame action. Consulting in the context of the public housework performed at the Institute is a special location for the practice of placemaking. We end this chapter with some reflections about housework and about the possibilities it offers to make beloved places while also contributing to organizational development agendas.

Approach

At the Institute our approach to placemaking always involved a mix of actions defined through collaboration with those people most affected by the project at hand. In all cases the question of who should participate became an early and open question within the dialogue. Often there was agreement that those most affected should be informed and given an ability to influence decisions. This turned out to be both a moral standpoint regarding the need for people to control their own lives and a practical standpoint directly related to the knowledges and commitment needed to get a job done well. The "who to include" question can then be answered through a review of stakeholders in the change process being considered, where *stakeholder* is understood to apply to both individuals and organizational units who need to contribute to the process of self-correction.[12]

The potential for self-correction must, of course, extend to management in a hierarchical organization. Most managers we encountered at the Institute agreed that projects most often fail because of errors in the implementation process. These same managers, however, also tended to remove themselves from such implementation because they believed in delegating authority and in staying out of the details. They did not want to be micromanagers. Often we would be retained to work in "the in-between," to connect the details of implementation with management decisions.

Within each project, the scope and approach to participation were carefully designed to relate specifically to the leadership style of those who commissioned us, as well as to those who sought the services of the Facilities Section. Some projects started with our being asked to avoid staff involvement. Yet, even in those projects where decisions were to be made by "authority" according to routine procedures, access was eventually encouraged by the same authorities as an essential part of the evolving scope of work. It simply became clear during the course of continued confirmation and interrogation that some types of information were needed but not accessible without involving staff. As consultants, we did not have the desire or power to force management to back down from previously held positions, but we often found they would expand on a limited-access directive based on the need for additional information.

Some of the commissions at the Institute did not appear "important" enough to involve a wide constituency or to affect a large number of people. All of these situations were handled through fairly routine "staff work" in which the senior leadership of each unit decided who would play a part and to what extent. Our approach to interrogating limited involvement is directly related to how much commitment to action is required from those who are excluded from participation. Our experience suggests that increased involvement and real ability to influence decisions leads to increased commitment to action and to the potential for self-correction.[13]

The idea that an "administrative decision" requires less collaboration than other types of decisions tends to dissolve during processes of confirmation and interrogation like those employed at the Institute. The metaphor of the telephone procurement as an administrative decision continues to be the most convincing story in support of avoiding such conclusions. At the same time, there are clearly some decisions that warrant wide involvement and others that require only a small number of participants.

Another aspect of our approach in facility management relates to the process of work itself. Initial data collection related to goal formulation becomes a way of confirming staff experience and an integral part of how the same staff comes to interrogate the nature of their place and their work. As often as not, the same data collection process becomes the action framing process. It is difficult to discern when the processes of information collection, confirmation, and interrogation become a detailed definition of project scope or a proposal for making a decision.

Most institutions that build, renovate, or move offices employ a simple sequential process that first develops a program of design requirements and then acquires approval for the requirements coupled with early cost estimates. The process then proceeds to the development of design responses to the requirements and budget. Such a process is consistent with many textbooks on programming and design that clearly demarcate the close of a phase of collecting information on requirements and the beginning of a design decision process based on "approved" requirements.[14] In the Institute work, we tried to suspend the end of the information collection phase of work until well into design development, so people would be informed about the design implications of their initial assumptions about requirements. It was important to give people an opportunity to adjust their understanding of requirements after seeing them used in design. For example, when some members of the Library staff saw the standard square-foot allocations to their workstations in a draft statement of the program, they were pleased to find what seemed a generous 90 square feet instead of the cramped 65 square feet of their existing conditions. They offered their tentative approval of the size of the new workstations. When they saw the furnished workstations in preliminary design, however, and diagrams that showed how book carts and other equipment might be used within the space, they adjusted their understanding of requirements upward and requested a total of 110 square feet. The examination of special functions through design became part of the justification for an increase in standard office sizes for several specific Library functions. This process of situating knowledge while designing and allowing the design to modify programmatic requirements is an important departure from more traditional decision-making processes in facilities work.

Projecting accurate cost estimates early in the development of a project may be seen as a barrier to suspending judgment on what is known until it is fully situated in the design. The Institute's approach to this process has been to start with a generous estimate based on the number of people moving, the types of workstations envisioned, and the volume of shared space and net-to-gross area ratios that can be roughly anticipated due to the available building envelope. The budgeting process is robust and flexible within each project and across projects. The estimate is revisited on occasion throughout design development in the project. In short, the Institute has adopted an approach to facility management that keeps both historical cost experience and well-documented requirements in sight throughout the moving process and allows design to be one of the ways to situate such information in the specifics of current conditions. Neither cost nor program requirements represent the absolute final word without the use of design development and discussion.

Still another aspect of the work approach is deciding what an intervention is really about. It is often difficult for professionals such as ourselves to suspend judgment about the nature of a problem, the aspirations of a given public, or the selection of the most fitting methods of inquiry. In the dialogic space there is a constant struggle to resist arriving at premature closure or classification of a problem. The discussion often invokes the metaphors of past practice in order to help select the goals and methods. But the metaphors are not employed in the manner of self-fulfilling prophesies. Instead, they are used to help differentiate the specific project at hand from ones that seem to be profoundly like it, thus confirming and interrogating the relationship. In this fashion, we are able to use the gifts of past practice without succumbing to the oppressive or demotivating characterization that "this project is just like that one." In truth, we have never found one project to be just like another.

Although we attempt to suspend judgments in our placemaking work, we are quick to move into speculation or tentative judgment. These tentative assertions become catalysts for dialogue rather than marking the end of dialogue. This has had the beneficial effect of extending the search for shared goals, finding the unique as well as common aspects of the presenting problem, and exploring the presenting problem's more far-reaching implications. The practice in our office is to decide on the nature of a project both early and often, remaking the decision frequently during project development.

We always attempt to keep the approach to work fluid and to offer the decisions regarding inclusion, goals, methods, and action as points of discussion. Placing these questions within the dialogic space has often avoided false distinctions between types of decisions, management and staff, and professional and layperson, thus contributing to the possibility that the work engaged is understood and self-correcting.

Goals

Goals and work approach tended to be the dominant topics of discussion at the beginning of every project at the Institute, and they were topics that were revisited often throughout the project. There was usually an initial series of interviews and workshops that developed and publicly tested goals for the effort. In preparing for small-group meetings to clarify goals and develop an approach, we often conducted interviews with the principals in the project and reviewed any background correspondence or literature that might further illuminate the goal structure of the project. As a result, a tentative beginning statement of goals was usually prepared as a catalyst for discussion, and some items that surfaced in individual interviews became public early in the process.

After the interviewing process, we usually began discussions on goals using small groups and brainstorming methods. Even at this point, we resisted making judgments about problem types or solution types that appeared to emerge from the initial exposure to the problem. We chose to wait for the problem and action framing to emerge in the dialogue. Inevitably, the process of generating expansive lists of possible goal orientations to a project or presenting problem revealed relationships to other ongoing work and hidden possibilities in the original presenting problem. When circumstances dictated that the scope be more narrow, precluding the addition of new agendas, we would record the additional presenting problems for address at a later date.

As our firm developed a history with the Institute, it became easier for us to interrogate the relationships between projects and the strategic development of the institution. The Integrated Procurement System project is instructive because of the way it involved several overlapping jurisdictions and revealed legitimate new agendas beyond the scope of the initial presenting problem. Parties to the discussion of the proposed system included procurement specialists, budget analysts, people responsible for inventory control, computer hardware and software specialists, contract managers, loading-dock administrators, and so on. As goals came to be revealed in the group discussions, it was clear that the accounting functions of the procurement system were only a small part of the return various units wanted from the effort. Coordination of computer, furniture, and workspace preparation procurement were cited as some of the possible products of a well-developed system. Minimizing the steps and records needed for inventory control was another. Several participants representing their respective organizations saw the procurement process as a way to coordinate or control more of the variables that affected their ability to do a good job. As a result, there was early maneuvering for a reorganization and consolidation of control that was implicit in the brainstormed lists of goals and was acknowledged by all participants when interpreted in the discussions following the brainstorming. An outgrowth of the effort was to name the tension between centralized control of the procurement process, and the corresponding need to put the procurement tool closest to those who needed it to conduct their work. Acknowledging the tension enabled work on the less ambitious procurement system goals related to accounting and invoicing to proceed while the tougher problems and acts of broader inclusion in the dialogic space progressed on a different time line. Prior to our commission, work on the specifics of the system was stalled because of relatively hidden control agendas.

An open goal–framing process at the beginning of a project has the benefit of offering a forum in which staff can offer their interpretation of a project, including discomfort, anger, and fears. In one commission, some of the staff expressed suspicion that a new technology in printing production was likely motivated by management's desire to reduce its vulnerability to labor actions (such as requests for sick leave and rejection of overtime requests). Making the fear explicit by naming it publicly made both the fear and the exploration of its implications a legitimate part of the project goals rather than the stuff of rumor and myth. The transformation of potential hidden agendas in goals clarification can occur at any time during the process of project development, significantly altering goals and methods of work and contributing to constituent commitment. [15]

However, not all issues can be open to discussion because some goals are "given" by the senior administration and are not open to negotiation. To the extent that the rationale for such goals can be presented, they become understood as part of the media with which the groups work. As such, mandated goals become integrated with the interests and concerns of participants and become related to the ongoing work effort of the participants.

For example, at the beginning of the Library project we interrogated the idea of the move, asking the Library director what could and what could not be influenced by the deliberations to follow. His response was clear that the question of whether to move was not open, in part because the decision to move was based on much broader concerns than those of the Library and its role in the Institute. His answer and the rationale were openly discussed with the Library personnel. Staff resisted the closed nature of the decision, and in early interviews and group work they presented their arguments to expand the Library in its present location rather than move to leased space outside of the headquarters building. These arguments were presented to management, considered, and accepted as legitimate even though management still directed the Library to move. However, the information and arguments presented during this exchange were very helpful in understanding programmatic requirements, acquiring further resources for the move, and in getting increased operational support resources after the move. As a result, the new facility has excellent access to daylight, large and well-furnished lounge and reading areas, new automation equipment, a custom-made circulation desk at its heart, and an expanded allocation of messenger service resources because of its remote location. Many offices are larger than the office standard in order to accommodate specific work tasks that do not fit neatly into conventional offices. There are numerous plants and prominent displays of international art throughout the new Library facility. Thus, even though the decision to move was not open, the implications of the decision were open to influence by the Library personnel. Discussion on the decision to move also helped management to be fully informed about the increased difficulty they could anticipate in the receipt of Library services; they better understood the importance of eventually reintegrating the Library with an expanded headquarters complex.[16]

Another aspect of the Library project demonstrates the power of influencing goals even in the context of not being able to change an administrative decision. After some discussion, staff came forward to express their discomfort with the apparent, but honestly unintended, denigration of their importance to the headquarters functions implied by the move. As a result of this perception, a goal emerged in the project, supported by the administration, to establish the conditions whereby the Library staff, the patrons, and the management would see the move of the Library as an enhancement of status. This goal named the issue and allowed participants to explore their perception of what constitutes status in their workplace. Status, per se, became a legitimate issue.

A scarcity of available resources for the Library move could have resulted in a very different physical arrangement, with fewer amenities, less address to status, and highly constrained or crowded physical conditions. Even so, the open process of goals formulation created conditions in which people could make the best of whatever situation they were given. The process also generated and shared enough information to frame projects of resistance if required. The open process does not promise a satisfactory result, only a very clear one that can help to frame future action. Comparing collaborative expressions of goals with available possibilities can create a tension that can be used to further identify who should be included in the ongoing planning process.

The process of goals formation and goals clarification is essential to self-correcting work. It facilitates repair by leaving the dialogic space open for participants to continually revisit and update goals, reconsider insights into the culture and circumstances of institutions, develop or modify methods of work, and decide what should be included or excluded from consideration for the moment. Making and remaking goals helps to establish a continuous, self-correcting, and critical practice that relates and redefines intentions and ways of working.

Methods

There is no single way of working—no method or group of methods—that can be used routinely to create an environment conducive to critical self-correction in placemaking, or that clarify goals and frame action consistent with the purposes of the participants in achieving environmental and organizational change. In our work with the Institute we often used existing methods, adapting them to specific situations, or invented new methods and ways of working. In each different context, a method was selected because it opened dialogue, clarified the goals relevant to each project through confirmation and interrogation, and facilitated the framing of action through processes of inclusion and exclusion.

Like other professionals, we employed contemporary social science, design, and/or engineering methodologies in our work. But we avoided simple applications in favor of *situating* methods, transforming them in collaboration with our clients. On occasion we would use a textbook questionnaire, observation, or interview method, but the resulting analysis was always made vulnerable to review in the dialogic space. Furthermore, methods, whether standard or socially constructed within the project, were not given sacred or privileged status as the most "technically correct."[17] They did not dictate what we or our constituents could do. Our methods of work evolved as the problems to be addressed were revealed in their full complexity and as the participants in the work exercised free and informed choice about a range of possible ways to proceed.

Deciding how to proceed, that is, which methods to employ, was part of the discussions in the dialogic space created at the beginning of each project. It often involved our immersion in the details of place, in the worldviews of project participants, and in their daily work life. At the Institute, we were fortunate in having established a relationship that permitted us to negotiate open-ended and general scope-of-work statements in which to begin work before the entire project was clear.

In the Library Move project, for example, it was necessary to relate the total Library mission to the individual unit missions, employee activities, and individual personnel job descriptions. Our work with the staff led to detailed descriptions of what was done on a daily basis, what materials were involved, what communication still had to occur, and how it would occur. One of the products of this immersion in the Library project was a rather complex work-flow diagram, the "Path of the Book." The path diagram, in matrix fashion, related the physical movement of any book to the various individual tasks being performed. Among other things, this analysis revealed what was, and was not, book-related. Contrary to our experience with ordinary libraries, this specialized library had many functions not directly related to the housing-of-the-books image traditionally associated with a library. The Library also served as the corporate mail and distribution center for the entire organization. The detailed path description revealed the need to enlarge staff workstations for material processing, to redesign the mailroom, and to relocate it in relation to other units. It further led to a reconceputalization of the desired "Path of the Book," which changed adjacency relationships between work teams within and between Library units.

No method told us to develop the "Path of the Book," how to do it, or how it should be collaboratively interpreted. The desire to document the process emerged from our collective intuitions about its relative importance. It was helpful for what it revealed about the management of materials, because it demonstrated how much Library staff time was consumed in other corporate support functions. These insights established the basis for reviewing the goals of the Library and its mission—to revalue and reconfirm that the Library did what it did on purpose or to suggest changes based on the same reflections.

Situating methods appropriate to context in a way that facilitates self-correction often challenges the perspectives of some partici-

TABLE 3.5
Example of using traditional social science methods. Participant comments on furniture to support Office Automation program.

| # RESPONDENTS | PRIVATE OFFICE | | | | | | OUTER OFFICE | | | | | | TERMINAL ROOM | | GRAND TOTAL | |
| | SINGLE N = 10 | | MULTI N = 2 | | TOTAL N = 12 | | SINGLE N = 6 | | MULTI N = 12 | | TOTAL N = 18 | | MULTI N = 12 | | N = 42 | |
	#	%	#	%	#	%	#	%	#	%	#	%	#	%	#	%
FURNITURE																
Inadequate work surface	2	20	0		2	17	3	50	8	67	11	61	4	33	17	41
Storage problems	7	70	2	100	9	75	5	83	10	83	15	83	10	83	34	81
Chair problems	2	20	2	100	4	33	3	50	4	33	7	39	3	25	14	33
Insufficient amount of furniture	2	20	0	0	2	17	0	0	0	0	0	0	1	8	3	7
Furniture does not meet requirements	2	20	0	0	2	17	1	17	0	0	1	16	2	17	5	12
Furniture does not fit workspace	1	10	0	0	1	8	3	50	3	25	6	33	2	17	9	21
Poor design of furniture components	3	30	1	50	4	33	5	83	8	67	13	72	10	83	27	64
LAYOUT / DESIGN PROBLEMS																
Poor relationship adjacencies	7	70	2	100	9	75	3	50	7	58	10	56	9	75	28	67
Inadequate floor areas	0	0	0	0	0	0	1	17	2	17	3	17	6	50	9	21
Wire management	5	50	1	50	6	50	5	83	8	66	13	72	3	25	22	52
Privacy	1	10	0	0	1	8	4	66	5	42	9	50	0	0	10	24
ENVIRONMENTAL CONDITIONS																
Lighting	6	60	1	50	7	58	3	50	6	50	9	50	6	50	22	52
Acoustics	2	20	2	100	4	32	4	66	7	58	11	61	9	75	24	57
OTHER																
Installation	1	10	1	50	2	17	2	33	0	0	2	11	0	0	4	10
Hardware equipment	3	30	0	0	3	25	2	33	3	25	5	28	3	25	11	26

pants. For example, some staff at the Institute were comfortable with the more empirical ways to measure preference in the Test Site project, while other staff distrusted the very same measures. Most were comfortable with the test-site protocol that employed both empirical measures and more open-ended and qualitative assessments, that is, different ways of working.

In each of our many interventions at the Institute, we employed, found, or invented ways of working that facilitated dialogue and action to achieve negotiated goals. In all cases, we attempted to create the possibility that the work itself would be self-correcting and open to the ongoing processes of environmental and organizational change.

Framing Action

The dynamics inherent in the aspiration for self-correcting work at times require a professional to suspend judgment, not only about goals and methods, but about action framing as well. What might appear to be a relatively straightforward project often becomes quite complex. It is our experience that the continually shifting world of managing a facility often demands the adjustment of goals and methods within a critical framework, but sometimes it requires the suspension of definitive action altogether.

A classic example of the latter is the decade of work at the Institute on Office Automation Workspace Standards. Standards for the Institute's offices were derived in part from the Office Automation program presented earlier. They have been rapidly evolving as understanding of office automation continues to emerge. However, there is tremendous resistance to their formal codification, and various attempts to produce standards have always been met with new discussions and dialogue. The direction for our continuing efforts on the Office Automation Workspace Standards projects shifts between the poles of maximum opportunity for the free and informed choice by employees, on the one hand, to the maximum of simplicity and economy of scale for the inventory, design, and installation process, on the other hand. At different times in this search for the "illusive standard," wide cross sections of the Institute have participated, while at other times there has been a tendency to adhere closely to the standards as an internal guide for the work of the Facilities Section.

The increased complexity of the office environment has taken the administrative officers of the Institute from the position of wanting a large amount of participation to wishing for the simplified application of routine standards without much consultation —"It all used to be so simple," is the nostalgic comment. The still-emerging complexity of equipment use and work-flow dynamics in the modern office establishes a continuing pressure for something more sophisticated than standard applications by rote. Facilities staff, like the administrative officers, are equally conflicted by the desire for the simplicity of standard applications, recognizing that the variables of the building architecture and infrastructure, the complexity of equipment use, and the changing nature of the kind of work performed by the staff all require close consultation with constituents. In other words, framing action on standards that might simplify work life for both administrative officers and the Facilities Section by reducing the amount of collaboration required is at odds with the ability to stay current with the dynamics of change.

When the pendulum in the open dialogue between the Facilities Section and the Institute swings explicitly in favor of standard applications, it is as if the administrative officers were saying, "Do the best you can without too much of our staff; if we don't like it, we will complain and renegotiate the standard." This position is in sharp contrast to the stand taken by the same administrative officers after what they still refer to as "the phone fiasco." Unlike the phone project, however, the open dialogue in the Office Automation program permits action and encourages reflection by naming the tension. All parties to the discussion seek to balance standard applications with opportunities for collaboration, keeping the standards question open while concurrently using de facto standards to help frame action.

This state of affairs could be critiqued as inefficient, but we think that the open question of standards and the experimentation with the current version of tentative standards keep the implications of a tremendous revolution in office work under constant scrutiny. The experiment continues just as the changes continue. The lack of closure on exactly what action should be taken is not reprehensible; it is inevitable and altogether appropriate.

Framing action in a changing organizational context is often difficult. At times it requires us to give feedback not explicitly requested about some aspect of the project because of the intimate relationship between environmental and organizational change. Our approach has been to be open about the implications we see, and at times we have prepared brief separate reports of the "in addition we also learned" type.

While programming space with the Computing Services Department of the Institute, for example, we were briefed on a new organizational structure for a division of the department. The structure was a matrix that organized work tasks on one axis and areas of expertise on the other. Because one kind of expertise might be needed in several functional areas, the new structure was intended to increase the flexibility to assemble teams as needed for a wide array of functions. This was a radical change from the previous approach, which organized work by phases of system development. The new approach represented what some staff sarcastically described as the "annual" reorganization designed to keep them from ever getting really good at one way of doing business.

Our mandate was to prepare a space program for the Computing Services Department. To provide physical support for the new organizational structure, we felt we had to know how the department proposed to do work; that is, how it functioned. And yet this request for clarity in functions and work flows appeared to contradict the new matrix organizational structure in which people in different knowledge areas could be assembled in different ways to meet changing functional requirements. As we described this dilemma to the staff in the department, they were happy to translate the knowledge areas into specific work tasks, and in fact, had largely already done so. However, these translations came to look very much like old organizational structure and, for many, seemed like a way of sabotaging the new matrix structure.

As we developed the work-flow diagrams and eventual space-allocation diagrams based on the group interviews, we had the opportunity to raise this contradiction with the head of the department, who had authored the new matrix organization. We asked if there were a contradiction between the general organizational philosophy of shared flexible knowledge resources that could go anywhere they were needed in the matrix, and the concurrent need, revealed in the work flow and space-allocation diagrams, for place-dependent machines and attending experts. We were testing the theory of the new matrix organization chart with the condition of physical planning and implementation in which we were engaged.

The result of the discussion was a clear expression of concern that some aspects of the matrix structure were not yet well understood by his staff, and that the physical zoning actually served well to illustrate where the matrix was very flexible and where it was not. Once this discussion was made public, staff no longer had to surreptitiously translate the "implications of the matrix" for their daily functioning. Clarity emerged from reducing the distance between the organizational matrix and the environmental requirements for work functions. This clarity validated the organizational designer's perception of the need for greater flexibility in the allocation of labor to the work-at-hand, and the staff's perception of the need for well-articulated functional responsibilities related to the location of physical resources that were inherently not flexible.

Once again, the process of framing action at the Institute was dependent on the idea of self-correcting work. During these projects there was a regular examination of work aspirations (the espoused theory) contrasted with the behavior that was actually occurring (the theory-in-use), helping to establish the conditions for critical inquiry into both the ongoing activity of workplace standards development and in the space planning for specific units. Using this particular form of examination kept the dialogic space open even while it framed the nature of the intervening and often self-correcting action. It revealed and legitimated hidden agendas related to fear, control, and status, and it found a way of proceeding in a rapidly changing context.

The office environment of an organization such as the Institute requires flexibility and repeated environmental and organizational restructuring. In light of this condition, the work of facility planning and management needs to be continually open to major changes and minor adjustments. We have found that an approach that focuses on self-correction creates a flexibility in establishing goals, selecting ways of working, and framing action in support of institutional objectives. We have also found that placemaking can become a powerful critical lens through which to view institutional agendas and work processes. All of our work with the Institute can be summarized as a form of public housework that elevates the ordinary acts of organizational and environmental change to the level of potentially strategic and central activities in the life of the organization.

Public Housework

The work of the Facilities Section in the Institute is to maintain and care for the facility and to nurture relationships with the staff, that is, to care about and for the staff and their "house." The Institute stories celebrate what are often stereotyped as the mundane acts of daily housework performed by facilities managers and consultants.[18] Stories about cleaning, move planning, renovation, security, technological support, administrative services, and caring for people make up the bulk of the daily lives of the Facilities Section. The term *public housework* reveals the tension between celebrating what can be liberating, caring work and recognizing its denigration within the dominant culture and its potential as a form of subjugation.

Because the Facilities Section works to maintain the house of the organization, it is not perceived to be engaged in the "real work" of the Institute, international banking. Rather, it provides the support that enables the rest of the Institute staff to work while not bothering about how their place functions. This work, like the work of the domestic sphere that maintains the home and community and that produces children, is essential, but not valued.[19] In modern institutions and organizations, the daily management of the facility is therefore assumed to be removed from the important life of the place.

The housework of maintenance and facility management can be characterized as formless work because there is no end product, or if there is one, it immediately begins to deteriorate or needs changing. The process of taking care of a place is never finished; it is a continuous activity that has no end until the building itself is demolished. The place must always be cleaned, offices are constantly being moved because of new organizational structures and shifts in organizational goals, things break and need to be repaired, and new technologies are introduced and somehow integrated into the ongoing work of the place. All of these activities must be accomplished without interrupting the flow of "real" work in the organization. Furthermore, the housework is rendered invisible by its relatively low status, becoming visible only when it is left undone or done poorly. The work is seldom appreciated or rewarded.

The nature of housework is that it not only cares for and maintains places but is also concerned with the care of people. In other words, it is not enough to keep the house clean or the facility running smoothly. Facilities sections must also maintain the web of relationships between themselves and the people using the facility because these people are intimately bound together by their place. As demonstrated in the "phone fiasco," it does no good to be "right" if the result is the deterioration of the relationship with the people whose place you are maintaining. To do the work of placemaking in a low-trust environment only confounds the possibility of doing the work at all.

If housework in placemaking is unappreciated and devalued, one might well wonder why anyone, given a choice, would choose it as his or her work. One might ask the same questions about why women and some men, in the face of their invisible, yet profound work of caring for and about the home and children, continue to do so. There must be—and there are—rewards that do not fit neatly within the framework of the market economy. Caring for and about places and other people in the domestic sphere is characterized by labor and love within a network of personal relationships in which responsibilities and obligations are intertwined with care and nurturance.

Feminist theorists write of the "ethic of care," which is a useful concept for understanding the nature of a practice such as housework. The ethic of care posits a moral system that is not based on the idea of justice and rights but rather embeds behavior in responsibilities and relationships.[20] The ethic of care is differentiated from an ethic of justice in that decisions are responses to concrete circumstances rather than to universal and abstract ideals. So attempting to answer an abstract question like "Is it ever acceptable to lie?" is rejected in favor of exploring the circumstantial opportunities for developing relationships that might make it necessary or unnecessary to lie. The decision of how to proceed is not based on principles but on human relationships and practices. The rewards of such work are intrinsic to the process of the work of parenting and homemaking—attending to others' emotional needs, providing nutritious meals, and maintaining a safe and secure place to live—rather than being solely invested in a product or in completion of a task.

Housework, like parenting, requires a double focus. One loves and cares for the child as she or he is now, attending to the immediate needs of dealing with a neighborhood bully, the first adolescent crush, getting teeth filled and clothes cleaned. Always, and simultaneously, one holds aspirations and hopes for the longer term, for what the child is becoming—a mature, competent, loving human being. Yet, as anyone who has engaged in these tasks knows, satisfaction is often mixed with resentment, and accomplishment with a sense of burden.

What occurs when caring is brought into the public sphere, as with the Facilities Section of the Institute? Again we find a double focus where one is concerned with the immediate needs of health, life safety, and conflicts between colleagues while simultaneously attending to the long-term social health and viability of the institution and its ability to change as the circumstances of the global economy shift and new technologies emerge. Unlike domestic housework, the labor is now explicitly compensated and carries the status of paid employment in the market economy. Yet it is still marginalized and viewed as secondary to the real work of an organization.[21] And unlike the work of caring in the domestic sphere, there may not be love to balance the labor of the housework. Being *required* to take care of and to care about a place and people creates the condition in which people become alienated from their own feelings—of love, and of frustration and anger at being unappreciated and invisible. The discourse on care also raises the question of what happens when the ethics of care become transformed into a more manipulative "emotion management." The hypocrisy of pretending to care—whether within the caregiver, the recipient of care, or both—results in very real human costs. Alternatively, burnout occurs if the person identifies with the job but sees the work as not being meaningful to others. High turnover rates in the "housework professions" suggest that the condition of requiring love or care may become intolerable.[22]

The reasons given by many for entering into public housework are often an extension of the ethics of care, framed in the language of wanting to be of service, to help others, to extend what they had understood as a value in the domestic world into the public world. The rewards are described in similar terms: Public houseworkers speak about the network of relationships that support the placemaking activities and about their willingness to engage in the double focus of immediate, often mundane tasks while keeping in mind the long-term care of the people in the institution that enables it to continue.

The people in the Facilities Section at the Institute with whom we have worked, many of whom have served with the section for years, are aware of their secondary status within the total organization. Yet they do not define themselves and their contribution in terms of the dominant culture's denigration of housework. They *know* the work they do is invaluable to the Institute; they *know* they are doing a good job; and they continually learn, correcting and adjusting their activities as they come to know better how to practice. They recognize that a critical aspect of their placemaking work is maintaining relationships and responsibilities within the place.[23] They operate from an expansive and public ethic of care in a kind of housework that sustains places and the institution.

It is possible within this public ethic of care to find that the Institute's interests are also being served through increased efficiency, improved corporate image, decreased turnover in personnel, self-correcting work performed by a well-informed staff, and genuine commitment of the workforce to the purposes of the institution. As the work by the Facilities Section became a metaphor at the Institute for how to do other kinds of work, it became a powerful organizational development tool. In the course of asking, "What do you do?" as part of the housework chore of new space planning, we are also able to ask, "Why do you do that?" The "what" question is a form of confirmation and the "why" question is part of the critical practice of interrogation. Using the nonthreatening standpoint of someone interested in housework, we can open a dialogue about the fundamental work procedures and intentions of the organization. The opened dialogue leads to a much broader exploration of intentions for work than might otherwise be possible. Housework is thus a very powerful form of inquiry, organizational development, and critical empowerment.

The same dynamics that make housework a form of organizational development can also make it a form of oppression for both those who do the housework and those for whom it is done. A staff member may be quite willing to identify problems and express frustration about work routine to a space planner but be much less willing to discuss it with the supervisor who invented the routine. If either the space planner or the staff are punished (explicitly or implicitly) for the resulting public description of a problem, then opening a dialogue becomes a source of real oppression. For example, the designer of the matrix organization in a division of the Computing Services Department could have become angry about staff concerns that this concept was dysfunctional relative to a fixed equipment inventory. The staff and Facilities Section report, developed and communicated through us as a constructive critique, could have become the basis for removing us for not being in compliance with the directive to implement the matrix organization. More seriously, this report could also have led to silencing the staff, forcing them to implement the new organization without addressing its problems. Explicit oppression of this type leaves the houseworker and constituent without the ability to confirm the experience of the other or to interrogate it.

A more subtle form of subjugation is also possible in the abuse of a broadly applied ethic of care in the creation of a dialogic space. Skillful managers can keep up the appearance of being open to the potential of critical practice, thus coopting the pressure for change and encouraging people to feel "cared for and cared about" when they are not. This kind of emotion management is more patronizing and oppressive than the clear exercise of overt power. It is a form of seduction in which the deceit emerges slowly over time, making those who helped open the dialogue in good faith a party to their own subjugation. Ultimately such cooptation of the dialogic space is revealed by a lack of commitment to the action framework, which is actually derived outside the space. But the manager may achieve short-term gains if those he or she included in the insincere dialogue willingly suspend their judgment. There may be no defense against such insincerity except confidence in its ultimate failure. In fact, any attempt to defend against it will also serve to collapse the dialogic space and preclude the possibility of a liberating critical practice.[24]

An alternative conception of housework, for which we have argued in this text, removes it from the realm of emotion management and uses a dialogic space to engage all participants in the conversation, empowering all in the space to work without fear of retribution. The first scenario stops dialogue and closes the space while the latter one opens it to a broader audience and to the potential for a shared critical practice.

In agreeing to open the dialogue, people always risk cooptation or worse, and there are no guarantees of benefit. However, in our experience with the Institute, we find that the personal and professional risks to those engaged in public housework—staff, managers, and consultants—are both unavoidable and rewarded. The risks establish the conditions necessary to open and maintain the dialogue, to confirm and interrogate the basic conditions of daily life work, and to frame action relative to that life. As such, the risks are precisely what establish the potential for both personal and organizational development.

The power of domestic housework and the practice of care done in support of maintaining a home—a place and its family—develops the potential of the members of the household as individuals and as a group. Our experience of public housework in organizations such as the Institute is that the same potential exists; well-conceived housework opens the possibility for individual and organizational development by establishing the stories that set expectations for future work. Such work is not, of course, limited to the realm of housework but also spills over into the daily work life and potentially into the strategic direction of the institution. Perhaps one of the reasons for the denigration of both housework and caring in our culture is that such work is an act of subversion with the power to transform oppressive circumstances. The public housework of placemaking has the potential to be a liberating and critical practice of care.

4

THE PRACTICE OF DEMOCRACY: THE ROANOKE NEIGHBORHOOD PARTNERSHIP

This is a story about Roanoke, "the star city" of the Shenandoah Valley in southwestern Virginia, which has struggled to create a structure of governance—a democratic project—in which neighborhoods are major participants.[1] The project's premise is that everyone cares about their neighborhoods and will take action on behalf of their homes, community, and city if the structure to do so is understood and accessible. The Roanoke Neighborhood Partnership (RNP), initiated in 1980 by the city's Office of Community Planning and by a steering committee of civic and neighborhood leaders, is a citywide neighborhood development program designed to bolster available community resources through an active partnership of neighborhood residents, local government, business, and nonprofit and volunteer organizations. Our work as consultants started in 1979 and has continued intermittently until the present.[2]

Roanoke, with a population of about 100,000 people, is the largest metropolitan area in the western half of Virginia and is the historic home of the Norfolk and Western Railroad. Like many small industrial cities, it experienced a period of decline through the 1960s and 1970s resulting from global economic restructuring and government policies that supported suburban over urban development. The result has been declining city neighborhoods and the

Figure 4.1 The city of Roanoke, Va. (Photo courtesy of the city of Roanoke)

subsequent problems that arise when the city is abandoned. Many inner-city neighborhoods were left with few resources, and the amenities—shopping, professional offices, and so on—followed people to the suburbs.

In the face of these major shifts, Roanoke struggled to maintain its business base and residential neighborhoods and made use of many of the federal programs of "the Great Society" project initiated by President Lyndon Johnson in the 1960s. But in the late 1970s and early 1980s, the difficulties facing cities were compounded by the beginning of an extended period of federal fiscal austerity, including a major restructuring of federal programs and support for community efforts. Financial assistance to local governments was greatly reduced, and communities were faced with the task of doing more with less.

In Roanoke at the end of the 1970s, there was a general feeling among many citizens that the city government was not spending the taxpayers' dollars efficiently. Parts of the city were beginning to feel "seedy," and there was a significant level of housing deterioration and abandonment. On the other hand, those in city administration were frustrated by what they felt was apathy on the part of the citizens, or worse, the beginning of an adversarial relationship in which they were being unjustly cast as "the bad guys." This story could have been the beginning of a long and frustrating battle between the city government and city residents, with accusations made on both sides and the most creative energies being spent on the conflict.

Instead, there were some insightful people in Roanoke who recognized that residents and officials shared the same goal of having a livable city made up of neighborhoods about which people cared and in which they chose to live. The leaders of Roanoke assumed that the responsibility of city hall was not to fix everything (an impossibility) but to provide a structure wherein all who wanted to could participate in the nurturing and care of the city.[3] This was a government that recognized that leaders do have responsibility— the responsibility to frame a space for dialogue so that all people may understand that they create their own history, and furthermore, that they are free to take action on behalf of themselves and their community.

In 1978 a new city administration took an aggressive stance toward the development of the city. They first addressed the most visible manifestation, its center, in a downtown urban-renewal project called "Roanoke Design '79."[4] This downtown revitalization plan was a major citywide venture into citizen and private sector involvement in planning through the inclusion of a citizen's advisory group, a storefront office, and a series of TV shows with an active, call-in format. The efforts in "public relations" and the resultant public responses were a lesson to city officials that people in the community did care about their city and, furthermore, that rather unconventional methods for reaching the public were effective.

The city's next step was to direct its energy toward the neighborhoods themselves. This was, of course, an incredibly complex task. Like many cities its size, Roanoke is an aggregate of diverse neighborhoods of radically different socioeconomic, racial, and physical characteristics, some with very serious problems. There was little communication among these geographically and racially segregated communities. The city's self-appointed task was to assist communities in becoming more self-directed with very limited resources and, at the same time, to create the opportunity for citizens to learn more about the city itself.

The RNP began in early 1980, not with a clear understanding of what it was but rather with a "utopian" vision of what it might become.[5] The vision was a call to the folks[6] of the city—that "we, a partnership of neighborhood people, backed by the resources of the public sector, volunteer organizations, and businesses, can identify and resolve many of the problems affecting the quality of life in our city." With the leadership of Mayor Noel Taylor, City Manager Bern Ewert, and Chief of Community Planning Earl Reynolds, the city found time in its continuing work to make a space for collaborative neighborhood planning. As Reynolds often said, "We don't have any money, but what we do have is a burning desire to work with you in terms of building this community."

The Story of the Roanoke Neighborhood Partnership

The Formation of the Partnership

Although the vision was clear, a course of action that would inform, involve, organize, and mediate all the subjects of this project was not. At the same time as the city manager was working administratively to facilitate the initiation of a new planning process and the mayor was creating a vision of what might happen, Reynolds, as chief of community planning, began meeting with local leaders to discuss what this partnership might be, gaining insights and suggestions from which he framed an approximate scope of work for the consultants. This scope was fleshed out through an ongoing dialogue among city officials, representatives from various organizations, and neighborhoods across the city. Because of our firm's proximity to Roanoke and our previous work with the city, we were involved in the earliest stages of Reynolds' investigations, thinking through with him how general ideas of neighborhood planning might be specifically suited to the context of Roanoke, Va.

The consultant team hired to structure and manage the initiation of the RNP was headed by Buckhurst, Fish, Hutton & Katz and included D.C. Collaborative, Margaret Grieve (an independent consultant), and the Caucus Partnership.[7] The consultant team was brought into the city to design and facilitate a planning process and to assist the city in structuring a neighborhood development program by confirming and interrogating their work and our intervention. Our tasks included discovering how to position this particular project in the context of the city's ongoing responsibilities, and designing an intervention strategy for deciding who plays, when, and how. Because a dialogue about neighborhoods depends on engaging the residents of the city in a critical reflection on their own communities, significant effort was expended in developing methods of communication to inform and engage the people of Roanoke; these included posters, fliers, television programs, radio talk shows, public issue forums, and more.[8]

As a beginning, a major public issue two-day forum, "The Partnership Forum" (November 1980) was designed to introduce the idea of the Partnership to the citizens of Roanoke. More than 700 people came to hear each other talk about what they loved about their neighborhoods and what they were afraid of. This was the first time many public officials and business leaders had heard neighborhood people speak about their communities—why they lived there and what they hoped for their children. An especially poignant moment occurred when Ms. Florine Thornhill of the Gilmer Avenue neighborhood stood up. She had never spoken to such a large group but was determined to tell other people in the city, business and civic leaders, and city hall about her area of the city. She took the stage and, although her voice shook, she told the group: "I love my neighborhood, but it isn't a good place for children to live. I want to talk to you about rats. I want to tell you about houses that burn down, killing young people, because the house is so drafty and the wood stove faulty."

Others told stories about many places in the city, about their parents' commitment to the neighborhoods in which they now lived, about the beautiful views of the valley, about special friends. There was a sense of excitement in this gathering. We designed the event in such a way that the participants could do serious work but also have fun. Bluegrass music played while city residents got to know each other by visiting the booths set up by some groups, and the process of voting about important issues was designed to be physically engaging. Having a good time together has remained a major characteristic of RNP events, and it has served to keep attendance high and help strangers get to know each other. The Partnership Forum was the beginning of a new relationship between the people of city hall and the people of the neighborhoods, a dialogic space for displacing assumptions, misunderstandings, and silence.

The Partnership Planning Workshops

We assumed that this partnership process must be able to work for the whole city, not just some sectors. The consultants and city officials decided to begin the citywide intervention by designing and implementing a neighborhood planning process in four racially and socioeconomically different neighborhoods as a way to test the robustness of the approach.

The thorny question "What is a neighborhood?" was handled through a process of self-definition. When a group came forward and said it was a neighborhood, they were taken at their word. This has resulted over the years in planning with neighborhood groups as small as five blocks, and with much larger allied groups of block clubs and business associations. The activity of self-naming to a large extent framed the kind of action agenda they set for themselves, with larger, more organized neighborhoods taking on more complex work and the smaller groups working to take care of immediate problems.

In this intervention we framed participation not by defining what a neighborhood was, and therefore determining who could play, but by giving the power of self-definition to the neighborhood groups, facilitating and perhaps forcing them to name the people with whom they would work. We both confirmed and interrogated their decisions, asking, "Why is this the boundary? Who lives over here, and are they organized? Who are the leaders of groups contiguous to your neighborhood?" and so forth. These kinds of questions sometimes led them to expand or constrict their original boundaries, enabling them to problematize their own definitions. If later it were discovered that the area was not collectively self-defined, we assumed that this situation would be addressed by the constituencies themselves. In the years since the beginning of the Roanoke Neighborhood Partnership, the idea of what a neighborhood is in Roanoke has emerged more clearly. There are now a set of questions asked of each neighborhood requesting membership in the Partnership about who they are and what neighborhoods bound theirs, again often leading to discussions and negotiations between groups.

A generalized profile of the first four neighborhoods selected to participate in the RNP planning process reflects the diversity of Roanoke's neighborhoods: Belmont, a poorly organized neighborhood of older, white people with few resources; Northwest–Gilmer Avenue, a very poor black neighborhood bordering the major urban renewal area of the city literally "on the other side of the tracks" from downtown; Raleigh Court, a middle- and upper-middle-class, fairly well organized white neighborhood in a gentrifying area; and Preston Park–Williamson Road, a white middle-class linear neighborhood organized along the major urban business road. We worked in all four neighborhoods simultaneously over a

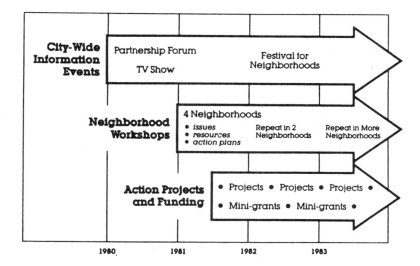

Figure 4.2 Diagram of the initial phase of the RNP process. (Courtesy of the city of Roanoke)

period of three months. The leaders of the communities were involved in setting up the meetings by contacting people and helping with logistics.

The structure of the series of workshops designed for Roanoke used the basic questions of most planning processes. We wanted to find out what the problems were, what resources were available, and how to solve the problems most pressing on community people. Using this very generic set of questions, we designed a sequence of three workshops, anticipating that they would be refined and modified in each neighborhood and subject to revisions as the process evolved. The three meetings—on issues, resources, and action planning—were designed to facilitate the neighborhoods' identification of their own issues, providing the opportunity for neighbors to confirm and interrogate each others' experiences and perceptions of their community, and to design ways that the issues could be resolved.

Many different methods were used in these workshops—group-process methods developed in the applied behavioral sciences, graphic presentations, and mapping—all readily available in a placemaker's toolbox. The meetings were intended to be participatory, and therefore were designed to use a small-group format so that all people would have the opportunity to be heard. An ongoing public record on large-format newsprint taped to the wall ensured that all comments and concerns were duly recorded by trained volunteer facilitators. In this way, each person had the opportunity to watch their words being recorded, usually in abbreviated and translated form; any misunderstandings could be corrected on the spot.

Each of the workshops was introduced by City Manager Bern Ewert, Mayor Noel Taylor, or Chief of Community Planning Earl Reynolds, bringing the highest level of city management to church basements and school auditoriums. Members of the Steering Committee, newly formed to oversee the process, were also in attendance in order to experience, firsthand, the process of the workshops and to hear for themselves about life in the neighborhoods. Attendance at the meetings varied with the size and maturity of the neighborhood groups, ranging from 150 to 200 people in Raleigh Court to 25 people in Belmont.

WORKSHOP 1: ISSUES

The first meeting in each neighborhood was introduced by the neighborhood's own leaders, who in turn introduced the city officials and consultants. People were sitting around tables in groups of six to eight with a very large map of their neighborhoods before them. The first question asked was: "What is special about our neighborhood?" The facilitators recorded responses and marked special places on the maps. Soon everyone had markers in their hands, talking to each other about the qualities of their neighborhood that they especially liked and wanted to preserve. The second question—"What are the problems, and what needs to be changed in our neighborhood?"—built on the first and continued the mapping exercise and comments on newsprint. There was often amazing agreement among the participants about the nature of the problems, even when the reasons offered for their causes were different. This intense form of interaction and the openness of conversation set the tone for all of the meetings and the homework assignments conducted between the large meetings.

At the end of the first meeting, each neighborhood had not only identified and confirmed its experience of why this was a special neighborhood, but had identified and rank ordered a set of problems that it wanted to work on. "Homework" groups were organized to work on priority problems such as trash in the alleys, abandoned houses, junk cars, and flooding. Between the workshops, these groups met with Maggie Grieve, the member of the consultant team who was living on assignment in Roanoke, or with other members of the city staff. These small homework groups were asked to come to the next meeting with as much information as they could gather on the nature and scope of problems identified

Figure 4.3 "What is special about our neighborhood?" A small group makes notations on a map of their neighborhood. (Photo courtesy of the city of Roanoke)

in the workshop, what had already been done to resolve them, and what resources they could find that might help them now. In addition, one group in each neighborhood researched on the history of the neighborhood and made a presentation at the second meeting.

This "in-between" meeting stage of dialogue among neighbors, and between neighborhoods and consultants, was one of the most important features of the process. Planning is a complex and difficult task that is learned by doing, and many of the people in the neighborhoods had no experience in systematically ordering and

Figure 4.4 "What are the problems, and what needs to be changed in our neighborhood?" A small group is working at an RNP workshop. (Photo courtesy of the city of Roanoke)

understanding the nature of this practice. They lived their problems and knew intimately how their lives were affected. But few had experience in organizing a group of people to take action, and most did not know how to move beyond recognition and complaint to framing an issue and problematizing it so that action might be taken. Creating the conditions wherein communities of people could eventually engage in their own placemaking work without professional assistance was critically important to the well-being of Roanoke and the Partnership.

WORKSHOP 2: RESOURCES

The second series of meetings focused on the available and potential sources of technical, financial, and organizational help for the problem areas. In preparation for this meeting, the consultants and city staff identified individuals and organizations from around the city who could help clarify and/or offer assistance with the problem areas. For example, if housing had been identified as a problem, we invited to this second workshop members of the city staff (planning, city inspector, and so on), members of the nonprofit sector involved in housing projects, architects, representatives from the real estate community, and people from the banking community. In the Preston Park–Williamson Road neighborhood where one of the problem areas was storm-water management, we invited the city engineer and a civil engineer from the private sector. All of these resource people generously volunteered their time.

This resource workshop began with reports from the various homework groups. In each neighborhood, the group researching its history gave an account of how the neighborhood had come to be and what changes had occurred since its beginning. The people of the Northwest–Gilmer Avenue neighborhood were reminded of the rich history of the area, which had been the historic center of black culture and community life until the 1950s and integration. Nationally important members of the black community had visited and entertained the community. In Preston Park–Williamson Road many learned for the first time that their neighborhood was built by community volunteers.

After the reports by the history group, the other working groups reported on what they had learned about the problem areas they had explored. These reports served as the framework for the discussion on priorities that followed. The format for this meeting was similar to the first: small work groups (seven to ten people) with facilitators recording ideas on newsprint. This time, however,

Figure 4.5 Making an additional note on newsprint during a small-group report. (Photo courtesy of the city of Roanoke)

each table was asked to discuss a different problem area, although more than one table could work on the same problem if more than ten people were interested. The selection of a discussion table was the first step in identifying which problem areas would be selected as most urgent or important—people voted with their feet. In these sessions, each group, using the resource people as participants in the dialogue, continued to frame the issues. They were asked to clarify the problem: to identify what had already been done to address this issue in the past, what could be done that had not been done, and who could help. The facilitators were charged with seeing that participants around the table engaged in conversations, that

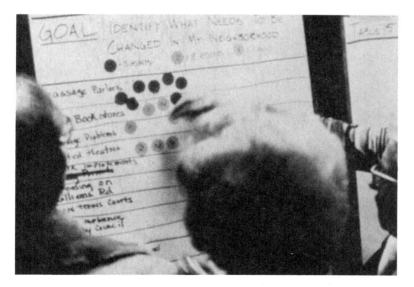

Figure 4.6 Setting priorities by placing a colored dot next to the issues most important to each participant. (Photo courtesy of the city of Roanoke)

the "experts" listened to the people and did not dominate the discussion, and that the issue was continually problematized, so that easy answers—which denied the complexity of problems and the richness of the context—could be avoided. At the end of this meeting, after each table had reported their evening's work, each of the four communities set priorities for the development of "action plans." Those priorities became the homework for the next series of "in-between" meetings.

Many hours of consultant, staff, and volunteer time were spent in dialogue with various homework groups of neighborhood people to develop a collaborative understanding of the nature and causes of the important issues. This work was particular and targeted to the different groups as each neighborhood framed its own concerns and ways of working. Some groups needed more assistance than others to learn how to access city hall, how to frame questions so that city staff could respond, and so on, but in each neighborhood some people learned to understand and access their local government. Groups tried to develop alternative strategies to resolve the issues; some of these "solutions" could be attempted within the resources of their own communities, and some required long-term commitment by many people and considerable resources.

WORKSHOP 3: ACTION PLANS

This last series of formal meetings used a process of proposal review.[9] The problem-area groups presented their work and the small groups reviewed the plans carefully, collectively identifying and discussing the strengths and weaknesses of the plans and modifying them according to the group's discussion. At the end of the meeting, having reviewed the three or four action plans developed, the entire group prioritized the plans it wanted to engage immediately and for which it would do further work. Before people left the meeting, a schedule for working on these issues was prepared, and people made a commitment to work on a specific aspect of one of the projects. In other words, these were not loosely defined ideas, but concrete proposals with actions to be taken by specific people to bring them about. Because these first meetings were structured around intact community groups, the infrastructure was already in place to carry out the project. As always, the meeting ended with refreshments to celebrate their collective work.

The action plans for each of the neighborhood groups were varied in terms of content and sophistication. All were thoughtful and careful—and had the active commitment of the neighborhood people who had participated in their creation. These plans were published in small booklets for each neighborhood. They were used as a tool for neighborhood development and as a "legitimate" aid to communication when requesting assistance of outside resource people.

These planning documents were not intended to be traditional neighborhood plans. They were organizing tools to facilitate immediate action by the city and neighborhoods around specific issues; they were the result of a process that engaged communities of people in the work of placemaking and reminding them of their power to work together to make their places better. The motto of one neighborhood association sums up this philosophy: "You don't have to leave home to live in a better neighborhood."

The three Partnership Planning Workshops had brought together people from each neighborhood. This process created the opportunity to work together during and between the workshops on various projects. The people who had actively participated now served as the nucleus for ongoing neighborhood work. Some of the leaders began serious campaigns of neighborhood organization to identify others who could become involved. By the end of the three months, one neighborhood leader had visited people on every block in her neighborhood and convinced someone on each block to become the "block captain." These networks continued the activity generated through the Partnership Planning Workshops.

The structure of this professional consulting was not unlike community development work characteristic of the late 1960s and the 1970s, in which local governments, mandated through community development legislation, were required to hold meetings to ask residents what they wanted. What was uncharacteristic was the intensity of work done by the consultants and city staff in preparation for each meeting and in debriefing sessions after each meeting to evaluate the work. Even though there was a general framework and meeting design, every contact with the neighborhood groups was conceptualized as a particular dialogic space; it was a special and precious time in which to engage in conversation about their community. We continually explored what had worked in the last meeting and what needed refinement before the next meeting, what was different about this neighborhood and what should be modified, how this particular process would generalize, who needed to be at the next meeting, what particular aspects of this group of people needed our attention, and so forth. The insights generated in these conversations were critical to the aim of situating the process and our knowledge in each context, and they helped us tailor what could have been a generalized planning framework to the special capabilities and needs of each neighborhood.

The city staff, neighborhood and community leaders, and consultants worked in an uncharacteristically open space to learn from each other how to generate, experiment with, and critique the Partnership process. What finally emerged was a homegrown version of neighborhood participatory action planning that has been successfully sustained for over fourteen years.

The First Projects

All of the projects in each of the four neighborhood action plans required some resources to implement, regardless of the extent of neighborhood planning and volunteer effort. As part of the project structure, the consultants recommended that the city implement a granting mechanism to help neighborhoods leverage funds for their projects. The Mini-Grant Program was developed to administer small matching grants of up to $1800. Groups wanting to take advantage of these funds prepared a brief proposal that outlined their objectives and the resources they would bring to bear on the project, including in-kind services. Both the city staff and consultants were instrumental in the preparation of these first proposals, in which neighborhood people learned how to access the funding program.

Each of the four neighborhoods selected a first project and worked in partnership with the city, the service agencies, and the private sector in implementing them. The Belmont Neighborhood Watch Group began serious restoration work on Old Firehouse #6, a symbolic structure that served as the community center. In June 1982, volunteers from Allstate Insurance Company, Shenandoah Life Insurance Company, the League of Older Americans, and city hall came to paint and fix up the exterior of this beautiful structure. For interior work on the heating and electrical systems, mini-grant funds were used to defray costs.

The Northwest–Gilmer Avenue neighborhood started on the two most visible aspects of its condition: perceived high levels of crime and the overgrown vacant lots. With the assistance of the police department and their newly established system of block captains, a Crime Watch was formed, and mini–grant funds were used for signs, dusk-to-dawn lights, and locks to help secure homes. With the help of a local construction company who lent trucks, the

Figure 4.7 Volunteer painting Old Firehouse #6 in the Belmont neighborhood. (Photo courtesy of the city of Roanoke)

Figure 4.8 Neighborhood volunteers spending a day cleaning up their alley. (Photo courtesy of the city of Roanoke)

city's public works department, businesses, neighborhood volunteers, and volunteers from Allstate Insurance Company, the neighborhood cleaned up its vacant lots. Furthermore, it was clearly understood that this was not a one-time activity but something that needed continuing attention. The group contacted the absentee owners of the vacant lots and, where possible, collected fees to help maintain them. And with two small grants from local private business, they bought a riding lawnmower; volunteers continue to mow the lots and collect fees to maintain the equipment.

This neighborhood began to understand its power to organize itself and take action on its own behalf. Fundraising through gospel concerts and local festivals forged the neighborhood spirit and brought people from outside the neighborhood to experience the warmth and generosity of the people who lived in what had been perceived to be one of the most distressed areas of the city.

Raleigh Court, interested in beautifying the neighborhood and marking one area as a special place, used mini-grants and volunteers from the Marines, Boy Scouts, and local businesses to landscape the neighborhood's commercial area with flowering pear trees. The Preston Park–Williamson Road group attacked their long-standing problem of inadequate storm drainage head-on. They worked with the city staff in collecting data to assist in the development of an engineering plan to correct the situation. A group of residents continued to meet with the engineers to see the plan to completion and to serve as a liaison to the community. The result of this coopera-

Figure 4.9 Tree planting days bring diverse community people out to work together. (Photo courtesy of the city of Roanoke)

Figure 4.10 One of many ribbon-cutting ceremonies shared by neighborhood people and city officials. (Photo courtesy of the city of Roanoke)

tive effort was a plan calling for $10.8 million in improvements, which was adopted by the City Council as part of the capital budgeting process. The sale of bonds began in late 1982.

These initial projects, large and small, were evidence of the power of neighborhoods to take action on their own behalf in partnership with other concerned members of the community and minimal government support. Many projects followed these initial ones, and each of the communities became more skilled at accessing resources such as information, collaboration, and funds. New neighborhoods joined and many participated in the Partnership Planning Workshops. Each grew in sophistication in the practice of planning.

Institutionalizing the Partnership

It was evident from the number of people who committed their time and energy and from their high level of excitement that the Roanoke Neighborhood Partnership had succeeded in capturing the imagination of the city: individual neighborhoods, city hall staff, people active in the nonprofit sector, and business people who wanted to be contributing members of the community. The placemaking practice had created an energetic conversation among the many sectors of the city who had come together to think about and envision their neighborhoods and their city.

The experience, attention, and compassion that the consultant team brought to the emergence of the RNP was indispensable, especially in creating the space for critical discourse about our collective work. Yet professional placemakers leave when their contracts are finished; they are often out-of-town consultants and almost always "out-of-place." This transition period is always a critical one, and many projects become nothing more than a feel-good experience for participants. Now the dialogic space that had been opened in conjunction with the consulting work would have to be kept open by others. How could Roanoke maintain the energy and structure of dialogue? How could the city government institutionalize the activities sufficiently to make it possible to continue but do so loosely enough that the fragile process might grow and change?

The transition was facilitated by the structure of the Partnership because of the openness and flexibility of the process and its focus on the educational aspects of the project. The space for dialogue and attitude of positive regard as a prerequisite to action were accepted as necessary in the conduct of work. The structure of interactive public meetings was also found to be very effective in generating constructive conversation among people who were working together on a project. Many of these processes were adopted and brought into city planning as standard procedures. However, other structures to facilitate access to resources on an ongoing basis had to be created and/or reinforced, and management of the RNP had to be transferred from the consultants to some other body. Part of our intervention as professionals specifically addressed the issue of institutionalizing the RNP. We helped the city develop a strategy that would serve to maintain the special space for the conversation about placemaking in the neighborhoods.

The City Council created and funded the Office of the Roanoke Neighborhood Partnership inside the Office of Community Planning, giving communities an access to city hall that they had not had. With the office came the position of neighborhood coordinator. This person was to serve as the contact between the neighborhoods and city hall, elected officials, and the Steering Committee. It was a complex job because the coordinator had to be able to interact at the management level at city hall, communicate with members of the community-at-large, and work closely with the folks in the neighborhoods. A national search was conducted, and from the candidates, Andrée Tremoulet was selected.[10] She served as coordinator until April 1986 and oversaw the institutionalization of this process into the daily business of city hall.

There was also the need to develop a management structure that connected the office of neighborhood coordinator in city hall to the partnership of neighborhoods, the nonprofit sector, the city government, and businesses. The obvious body to do so was the Steering Committee, which had been created at the beginning of the process to oversee the RNP's management. Its membership had been drawn from all participating sectors and given staggered terms of one to three years. During the time when attention had been focused almost exclusively on work in the neighborhoods, the Steering Committee had met and been kept informed of all activity, and certain members had been very active in the Partnership planning process. However, as a body, the Steering Committee had not received the same attention as had the neighborhoods themselves. Therefore, the next major project was the organizational development of the Steering Committee as a working team to oversee management of the Partnership and to work closely with the neighborhood coordinator. Because some members' terms were to end after one year, the Steering Committee membership was reinforced with people who were willing to work and with new people who became involved as volunteers. Also, neighborhood leaders who may not have been known during the initial appointments and who had become active in the RNP were included as candidates for the Steering Committee appointed by City Council.

The functioning of this body was problematic because it represented different cultures and styles. For purposes of illustration only we will generalize "types," recognizing that such generalizations never reflect the complexity of people's action and motives. However, there was a general tendency for neighborhood people and representatives from the nonprofit sector to favor consensus decision–making processes. Most of them had had experience in volunteer organizations, where it is critical that people have the opportunity to sufficiently talk through issues before the group decides to take action. On the other hand, there were executives and business people used to making quick decisions and having others execute them. These different styles initially created difficulties in communication among members of the Steering Committee. It was very important in the early stages to have people who could bridge the different cultures to confirm the different ways of working and to ask questions to move the group through what could have been impasses in the development of the body. Establishing a collaborative framework within the Steering Committee, and between the Steering Committee and the Office of the Roanoke Neighborhood Partnership, was critical in the early period of the RNP.

One of the most problematic aspects of the Steering Committee was its structural position both within and outside of city hall. This body did not fit into traditional governing structures such as the board of directors of a nonprofit corporation. They did not hire and fire staff, approve budgets, or raise funds. However, they did make policy, set priorities for work, assist with the implementation of projects, develop contacts and do networking, and, importantly, serve as spokespeople to the city-at-large. This in-between character of the Steering Committee was both its limitation and its strength. It did not have the legitimation that comes from being within a governmental structure, but this also freed the body and its members to be publicly critical when they felt it necessary to speak out. The Steering Committee was located between city hall, the neighborhoods, and the nonprofit and private sectors, and although sometimes uneasy in this situation, was able to move freely among them.

This boundary confusion, however, created another structural complexity with respect to the position of the neighborhood coordinator. Hired by city hall, this person worked within the Office of Community Planning. As an employee of the city, the coordinator obviously had a commitment to that institution and had to follow city procedures. Yet, because of the nature of the work, the coordinator's allegiance was to the neighborhoods as an advocate and mediator. Furthermore, the coordinator was both responsible to, and director of, the Steering Committee. As Andrée Tremoulet said of the position, "The coordinator wasn't sure who she was responsible to. Actually, you just wore whichever hat fit at the moment, and there weren't really many conflicts."[11] This attitude, this willingness to engage in an ambiguous environment, has been a powerful way of being in the world, of being able to work within a democratic framework.

To everyone's credit, the Steering Committee and the coordinators have continued to struggle with these issues and have developed strategies to validate everyone's perceptions while designing methods of work. The Steering Committee and the RNP engaged in several intensive self-evaluation processes in 1981, 1985, and 1989. At various times, the Caucus Partnership, Margaret Grieve, and/or Michael Appleby have assisted in these reflections and helped the committee clarify the shifting relationships between themselves, the expanding neighborhoods, and the city.

The structure and governance of the Steering Committee has never been totally resolved and possibly never will be. In the most positive sense, the issues of the self-governance of the Steering Committee and the structural ambiguity of the RNP in relationship to the city point to a site for struggling with new ways of understanding and taking action in a dialogic space, expanding traditional forms that constrain as well as facilitate work. This willingness to engage in dialogue reinforces the concept of the Partnership and has been significant in maintaining its viability.

The Middle Years

By 1982, two years after the Partnership Forum event that started the Roanoke Neighborhood Partnership, Roanoke was named an All American City by the National Municipal League, in part because of the transformative experience of the RNP. Many neighborhood people who had participated in the Partnership gave testimony to the power they now felt to make changes in their lives. A vision, a utopian project, had been presented to the people, and they, thirsty for significant participation in the governance of their own lives, joined with others in their communities to make Roanoke a better place to live. The survival of the RNP had been carefully considered so that new neighborhoods might join, and communication between neighborhoods about shared issues has become a common practice.

Lewis Peery, one of the chairs of the Steering Committee, spoke of the Partnership:

> The real story of the Partnership centers around the new spirit of hope and optimism in Roanoke's neighborhoods. We think that people have begun to believe that they *can* shape their neighborhood's destiny if they are willing to invest their time and energy. Every newly mowed vacant lot in the Northwest, every recently painted house in the Southeast, every monthly edition of the *Forum* in the Northeast, and every tree planted in the Southwest is a testimony to people's faith in themselves, their neighborhood, their city. This faith is what makes complex projects possible and helps people find the courage to form new groups.[12]

In 1984, volunteers spent more than 27,000 hours working for neighborhoods through the RNP.[13] This volunteer time during one year reflects a commitment equal to thirteen full-time staff people. Through the Office of the Roanoke Neighborhood Partnership, new programs, in addition to the Mini-Grant Program, have been

Figure 4.11 Mr. Peery as chair of the RNP Steering Committee meeting with a local neighborhood group. (Photo courtesy of the city of Roanoke)

instituted to respond to the needs of neighborhood people. One example is Operation Paintbrush, which manages summer crews in painting houses for people who meet certain requirements of eligibility. Another is Eyesore Alert, in which each neighborhood organization submits its top two building problems each month to the building commissioner's office for priority consideration. In 1985 the RNP created the first Virginia Neighborhoods Conference in Roanoke to provide a forum for the sharing and exchange of neighborhood work.

Not only are more projects being managed because there are more neighborhoods involved, but the projects developed by each neighborhood continue to become more complex, reflecting the increased sophistication of the neighborhood people and their ability to access resources in the public and private sector. Neighborhoods have adopted parks and developed and preserved these neighborhood resources. Northwest–Gilmer Avenue, one of the more distressed neighborhoods, has begun to engage in housing renovation and new construction. The Williamson Road Association joined forces with local businesses to execute significant improvements to their main street, and worked with city hall to develop new zoning ordinances.

The increased level of complexity in neighborhood projects has been a subject of continuing discussion between the Office of the Roanoke Neighborhood Partnership and the Steering Committee. It has put an enormous burden on the neighborhood coordinator and the Steering Committee to work with all of the projects and

Figure 4.12 Housing renovation and newly constructed houses in the Northwest–Gilmer area, a project of the Northwest Neighborhood Improvement Organization and the Roanoke Neighborhood Partnership. (Photo courtesy of the city of Roanoke)

with the over twenty-five neighborhoods who want to be active—surely an indication of the RNP's success. One of the original ideas was that neighborhood leaders who had gained effective skills and abilities in managing projects would need less time and assistance and so could "graduate" to working more independently. What has emerged, however, is that neighborhood groups, as they gain competence, take on more complex and difficult projects on behalf of themselves and so continue to need guidance. And new neighborhoods that join need the same careful and thoughtful attention that the earlier groups needed in order to be reminded of their own placemaking abilities. Neighborhoods with older membership in the RNP can and do assist newer neighborhoods through shared experiences and many stories, but because the former are thoroughly engaged in their own neighborhood work, they do not have sufficient time to devote to new groups. This puts an ever-increasing pressure for face-to-face contact on the RNP staff.

THE PARTNERSHIP CREED

Whereas we are an organized neighborhood in the City of Roanoke, Virginia;

Whereas our neighborhood subscribes to the policies and supports the objectives of the Roanoke Neighborhood Partnership;

Whereas we agree to observe the restrictions placed upon all nonprofit organizations as they relate to the endorsement and/or support of politicians and political campaigns;

Whereas we agree to participate in at least one Partnership-sponsored workshop per year;

Whereas we agree to keep the Partnership Office informed about the officers of our Neighborhood organization by submitting a list of their names annually;

Whereas we agree to promote awareness of The Partnership by distributing communications, publications and newsletters from it to our members;

Whereas we agree to use the Partnership approach to resolving and working through concerns with local government;

Whereas we agree to maintain a membership which is open to all who live and work in our neighborhood;

Whereas we agree to hold at least four properly announced Neighborhood meetings per year and to conduct our meetings in conformance with Robert's Rules or other Duties of Order, and to welcome a visiting Steering Committee member who may wish to attend said meetings;

And, Whereas we have filed a list of up-to-date by-laws and/or articles of incorporation with the Partnership office:

It is deemed to be good, wise, and proper that your neighborhood be recognized as a member in good standing of The Roanoke Neighborhood Partnership.

In 1992 the RNP office and the Steering Committee asked for assistance in addressing this condition by exploring with us how they might facilitate work on the kinds of problems, issues, and projects that occur repeatedly in most neighborhoods. They felt that the experience in dealing with many issues could be passed on in a written format to a new neighborhood groups, along with information on the various programs and how to access them. In collaboration with the neighborhood coordinator, Stephanie Cicero, other city staff, and neighborhood leaders, the Caucus Partnership prepared the *Roanoke Neighborhood Partnership Self-Help Manual* for distribution to all their neighborhood organizations and to groups who were considering membership in the RNP. This book explains the RNP and its history and programs, and serves as a primer on neighborhood organizing. The *Manual* is being used as a training tool for neighborhood leaders who want to learn more about engaging in planning efforts, and as an evaluative tool to assess where they are. The codified text is not intended to substitute for the face-to-face encounter so necessary for a dialogic conversation about making communities, but it is being used to support that effort. The *Self-Help Manual* is a continuation of the Partnership process began fifteen years earlier when the city—government officials, neighborhood people, businesses and nonprofit organizations —joined in the struggle to find the best way to situate planning and neighborhood empowerment in Roanoke.

Reflections

Right Time, Right Place, Right People

It is never easy to respond to the query about why the Roanoke Neighborhood Partnership, as an experiment in local democracy, worked in that city at the beginning of the 1980s while many other programs in community empowerment did not achieve their goals or fell into a form of token participation. Many conditions contributed to the placemaking activity at that time: the people in leadership roles both in government and in community organizations; the history, scale, and condition of the city; the particular consultants who participated; and the ideas of the times. The Partnership made a significant difference in the lives of many people in Roanoke and, indeed, in the lives of those of us who participated with the people of the city. Some aspects of the RNP were very successful, such as a new sense of accessibility to city hall among neighborhood folks, and the transformation of reward systems within city hall that made that possible. Other aspects were more problematic, such as the active inclusion of the private sector. In addition, some unplanned things happened because of the restructuring of community life precipitated by participation in the RNP. In this section we present some of these factors and consequences.

The conception and implementation of the RNP at the beginning of the 1980s—the Reagan-Bush era—was timely. One characteristic of this period was a restructuring of federal assistance programs, which shifted the financial and administrative responsibilities to local government, and a radical cut in community development block grants. Local governments had to continue the same level of services and take on expanded responsibility, both with fewer resources. The idea that the citizens would have to assume more responsibility for their own well-being was not new—this is a "normal" response to budget reductions. What was creative on the part of Roanoke was its recognition that the local government was situated among various constituencies, individuals, and *intermediate institutions,* such as churches, schools, and civic clubs.[14] Because of this positioning city hall had the power to influence and structure these resources for better governance of the city.

The RNP used existing intermediate institutions as a way to work in the neighborhoods, and worked to develop and maintain these public spaces as spheres for democratic action. For example, an important social network in Roanoke was maintained by the churches; these institutions were important to many residents' social as well as spiritual lives. The churches were spheres for the practice of self-governance, regardless of an individual's or a community's social or economic standing. Many ministers actively supported the idea of the Partnership, and the churches in each neighborhood provided contacts, space, communication channels, and other forms of help. Because the social context was familiar, it was easier for people to be comfortable working in new ways on new ideas.

Another factor was Roanoke's small size: Direct contact with neighborhoods was easy, and civic leadership in various sectors knew one another. Also, the scale of the initial intervention was limited to four neighborhoods. This facilitated face-to-face interaction, which was the essential communication channel in Roanoke. The limited intervention allowed time to build important relationships within the communities and the city as a whole, and gave space for the fragile process to grow and develop. The attention to this intimate scale was balanced with the concern for structuring the comprehensive citywide model so that it could be grounded in both the concrete realities of the everyday lives of the people and the abstract governance structure in which such concrete experiences could be given voice.

The late 1970s brought together a group of people in Roanoke in leadership roles that conceived of and supported the idea of a democratic partnership. Although Roanoke was not unique in having a serendipitous meeting of people with a vision for working together on a democratic project, it did take advantage of the specific historical moment. The mayor, the city manager, and the chief of community planning shared a view of the nature of the public as being composed of individuals and organizations who were competent to engage in community making. These folks were willing to risk a new way of working in the neighborhoods and with the people. It was not good enough, in the words of Mayor Taylor, to "Go ye therefore and don't screw up too bad." City government was expected to take positive action on behalf of, and with, its citizens.

Bern Ewert, as city manager, viewed his position as structuring conditions in such a way that things could happen. He was restless, quick, abstract, and intellectual; in many ways, he was rather out of place in the southern dance of politics. He believed that his office was the seat of what he called a "basket of power" and that it was his responsibility to distribute power, not to gather it.[15] Therefore, his management style, though demanding, was based on trust and a belief that people wanted to be involved. As he said, "I believe we can touch people's spirits and souls and create social change without laws and legislation."

Ewert was not consistently involved in the RNP program nor its formation, but he was willing to give the idea sufficient time and space to make it work. He was willing to suspend judgment and to watch while Chief of Community Planning Earl Reynolds and others experimented with a new form of democracy for Roanoke. He did believe that democracy could work if sufficient public space could be generated, partly because everyone needs a place in which to exercise control.

Reynolds was a Roanoker, born and raised in the city. He knew it intimately, loved the people, and was trusted. His experiences in his church and community grounded him in knowledge of the place, and he had confidence that people wanted to take action on their own behalf. He had watched this occur informally his whole life. He often spoke of his "theory of mitigated confusion," that is, the more people understand something—in this case, city government—the less confusing it is and the more able they are to move through it and take action.[16] For Reynolds the main focus of the Partnership was communication and dialogue. It was the responsibility of local government to make itself transparent to the citizens, for, after all, it is the government of the people. Under his leadership, the members of the Office of Community Planning continued their traditional 1980s role of economic development but also emphasized the political nature of their work; that is, they identified and structured dialogue and negotiations about power in the conduct of their work.[17]

Along with their loved four-term Mayor Taylor, who was the minister of one of the larger black Baptist churches in the city, Ewert and Reynolds were able to gather the resources to create and implement the RNP. The three shared an assumption about the basic competence and nature of people. From their perspective, what needed to happen was that the barriers to action had to be identified and then transformed or removed, and the process had to be carefully structured so as not to create new obstacles.

These three had the vision and energy to involve others in the experiment, even though at the beginning they really did not know what form it would take. They made a commitment to engage with others to find a way to make what could have been a vacuous dream into a reality. Their energy made it easy to gather together folks in the community who shared their basic assumptions about human competence to join in thinking about the city. Moreover, Reynolds had an expansive network of people he had already worked with, who trusted him, and who entered into a conversation about how neighborhoods might be more fully engaged in city governance.

Reynolds also knew that the consultants selected to work with the city on this project could facilitate the creation and establishment of a unique neighborhood development process and assist in restructuring capital improvement decision making for community development block grant funds. And he knew that the wrong consultants could make it impossible to reinvent governance in the city for a long time. The request for proposals developed through Reynolds' office with the input of many others was carefully worded to seek professionals who not only had technical competence and experience, but who shared his view of human nature. These basic assumptions would be self-fulfilling prophecies and would, to a large extent, determine what happened in the next few years. The consultant team resulting from this interview process willingly joined the experiment. Through use of the dialogic space and the practice of confirmation and interrogation, city staff, the consultant team, and interested others were able to bring form to an idea and to sufficiently structure it so that action in the neighborhoods was possible.

Because Roanoke did not have a history of bitter conflict between neighborhoods and city hall, trust was easier to establish than in many cities. Ewert, Taylor, and Reynolds, rather than demanding that the residents trust them first, initiated the relationship of trust, communicating their belief that the people of Roanoke wanted to be participating citizens.[18] Furthermore, the city continued to maintain the relationship by keeping the expectations for this project modest and by always presenting the aim of the RNP as the discovery of "what the neighborhood can do for itself with the help of others." There were no false promises. Small successes were celebrated and new actions encouraged. This incremental process was easily adjusted to specific people and place situations and new insight. The tension between the utopian view of the democratic project and the actual small-scale incremental changes was viewed as a transformative element and was part of the energy that fueled those engaged in the dialogue.

This is not to suggest, however, that all of the goals of the Partnership were successfully engaged. Private sector involvement has always been an aim for the RNP—a partnership of neighborhoods, government, the nonprofit sector, and neighborhood businesses. This goal continues to be problematic because it is not always obvious how businesses might participate. The private sector operates under a very different reward system than the public sector.[19] In order to encourage the private sector to participate as a community, one must understand their reward system and structure opportunities for their participation that coincide with their other objectives.

The RNP has developed the Business Partner Program, arguing that improved neighborhood quality creates a favorable image for Roanoke, attracts new businesses, and keeps customers in the city. Good neighborhoods make good business. In some areas, such as Preston Park–Williamson Road and Raleigh Court, which had healthy business districts, local people were very successful in developing collaborative frameworks with neighborhood businesses. A few of the large businesses, such as Allstate and Shenandoah Life, became active in providing labor as company projects, and in giving small grants. Contractors found ways to contribute within the

limits of their resources, and other small businesses began to understand the value of developing good community relations. As volunteers, individual business people facilitated communication within
the private sector structure. However, sustained private sector involvement in neighborhood development has been difficult to
maintain because of the radically different social, political, and economic structure within which the private sector is located.

Transformed Reward Systems

Neighborhood planning processes are usually begun with great
excitement but often fail to sustain themselves because they are
added to already existing city programs and to the workload of city
staff, who feel that they are already fully employed. In order for this
placemaking effort to continue to make a difference in people's
lives, the consultant team realized we would have to understand
how the Roanoke Neighborhood Partnership fit into and/or could
transform the current organizational structure and standard operating procedures of city hall, and how it could belong to many
people, not just the Office of Community Planning.

This critical practice involved confirming and interrogating the
work of the city in neighborhood issues. We identified and suggested ways to reinforce the rewards that city staff currently got
from meeting the needs of neighborhoods groups, and we identified and attempted to remove the "demotivators," those structural
and institutional impediments to creative placemaking in the city
and neighborhoods. The RNP, although couched in the language
of utopian possibilities, was nevertheless realistic and critical. The
work around the idea of demotivators was one of the most important tasks of the project, and many hours were spent uncovering and reframing the work of city hall in relation to the neighborhoods and, conversely, the work of the neighborhoods in relation
to city hall.

It was often repeated at neighborhood meetings that one of the
major obstacles to getting things done in the neighborhoods was
"city hall." Like all institutions, the local government had over time
organized itself to be internally accountable. As with many bureaucratic structures, people were rewarded for getting their work done
efficiently, not by complicating their work and creating new problems. In this context, the idiosyncratic demands of neighborhoods
were often interpreted as interruptions and complications that kept
one from doing a good job. It is easy to develop structures and a
manner of work that demotivates community people from making

demands. It would have been convenient to declare city hall to be truly "the bad guy," to insist that the reason this or that neighborhood was not everything people wanted it to be was because of "those people" who work there. This scapegoat strategy is often used as a community-organizing mechanism in advocacy planning and is very effective as a short-term strategy. But we had started with the assumption that people are competent placemakers—people in neighborhoods and people in city hall. The consultants involved in the intervention refused to use scapegoating as the way to unify neighborhoods, recognizing the liabilities of such a method. If the RNP were going to work, it needed the people in the neighborhoods and all the folks at city hall. We had to find the demotivators that prevented engineers, social workers, administrators, secretaries—everybody—from engaging community people, and we had to create rewards for working with the neighborhoods.

We engaged in careful and specific work in deconstructing current processes and procedures to understand the existing reward system, which inadvertently demotivated city hall staff from working with neighborhoods. This work was not always easy; it demanded honesty and openness on the part of all participants. But framing the work within a discourse that affirmed people's good intentions made difficult conversations easier and facilitated a willingness to explore other forms of working. Furthermore, through the various planning projects representing the action plans of the four beginning member neighborhoods, we demonstrated to city staff that neighborhood people could be allies in getting done things they knew had to be done; they could even help in gathering data for certain efforts, as was done in the Preston Park–Williamson Road area on the unremitting flooding problem.

The removal of demotivators started at the top. When the mayor, the city manager, and the chief of community planning focused their attention on neighborhoods and were willing to spend their evenings at community meetings, this signaled a change in business as usual. City staff were at first instructed to attend to the four neighborhoods engaged in the initial RNP process. ("If Ms. Thornhill or Mr. Peery calls from the neighborhoods, I want you to take care of them!") Staff were encouraged to engage neighborhood folks and spend time helping them resolve identified problems. Once city employees gained experience in working with neighborhood people and were publicly recognized and rewarded for their efforts on behalf of individual neighborhoods, they began to reconceptualize this practice as part of their work. The changed reward system enabled them to conceive of their work differently: Many began to see themselves as educators and communicators, rather than as hassled employees. Through the newly created space for dialogue in which conversations between city officials and the people in the neighborhood occurred, the workings of city hall became more transparent to the citizens, removing a major demotivator to calling on the city as new understanding and competence developed. Reynolds' "theory of mitigated confusion" was confirmed—the more the neighborhood folks understood how city hall worked, the more they could move through it and take action in relationship to it. Lou Ellis, a member of the Steering Committee, said that "[t]he Partnership has proven to be an excellent problem diffuser, and has been very successful in bringing together city services and neighborhood needs."

It did not take long for the people in the neighborhood to learn that if they worked hard together and made clear what they wanted—whether information or assistance—they could get it, or at least know why they couldn't get it. Neighborhood leaders became adept at accessing city hall through the RNP office. They began to make judgments about what were reasonable requests; they began to understand more clearly what city hall could and could not do, what they could do for themselves, and when they needed other assistance from the private sector (access to bank loans, person–power to help on a project, and so forth). The initial demotivators to taking action on behalf of their community—getting organized, framing issues, being heard, taking concrete action, and seeing results—were addressed through the RNP workshop process, through a new relationship with city hall, through personal contact, and through the visible results of their labor.

Furthermore, the city assumed not only the responsibility of removing demotivators that had kept citizens from participating in local government, but also the responsibility of rewarding them for such work. Neighborhood leaders were asked and funded to participate in conferences and presentations of the Partnership. For example, when Roanoke sent in its bid to become an All American City, neighborhood residents traveled with the city officials to make the presentation. Citizens were given space on the city agenda to make presentations for their work, and some of the players were honored as Citizens of the Year. Within the RNP itself, the process of celebrating successes and spreading the credit for hard work was given a significant place in Partnership events. One volunteer expressed

Figure 4.14 Neighborhood leader receiving a Certificate of Appreciation. (Photo courtesy of the city of Roanoke)

the feeling of accomplishment shared by many others when she said that the RNP "has been the most rewarding experience that I have ever had. I am very fortunate in that I really have made a difference in the quality of life in Roanoke by simply giving a little time and effort."

The folks in city hall, for the most part, have been continually rewarded for their courage in initiating and maintaining the RNP. Not only were they successful in facilitating neighborhood development, they were able to do so while maintaining accountability within the constrained economic situation. Unlike the experience of many cities, the participatory process was a good experience, not a terrifying one in which the city perceived it had lost control and unfair demands had been made on it. City hall learned to trust itself to manage planning processes that involved people as partners, and to trust community people to be thoughtful and critical collaborators. For example, in 1985, when the city developed the master planning process put forth in *Roanoke Vision: Comprehensive Development Plan for Roanoke, Virginia, 1985–2005,* it used a participatory framework similar to the RNP planning workshops to develop goals and priorities for areas of the city.[20]

The Roanoke Neighborhood Partnership, by changing the way the city did business, empowered the neighborhoods to be real participants in the governance of the city. In a relatively short period of time, hundreds of people became active in issues directly affecting their neighborhoods. This practice changed the perception of city hall as "an obstacle to getting things done," and effectively made governance more accessible to the citizens.

The Practice of Democracy

Democracy in a postindustrial society like the United States is increasingly characterized as a system of governance orchestrated by the media to shape a mass of passive consumers. Because of the scale and structure of the political economy, we have come more and more to understanding the body politic as an adversarial democracy, in which the primary responsibility of the citizen is to vote. If one is committed to democracy as a social structure of human organization and politics, the question must be asked: Where does one learn to be a citizen? And how do groups of people communally engage in democratic action and develop community intentions?

There are those who argue that public schooling is a primary site for the active engagement of democracy because it provides a public space for exploring political and social relationships.[21] Giroux (1988), writing on the practice of education, describes the educative public space in a manner similar to our proposed dialogic space:

> By public space I mean . . . a concrete set of learning conditions where people come together to speak, to dialogue, to share their stories, and to struggle together within social relationships that strengthen rather than weaken the possibility for active citizenship.[22]

We would like to suggest that placemaking, like public schooling, offers a unique public space in which to weave a web of relationships that interact to create a common world. This is neither a space of "public opinion" nor solely a collection of individual votes, but a sustained and shared public dialogue about who we are and where we want to live.

The conception and formation of the Roanoke Neighborhood Partnership was predicated on a view of humans as citizens who are willing and able to take collective action on behalf of their own communities, and the belief that this action would strengthen the city as a whole. The distributive-power framework created a structure that permitted—in fact, demanded—the active participation of citizens to make it work. Moreover, by locating the neighborhood

Figure 4.15 Neighborhood people celebrating their community in an RNP parade. (Photo courtesy of the city of Roanoke)

coordinator of the Partnership in the Office of Community Planning, the group responsible for the economic development of the city, the city gave evidence that it recognized it had a responsibility to facilitate democratic action.

All placemaking activity in the practice of planning is about the process of action framing, and action framing is always about the use (and abuse) of power—who can play, what are the boundaries for action, and how the players shall act. The answers to these queries in any placemaking intervention can be framed by a few, or by many. The approach can be dictated, or it can emerge from a collaborative engagement with the resulting process accepted, contested, or negotiated.

The folks in Roanoke who participated in the RNP over the years have sought control over their everyday lives—over the things closest to them, their families, and their community. They have worked on the condition of their neighborhoods and the spaces where their children play, such as the streets, vacant lots, and parks. They have improved the quality of the housing and created places to gather as a community. They have sought ways to control crime through physical interventions, such as improved street lighting and the distribution of special locks, and through collective action such as crime watches. One neighborhood eliminated all of the crack houses through twenty-four hour watches and by developing better relations with the police; they refused to be intimidated as individuals and took a stand together. The focus of the work in the Partnership has been on the making and unmaking of the everyday world, a recognition that when our places are endangered, when they are not cared for, we are endangered, and our children will not prosper.

Some aspects of the RNP's work went beyond the neighborhood level. The Partnership process has had the apparently paradoxical effect of acknowledging and empowering individual neighborhoods as discrete places, while at the same time forging an image of the city as a whole. The neighborhood is a real, concrete place in which one's life is lived, a physical locality that is known intimately. The city is an idea, a concept, which depends on understanding relationships—economic, social, political, and so forth—in the abstract. Both the neighborhood and the city have meaning, real and symbolic, in people's lives, and are reinforced and strengthened in the dialectical relationship. As Roanoke people came to know their neighborhoods more intimately, as people in dialogue worked to construct and transform their beloved places, and as neighborhood leaders began to know people in other neighborhoods who were actively working to do similar things, the concept of city, particularly the city of Roanoke, Va., took more substantial form. Not only did the partnership process result in real, physical changes in their neighborhoods; it concretized the image of the city of Roanoke for residents. Ginni Benson, a former neighborhood coordinator, put it this way: "The Partnership means getting to know people from different parts of the city and city administration. It made the city feel much smaller and literally, just like a big neighborhood."

One other change merits attention. A subtle, but significant, transformation in race relations occurred among participants in the Partnership. This was not an RNP goal, but rather an effect of the dialogic nature of the Partnership process. City neighborhoods in Roanoke, as with many cities, were and still are, very segregated by race and socioeconomic conditions. The movement to the suburbs had, to some extent, integrated the suburbs racially, but the structure of the city neighborhoods remained intact. In fact, some of the elders in the black community felt that integration had destroyed their communities by facilitating the movement of black middle-class leaders from the city neighborhoods into the suburbs. Moreover, because the life in many city communities is in the neighborhoods—the street, the church, the neighborhood association—there was little opportunity to meet people in other areas of the city.

What the RNP did was to legitimize contact between people simply because they were people working to improve their neighborhoods, a process not grounded in race or class. It created a structure that facilitated communication between black and white neighborhood residents who were addressing common problems. It may be easy to critique this aspect of change in race relations because the contact between blacks and white has not resulted in a radical restructuring of social and/or economic conditions. However, the RNP did make significant changes in the lives of some people; therefore, it warrants attention as a way in which placemaking creates the possibility for transformed relationships. White people who had never had the opportunity to visit a black neighborhood came to gospel concerts to show support for colleagues; small celebrations were attended among neighborhoods, such as the dedication of the tractor mower or the ribbon cutting ceremony to celebrate the beginning of the storm-water management project. Hannah Arendt wrote: "Action . . . establishes relationships and therefore has an inherent tendency to force open all limitations and cut across all boundaries."[23] Blacks and whites, who may have professed integration, now had the chance to live it in a way that gave form and meaning to their hopes for improved relationships between the races, and a more democratic society.

The RNP, as an organization concerned with the quality of life in neighborhoods, takes time for reflecting on its work, and considers how it must be modified to meet new challenges and ongoing changes. There are always new neighborhoods joining, new leadership in city hall, and new people involved. Furthermore, there are new programs in city hall. For example, the neighborhood planning process initiated through the Visions Project in many ways overlaps the RNP process. Understanding the relationship between these efforts is one of the current tasks of the Steering Committee, the Office of Community Planning, and the RNP Coordinator. Another issue that demands attention is the increasing complexity of the neighborhood projects. Some are moving away from physical planning to social issues—things that are less visible and require a long-term commitment of energy and resources. This kind of democratic work requires a maturation of the organization and a more sophisticated relationship among the participants. These types of complex questions are the subject of the continuing dialogue of the Partnership.

The Roanoke Neighborhood Partnership demonstrates that placemaking can be a forum for the practice of democracy. Professionals working in the public domain can enable people to practice citizenship within a dialogic space in which neighborhoods and cities can be discussed, critiqued, planned, and changed. Lenora Williams, one of the neighborhood leaders of the Southeast Action Forum, commented that she "see[s] the Partnership as a professional guide in helping with communication with the city and business organizations." The ability to communally communicate needs, desires, concerns, and hopes in a public forum is a democratic struggle. All who participate in this form of critical practice must attend to small details, such as how and where meetings happen, and also to much more complex issues, such as neighborhood organizing and governmental bureaucratic reward systems. This is the work of creating and maintaining community intentions and framing action on behalf of larger public groups.

The Roanoke Neighborhood Partnership has changed greatly since the early 1980s, reflecting new times and new people.[24] But continuation of the RNP in its initial form is not an appropriate measure of its viability as a democratic project. Quite the contrary: If the RNP existed today as it did in 1980, one might say it had

Figure 4.16 Barbara Duerk as chair of the Steering Committee leading the celebration at the Partnership's tenth-anniversary gathering. (Photo courtesy of the city of Roanoke)

become a static institution, demonstrating that it was not respond-ing to the dialogue of its participants. It was never conceived as a project that would be completed; rather, it became a way of work-ing. As the Partnership moves through its second decade and faces even more complex issues at a time of even further reduction in public spending, the viability of this particular form of community structure will be tested.

A critical aspect of a utopian project such as the one initiated in Roanoke is not the achievement of an end goal, but the struggle to engage. All of us who participated in the inception, growth, and transformation of the Roanoke Neighborhood Partnership have joined in a process of community building. This story, which de-scribes the attitudes, capacities, judgments, and values of a demo-cratic project, confirms a dynamic act of human construction. The Roanoke Neighborhood Partnership planning process reveals the potential power of placemaking as a democratic project when there is a willingness to engage in a sustained dialogue about how places are made and remade by people in places.

5

REDEFINING EXCELLENCE IN THE URBAN ENVIRONMENT: THE RUDY BRUNER AWARD PROGRAM

In the previous chapters we have told three stories of placemaking: the making of a new church building, the ongoing maintenance of an office environment, and neighborhood planning in a small city. Each story describes situations in which professionals and people with a long-term stake in their dwelling, church, or work circumstances collaborated in placemaking events and sustained conversation and action on living well. Although each situation had unique aspects, it is important to remember that these stories are not idiosyncratic: Competent and empowering placemaking happens every day in many ways.

The Rudy Bruner Award (RBA), our fourth story, reveals the both common and extraordinary nature of placemaking in many different settings.[1] The RBA is an inquiry into urban excellence established to identify and honor urban places that effectively integrate economic, visual, and social perspectives and that are considered "excellent" by the many people involved in the process of making and maintaining them. In the words of the call for participation brochure, this nontraditional award was established to illuminate "the subtle and difficult process of creating excellence in the urban environment." As such the program is designed to bring recognition to the *place,* and in so doing, recognizes all the participants involved in its making and management. Its intellectual intention is to directly address the question "What is urban excellence?"[2]

In this chapter we analyze stories from the Rudy Bruner Award Archives to demonstrate the power of placemaking in different settings and to confirm that our experiences in the first three stories of this book are not unique.[3] Unlike other stories in the book, we were not involved in placemaking activities with the RBA program applicants. Rather, our involvement was to gather and reflect on the work of others, confirming and interrogating assertions about the nature of excellence in each place and attempting to understand how various knowledges and worldviews were situated. The awards process serves as an example of how the intellectual work of reflecting on placemaking events can be an integral part of critical practice. Furthermore, it illustrates what one might do with the intellectual result of this critical activity through situating the placemaking stories in another contemporary setting, a conference on urban violence co-sponsored by the RBA. We use it as an example of one way stories like those offered in the extensive RBA program applications become part of the practices of placemaking in other communities.

In 1994 the RBA program began its fifth cycle of recognizing excellent urban places and reflecting on how they came to be. Between 1987 and 1993 twenty-one projects had been short-listed as finalists out of a total of 339 applicants. We concentrated our analysis on the first five years of the program (1986–1990), during which eleven projects were designated as finalists and were reviewed in depth. They demonstrate the range and complexity of projects considered by the program's Selection Committees. Our analysis also employs a less detailed review of all the initial 176 applicants to the 1987 and 1989 program cycles, both to test what we see as general trends emerging from places designated as finalists and to establish an intellectual framework for our search for tentative answers to the question of what is urban excellence.

Perspectives on Excellence

It is no surprise that beauty and economy, or at least self-sufficiency, are perceived to be essential to *excellence*.[4] This conclusion is unmistakable from the results of 140 individual interviews conducted during Selection Committee research team visits to

TABLE 5.1
Eleven projects: The Rudy Bruner Award short lists—1987 and 1989.

THE 1987 RUDY BRUNER AWARDS

The 1987 Rudy Bruner Award Winner
Pike Place Market: "PRESERVING A SOCIAL ECOLOGY" (Seattle, WA)
  A 7.5-acre preservation district, Pike Place Market in Seattle, Washington, is an unusual complex of buildings overlooking the Puget Sound serving a very diverse population including wealthy residents, tourists, produce merchants, craftspeople, farmers, the elderly, and low–income as well as indigent populations.

The 1987 Rudy Bruner Award Short List
Casa Rita: "SMALL-SCALE SOLUTIONS TO BIG PROBLEMS" (New York, NY)
  Casa Rita is an emergency shelter for sixteen homeless women and their children in the South Bronx.
St. Francis Square: "NOT JUST HOUSING, BUT A WAY OF LIFE" (San Francisco, CA)
  West of downtown San Franciso next to Japan Town lies a three-block development of cooperative low- and moderate-income family housing built in 1963 (299 apartments, two/three bedrooms) through the sponsorship of the International Longshoremen's and Warehousemen's Union and the Pacific Maritime Association.
Fairmount Health Center: "AN OASIS WITHIN A DECAYING CITYSCAPE" (Philadelphia, PA)
  The Fairmount Health Center brings affordable health care to underserved Hispanic and black populations, who struggle with high unemployment, a decaying housing stock, and some of the highest maternal risk and infant mortality rates in the nation.
Quality Hill: "THE RISKS OF BEING FIRST" (Kansas City, MO)
  Quality Hill is a story of "firsts" for Kansas City: the first successful downtown housing in forty years, the first major effort at the adaptive reuse of historic structures, and the first use of private foundation money in Kansas City for downtown housing development.

THE 1989 RUDY BRUNER AWARDS

1989 Rudy Bruner Award Co-Winners
Portland Downtown Plan: "CITIZEN PLANNING FOR THE LONG TERM" (Portland, OR)
  The creation and implementation of the Portland, Ore. Downtown Plan and Program is a cooperative partnership of interests and citizens aimed at making downtown Portland a vibrant people-oriented urban center.
The Tenant Interim Lease Program: "COOPERATIVE LEARNING AND LIVING" (New York, NY)
  The Tenant Interim Lease (TIL) Program is an innovative project to help tenants rescue buildings abandoned by their owners in New York's low-income neighborhoods.

The 1989 Rudy Bruner Award Short List[a]
The Southwest Corridor Project: "PEOPLE AND TRANSIT BEFORE HIGHWAYS" (Boston, MA)
  The Massachusetts Bay Transportation Authority (MBTA)–Southwest Corridor Project is a long-range transportation planning effort that helped save and revitalize three neighborhoods stretching from downtown Boston to the southwest suburbs.

(continued)

TABLE 5.1 (*Continued*)

Cabrillo Village: "THE FAMILY FIRST" (Saticoy, CA)

Cabrillo Village, an innovative housing cooperative in Ventura County, California, located on the site of a former camp housing migrant workers, was developed through the efforts of the low–income farmworker families that now own it.

The Radial Reuse Plan: "NORTH OF O IS GREAT" (Lincoln, NB)

The Radial Reuse Project in Lincoln, Nebraska, an example of neighborhood revitalization through the cooperative efforts of government officials and concerned citizens, redeveloped a four-mile corridor of vacant and underutilized land stretching through three of Lincoln's older inner-city neighborhoods all north of "O" Street.

A Recreation Path: "THE COMMUNITY BACKYARD" (Stowe, VT)

The Stowe Recreation Path is a community greenway that provides a safe and attractive path for biking, walking, cross-country skiing, and socializing.

*a*The 1989 Bruner Award short list included projects that tended to carry more emphasis on large-scale planning. Several of the projects were more complex and had large numbers of participants. The Southwest Corridor Project in Boston, Mass. for example, was that state's largest capital construction program ever, and the Portland Downtown Plan and implementation included over $1 billion in construction. The Selection Committee identified six projects out of ninety-two for the review team to investigate.

short-listed project sites and also evident from our analysis of the almost 2000 perspective sheets completed by individuals as part of the 176 RBA applications for the 1987 and 1989 awards. Other criteria for excellence evident in the material are perhaps more surprising and useful. Both the people interviewed and the perspective sheets report that excellence is dependent on the relationship that constituents establish with each other, with the place, and with the processes by which the award was and is continually created. All of the characteristics of excellence merged as applicants described two primary aspects of the places: (1) their origins, and (2) the organization and management of these places after occupancy.

Submissions to the RBA tell the story of project beginnings and appear to be rooted in one or more of three factors: crises, opportunities for empowerment, and acts of political and personal courage. It is not possible to rank order the importance of such broad factors, or to suggest that any one is more important than the other. In each place, the roles played by crisis, empowerment, and/or courage were uniquely situated.

All RBA project applicants are also asked to reflect on the organization and management of their place, relating their perception of excellence to its long-term viability. The continuation of excellence in a place most often correlates with the existence of factors like the emergence of the place as a symbol of the social health in a community or city, the existence of a system of checks and balances that precludes any single interest from dominating, and the use of each problem presented to the place as an opportunity for critical reflection and placemaking action. Many of the RBA applications we analyzed gave evidence of all these factors, and some identified at least one or two of them as significantly contributing to their ability to maintain excellence.

The factors that make up the origins of an excellent place also contribute to its ongoing maintenance. For example, the crisis theme in the origins category is conceptually similar to finding an opportunity in every problem in the organization-and-management category. Both are fundamentally about "never wasting a good crisis" or problem, but crisis in the origin story has intensity and power, enabling it to focus the energy of a large constituency almost immediately. The idea of finding opportunities in problems is often less dramatic; it is more akin to an attitude that gets incorporated into the system of management and maintenance of a place. A similar difference exists between the idea of empowerment as a focus for an origin story, and the idea of checks and balances set in a place to sustain it, keeping different groups empowered. The courageous acts of key participants in an origin story are codependent with the activities engaged in to sustain a place as a symbol of continuing social health and to manage the checks and balances. Our analysis in this chapter of the RBA applicants focuses on both themes: the characteristics of project origins as well as the organization and maintenance of places after occupancy. We cite individual placemaking activities in order to demonstrate the interrelated characteristics of the origins and of the organization and management of excellent places.[5]

Crises as Catalysts

Environmental change in the twentieth century is often the result of converging forces that reach near-crisis proportions before action is taken. Relating physical and organizational change to the historic event of crisis appears to establish the origin story of a project and sets a consistent basis of comparison that stays with the project throughout its life. Sometimes the crisis is based on an almost violent citizen opposition to a proposed change, such as the demolition of a building or the construction of a highway through a neighborhood. At other times the crisis derives from an aggregation of uncomfortable dynamics related to such things as the gradual flight of the middle class to the suburbs, increasing ranks of people without homes, and the slow but devastating process of neighborhood disinvestment. The crises take many forms, but all appear to have the ability to focus opinion and effort in response.

The Coates House Hotel fire on Quality Hill in Kansas City, Mo. is a good example. It was a serious fire, adding insult to an already blighted entrance to downtown and putting the historic structure at risk. What was once just one more eyesore in a field of many was now a health hazard, a liability that, according to many people, had to be demolished before it endangered more lives. The newly emerging Historic Kansas City Foundation contested this solution; they brought a great deal of public pressure to bear on saving the structure by starting a carefully conceived cleanup program at the site of the fire. Press coverage of the event headlined wealthy "Mink Coats" working side by side with local resident "Denim Jackets" and spoke to the shared perception that an important part of Kansas City was threatened.

The fire and resulting "Save the Coates House" campaign brought new life to several years of low-key land acquisition and raised hopes for a renovated Quality Hill that could include, but would not be limited to, the restoration and reuse of the Coates House. Yet, even as a development package was being put together, most of the commercial and business interests in town thought it to be an unrealizable dream. One bank chose to donate money to the project but did so as part of a community gesture, rather than taking an equity position in the project for fear of showing a bad investment when the project failed. This pessimism may have been caused, in part, by the perception that the devastated Coates House was only a small part of a much larger problem. When McCormick Barron, developers from St. Louis, started to put the development package together, they added to the pressure by defining the crisis as involving more than preservation and safety; they reinforced growing concerns that no new middle-class housing had been built in Kansas City in decades and that the downtown was slowly dying. Housing was to be part of the strategic effort to save historic property and also the life of the downtown area.

For many in Kansas City, the real crisis was seen as the lack of a middle- and upper-income presence downtown, and the Quality Hill project was seen as a useful catalyst to focus attention on this. The preservation of the historic stock of buildings, the infill housing, and commercial development proposed for parts of the project were to pioneer an increase in the diversity of the downtown population, and to add to the power and economic clout of the area in the competition for city resources.[6]

Concerns about human safety, saving the historic building stock, bringing the middle class back downtown, and changing the eyesore entrance to the city all reveal the complex nature of the crisis. In fact, most of the stories in the RBA Archives are authored by a range of special interests with very different perspectives on what the real crisis is and what action should therefore occur. Nevertheless, the energy gathered by such multiple interpretations of crisis conditions often becomes transformed into collective action, leading to the dramatic improvement of places.

In another story, Boston's Southwest Corridor Project, the crisis for the residents of three neighborhoods was a proposed highway cutting through their communities. The highway plan brought people together to fight for and against it. "People before highways!" was the populist slogan. For others interested in the regional economics of the area, the crisis was defined as a lack of access between the suburbs and downtown and the need to open up the neighborhoods in the corridor to economic development. Business and other interests worked more quietly in support of the highway construction. Ultimately, mass transit replaced the elevated highway plan, satisfying the needs of the business interests, while the transit corridor was decked over in several places to create a linear park linking the neighborhoods. This process of transforming conflicting and often negative, angry protest into positive action for a project occurs frequently in RBA projects.

In the Southwest Corridor, the level of consortium energy supporting the resulting transit and park plan became very strong and continuous. For example, when the project was threatened with serious budget cuts, the neighborhoods and business interests worked through an elaborate system of committees and organizations in order to maintain the integrity of the solution they had derived. The origin dynamics established a system of checks and balances and a history of successful collaboration that later protected the project.

Another example of crisis involved a San Francisco project. In

Figure 5.1 Part of the origin story of the Southwest Corridor project was an aggressive campaign to stop a planned freeway through three Boston neighborhoods. (From the files of Stull and Lee, Inc.)

the late 1950s the San Francisco Redevelopment Authority identified an urban exodus to the suburbs, which they defined as a "crisis," comprising many small acts of migration over a number of years. The planners believed these migrations would, over time, erode the residential base of the city. A second perception of crisis involved the increased cost of housing, which was excluding a large part of the in-city population from decent housing. As part of their effort to reverse both conditions, the Redevelopment Authority issued a Request for Proposals for an area of the city off Geary Boulevard near Japan Town, cleared under an urban renewal program in the early 1950s and still largely vacant. They asked for developer/architect teams to propose medium-density and low- to moderate-income housing that would be able to compete with suburban characteristics. The Redevelopment Authority hoped for a model of housing development that might be repeated elsewhere in the city to stem the outward migration of residents. The result of their efforts was the 300-unit St. Francis Square Housing Cooperative, which has since become a national model for garden apartments in urban areas.

Another variation on the crisis theme is illustrated by the still extant condition of high infant mortality and maternal risk in North Philadelphia. The crisis is explicitly medical, but it also deals with the hopelessness and desperate poverty of a large segment of Philadelphia's population. In the early 1980s, North Philadelphia Health Services, a nonprofit health services corporation, saw these

Figure 5.2 St. Francis Square was originally part of the San Francisco Redevelopment Authority strategy to address what they saw as the crisis of white flight to the suburbs by creating, in the inner city, viable mixed-race housing. (Photo courtesy of the Rudy Bruner Award Archives)

and other problems in the area as being interrelated and at a crisis stage. Over time they developed three health centers which now collectively serve 80,000 clients a year. The 16,000-square-foot Fairmount Health Center, the third facility provided by the corporation, is specifically designed to go beyond the delivery of health care, addressing the crisis of despair and hopelessness in the area. It encourages community groups to use its conference facilities for meetings after hours, offers education programs in the auditorium, and makes its vending and waiting area open to the general public during regular hours. The community pride in the facility is demonstrated by the large number of people who pose for graduation or wedding pictures in front of what they consider the nicest building in the neighborhood. It is one of very few buildings in the surrounding area not covered with graffiti or otherwise vandalized.

Adopting the Hispanic metaphor of the "village church," its director and staff set out to make it a symbol of hope, a place of pride, and a place of community.

The Bruner Selection Committees over the years have tended to select projects that took full advantage of crisis conditions. Quality Hill used the energy behind the historic preservation movement and a fire in a significant building to help focus the energy of people concerned about the lack of housing downtown, the ugliness of the entrance to downtown, and the health and life safety in that area of the city. The Southwest Corridor project used the crisis of a proposed highway scheme and its attendant "stop the highway" movement to address an immediate threat to neighborhood preservation, as well as to argue for better public transit and the need for regional economic development. The St. Francis Square project sought to stop the crisis of migration to the suburbs, to address the crisis created by acres of land laid waste by the city's urban renewal program, and at the same time to ameliorate the crisis defined by the lack of affordable housing for large segments of its population. The Fairmount Health Center was a response to the crisis created by poverty and its associated poor health conditions and loss of community cohesion.

In general, our analysis of applications to the RBA shows that over 75% of the places submitted for award had their origins in what applicants described as some form of crisis. Most of the projects chosen by the Selection Committees for more detailed evaluation were motivated by the related energies of more than one crisis, and these continue to serve the interests of places made. The origins become popular folklore, and these stories establish continuing interest in placemaking activity.

Empowerment

Often projects that have their origins in the power of crisis conditions are also stories of empowerment. Most of the projects identified for further study by the Selection Committees engaged participants from divergent perspectives in a manner that enabled them to significantly influence each other and the place-becoming. The crisis was often found in the divergence; the empowerment lay in translating disagreements into positive action through discrete acts of inclusion that enlarged project constituencies. Usually this form of empowerment was not a gift from one participant in the process to another, but rather something either fought for and won, or revealed in the dialogic space created during project development.

In several cases, the RBA applicants clearly stated that the project was intended to enable individuals to develop the skills and facilities needed to become coauthors of their places and lives.[7] Empowerment also often extended itself beyond the bounds of a single project and took the form of project constituents acquiring a voice in the conduct of city and regional governance.

One of the more moving examples of an empowering place and process in the RBA program is the story of Cabrillo Village in Saticoy, Calif. The place was built as a private farmworkers' camp in the 1930s for single men who came on a seasonal basis from Mexico to pick fruit for the Saticoy Lemon Growers Association. There were originally about 100 houses, most of them about 480 square feet in area. The company maintained an office on the site and took minimal care of the houses and dirt streets. For most of its life the camp was a depressing place, characterized by years of deferred maintenance and enclosed by a chain-link fence topped with barbed wire. The houses were shacks of single-wall construction: two-by-two-inch studs with board and batten on the exterior. The plumbing was simple—a toilet and a kitchen sink. The septic system for the community emptied into two open settling ponds next to the river. The camp in Saticoy was one of a number of such camps, which collectively represent an ugly chapter in the history of exploitative agricultural practices in the United States.

By the 1960s, families were living in the camps. Laws against the exploitation of migrant farm labor had stiffened slightly, and immi-

Figure 5.3 A typical farmworker shack at the Saticoy, Calif. camp in the 1930s had 480 square feet of living space built for men, with a toilet and kitchen sink. (Photo courtesy of the Cabrillo Economic Development Corporation)

gration practices changed correspondingly; married men brought their families to the camp, working to keep up the houses on their meager incomes. By 1974, significant changes were beginning to occur in agriculture: the development of global markets, successful union organizing, and the realization among growers that profit margins were getting very thin. Many of the residents of the camp had permanently immigrated to the United States to work for the Lemon Growers Association and had their rent deducted from their paychecks.

In October 1974, working and camp conditions had deteriorated to the point where the farmworkers went on strike. They were inspired by the union organizing work of the Mexican-American Caesar Chavez, who was successfully getting national attention focused on the plight of migrant farmworkers. The October strike was organized locally by the people in the camp through the efforts of a union organizing committee. It lasted for one month, after which time the growers accepted the terms of settlement and the people went back to work. The Lemon Growers Association, however, proceeded to ignore the terms of the settlement, and the workers began to organize another strike, this time enlisting the support of Chavez's United Farmworkers Union (UFW). The crisis came to a head in the late summer and early fall of 1975, when the workers were to vote to certify the UFW as their union. A series of strike-breaking moves by the growers was initiated, including laying off 190 union-eligible workers and sending eviction notices to camp residents in an effort to disperse the remaining union-eligible members and to close the camp. These moves precipitated the crisis that ultimately led to further empowerment of camp residents and to complete transformation of the place into what is now called Cabrillo Village.

As a part of the eviction process, camp residents were offered $500 each for family relocation expenses and were given thirty days to leave. The reason the growers gave for closing the camp was the extraordinarily large number of health and safety violations (estimated at 1600), which would cost them more than $1 million to repair. Of course, many of these violations were directly attributable to over thirty years of deferred maintenance by the growers. Even though it was clear to many of the families that the growers were trying to prevent the workers from organizing by dispersing them, a few took the money and left their homes, attempting to find housing elsewhere in the county. Most of these workers discovered very quickly that there was little available affordable housing for large families.

When the majority of families realized they did not have the option to move, they decided to fight, staging protest marches, conducting all-night vigils at the home of one grower, and generating media coverage regarding their conditions. Both the Catholic church and the UFW stepped in at this point to lend their support. The UFW offered training in leadership and organizing while the church offered its Saticoy facility for meetings. It was a priest from the church's Migrant Ministry who initially suggested that the workers buy the houses. Meanwhile, the growers had signed an option to sell the whole camp for real estate development, brought a bulldozer to the site, and destroyed the houses vacated by those who had decided to move. The workers continued to exercise their power, waging a letter-and-picketing campaign that eventually convinced the potential buyer to abandon his plans. When the growers escalated the situation by returning with bulldozers to raze the camp's preschool, the residents formed a "human circle," holding hands and surrounding the building.

The human circle around the preschool was a gesture of defiance that further united the community and brought widespread attention to conditions at the camp. The preschool employed workers funded by the federal Head Start program, which was administered by the local school district and a local elementary school. Both the principal of the school and the president of the school board were at the site during the showdown with the bulldozers, ostensibly to protect their employees, but also to bring some political pressure to bear on the camp owners to force them to back off. Public reaction indicated that even the most conservative people in the country identified with the American ideal behind the resistance.[8]

Over the next six months the workers organized into a corporation, chose a board of directors, and met with the Saticoy Lemon Growers Association to negotiate a purchase price for the camp. They were assisted in opening this dialogue by the UFW, the Catholic church, and a number of nonprofit groups, including the Campaign for Human Development, the Housing Assistance Council, and Self-Help Enterprises. Government support from Ventura County was provided by its Director of Human Relations, Rodney Fernandez.

From these beginnings, the new owners of Cabrillo Village developed their twenty-five-acre site as a limited-equity stock cooper-

Figure 5.4 One of the renovations at Cabrillo Village following the purchase of the camp by the farmworkers' cooperative. The largely self-help renewal of the original farmworker shacks at Cabrillo Village in Saticoy, Calif. was a tremendous source of pride for the residents. (Photo courtesy of the Cabrillo Economic Development Corporation)

ative for low-income farmworker families. The development includes 154 units of renovated and new family housing, eighty units of which were the existing shacks made into single-family homes by the farmworkers. New construction was contracted in two phases, involving first thirty-five new multifamily units in quadraplexes, and then thirty-nine additional new townhouse units. Cabrillo Village now supports over 150 families with about 600 children. The cooperative also constructed the village office building, a convenience store, a church, a laundry, a community center,

Figure 5.5 New townhouses, built as part of the latest developments at Cabrillo Village, provide low- and moderate-income single-family housing. (Photo courtesy of the Rudy Bruner Award Archives)

playing fields, and new infrastructure including sewer, water, and road improvements. All of this was done with broad participation by village residents every step of the way, as they turned what was once known simply as "the camp" into a place of intense family pride.[9]

The empowerment first revealed in the fight to open a dialogue between camp owners and camp residents continues in the Cabrillo Village story. They widened the dialogue to include Ventura County officials, the UFW, several nonprofit groups, and the local school district, which has changed the unequal power dynamics of the earlier conflict and increased the potential for residents to take control of the housing, education, and employment circumstances of their lives. The residents have used their years of camp meetings, the union organizing process, their discussions with social service providers, and their interactions with government officials as opportunities to develop the leadership of their community. Gradually residents have become more and more independent of these support organizations, establishing their own employment base and new low-cost housing development. Several of their children are now college graduates, others are in trade schools, and most are graduating high school. The employment base of the community has diversified so that it is no longer solely dependent on farm labor. Residents of the village are fully aware of their power to influence the circumstances affecting their lives, and they are fully engaged in the struggle to live life well.

Other projects identified for review by the Bruner Selection Committees are also about people empowering themselves to take control of the most basic elements of their lives by governing their housing. The Tenant Interim Lease (TIL) program in New York City, winner of the 1989 RBA, facilitated the renovation of over 500 buildings, most of which are now operated by tenant-owned cooperatives. St. Francis Square in San Francisco remains a classic project in low- to moderate-income tenant-owned cooperation. It is clear from the on-site interviews and application perspective sheets from the Cabrillo Village, TIL, and St. Francis Square projects that housing of last or almost last resort became the housing of choice. The liberating effect of such housing choices is illustrated through the transformation of both personal and group life during the process of placemaking.

Sometimes the empowerment theme in the Rudy Bruner Award Archives has repercussions for governance that extend well beyond the confines of a single housing project. For example, as the residents of St. Francis Square matured as a cooperative organization, they also gained political clout and represented their own and their neighborhood's interests in acquiring city services. The participants in Boston's Southwest Corridor Project used their involvement in the collaborative process of development as a kind of school, in which whole communities and government agencies learned how to cooperate. The lessons of their work together are now legends in Boston and continue to influence projects all over the city and region.

In one RBA case the process of placemaking actually helped to change the governing structure of an entire city. The complex story of the Radial Reuse Plan in Lincoln, Neb. involves the empowerment of three relatively poor communities in the north-central part of the city. The radial highway was part of a 1952 master plan for the city but was never built. By the early 1970s, however, the plan was still considered viable by many. There had been over twenty years of gradual land acquisition and disinvestment in the three communities anticipating highway construction, leaving the areas with no infrastructure improvements, many vacant lots, and a large backlog of deferred maintenance on their building stock.

The empowerment of Lincoln's neighborhoods grew out of their confrontation of the conditions of deterioration in the three communities. Prior to 1970 few neighborhoods played a significant role in the city's governance. However, from 1970 to 1980, a consortium of eighteen neighborhood associations in the affected area, called the Neighborhood Alliance, was formed to fight against the highway. The Alliance was aware that the highway plan was monitored by a citizen's goals and policies committee appointed by the mayor that, in turn, reported to both the mayor and to seven City Council members elected at–large. The Neighborhood Alliance was concerned that the at–large structure of the City Council did not give the neighborhoods a significant voice in the planning: They could not influence the City Council delegates who tended to come from the more affluent sections of the city, and they had no real access to the mayor. As the neighborhoods consolidated their interests in the radial land, they developed solidarity. A group of political activists led by a VISTA volunteer, working in the most distressed of the impacted communities, successfully organized a revision to the council makeup. The resulting council structure called for four district representatives and three at-large representatives to replace the seven at-large City Council seats. This redistribution of power on the Council assured better geographic representation. Eric Youngberg, the VISTA volunteer, was elected as the district representative from the radial reuse neighborhoods. The political restructuring was also reinforced when Helen Boosalis, a staunch supporter of citizen involvement, was elected mayor in 1975. Thus the initial work of empowered communities to influence a long-standing highway plan became the vehicle to challenge and redesign city government in Lincoln. The new political infrastructure established the basis for defeating a 1981 ballot initiative to finally build the radial highway, and helped establish the importance of neighborhoods in city government.

One attribute of a good placemaking process is that it builds relationships to the place being made and creates relationships between the participants. These same participants then carry the lessons learned from the process into other planning and design projects. In the case of Lincoln, the Radial Reuse Plan process has dramatically improved the relationship between the city and its neighborhoods by establishing mechanisms that give the neighborhoods a stronger voice in issues directly affecting them. No one makes a neighborhood or city development move in Lincoln without first finding out and carefully considering what the neighborhoods think.

Empowerment, like crisis, takes on different dimensions in different projects. It is often a by-product of very pragmatic problem solving, occasionally surfacing as a specific response to oppression, and sometimes beginning as a matter of form or ethical principle. However it begins, it takes on a life of its own: It is literally "out of control" while it redefines what control means in placemaking processes. At its best, empowerment establishes a continuing basis for integrally involving people in the placemaking tasks central to their lives.

Courage

Wherever there is crisis and the process of empowerment is taken seriously, there is courage. The RBA Archives are rich with examples of politicians, neighborhood activists, and whole communities exhibiting courage under difficult circumstances. Massachusetts Governor Frank Sergeant turned down $650 million in interstate highway funds earmarked for the Southwest Corridor highway without assurance that the state would get it back in transit funds for the Southwest Corridor transit and park project. The city of Seattle put $64 million in federal urban renewal funds at risk when it declared the Pike Place a Preservation District; it would be over ten years before Senator Magnasun could negotiate replacement funds to help in the restoration of Seattle's famous market. In an election year, Portland's first-term Mayor Goldschmidt, when faced with a dying downtown, started a transit project and all the construction disruption that entails. It was not a project that would yield strong return while he was in office. One of his campaign posters shows him in the rubble of a torn-up commercial street with his hands outstretched asking, "Would you do this in an election year?" The answer was clearly "yes," even with considerable early resistance from some of the more conservative business interests in town.

Besides politicians, others exercise courage in making excellent places. The International Longshoreman's and Warehouseman's Union and the Pacific Maritime Association developed the St. Francis Square housing project, successfully pushing for mixed-race housing when it was decidedly unpopular, financially untried, and, some thought, illegal to work for racial quotas in housing. The financial risk in the housing project created significant apprehension due to the investment of union pension funds. Rita Zimmer and her New York City–based Women in Need organization went to New York borough organizations with proposals to establish housing for homeless women and children at a time when the prevailing wisdom was that such facilities tended to destabilize rather than contribute to their surrounding neighborhoods. Women in Need took the unpopular and courageous position that such facilities could actually contribute to the stability and development of transitional neighborhoods, and then proved it with the development of Casa Rita in the South Bronx. Also in New York, we see the courage of one tenant organization after another learning how to cooperate on the complex processes of building management and eventual tenant ownership in the TIL program.

A facet of courage is the deep personal commitment needed to originate an excellent place. The very act of taking time from already full lives for placemaking often requires courageously choosing to give up something in favor of the often uncertain potential of a place-becoming. Most of the projects in the Rudy Bruner Award Archives told of several people who gave much of their lives for extended periods of time to make the projects successful. Anthony Pangaro, the Governor's project coordinator for the Southwest Corridor, speaks of giving the effort ten years of nights and week-ends in addition to sixty-hour work weeks. The community organizers who initially worked to stop the highway in Boston and then became involved in the transit project worked for fifteen years to transform the crisis into a positive force in their communities. The volunteer community and neighborhood group work in the Radial Reuse planning in Lincoln, Neb. was a fifteen- to twenty-year project for many. Anne Lusk is credited with almost singlehandedly bringing the neighborhood greenway in Stowe, Vt. into existence through a largely volunteer effort over a period of several years. The Citizen's Advisory Committee for the 1972 Downtown Plan in Portland, Ore. was still active with some of the same leadership seventeen years later to continue facilitating the plan implementation, keeping the citizens informed of new issues, and assisting in the review of projects. The origin stories in the RBA Archives reveal that a courageous commitment of time and energy is often an integral part of making excellent places.

Time commitments, political vulnerability, and financial risks are just some of the indicators of the courage people exhibit in making excellent places. The conditions created by crisis and the aspiration for empowerment also call for people to take positions and act without certainty or sometimes even clarity. Creating excellent places may well be fundamentally about accepting the personal, professional, political, and financial risks demanded by the circumstances of place and about trusting in the possibility of forgiveness and correction.

The Organizational Dynamics of Excellent Places

The same interrelated processes that create a place also serve to sustain it over its lifetime. Often, however, the origin stories are intense or even explosive when compared with the daily acts of management and maintenance that must follow them. An analysis of the operations and maintenance of places thought to be excellent by RBA applicants demonstrates that several patterns are similar from story to story. Many place constituents had adopted the attitude that daily problems could be opportunities to further secure support for their place. There also tended to be a strong system of checks and balances in the organization of many places, insuring that the empowerment of place constituents was not compromised by the accumulation of too much power by any one vested interest. Finally, the ongoing management and maintenance of a place was conducted in a manner that continued to reinforce recognition of the place as a symbol of social health. The places are nurtured and change over time even as they continue to acknowledge the crisis, empowerment, and courage demonstrated in their origins. Places, as symbols of social health, must continually be reinvented to contribute to the processes of living life well, as people discover and solve new problems and continue the process of empowerment through checks and balances.

The 1987 Rudy Bruner Award was given to Pike Place Market in Seattle, Wash. A study of the transcripts of the RBA Selection Committee deliberations, the on-site evaluation reports by the research team, and the application materials provided by the Pike Place Market Foundation all give evidence of what we describe as the characteristics that contribute to the origins and maintenance of excellent places.

In many of the interviews, the Selection Committee research team was told that the Pike Place Market is a real and vital place, a living symbol of the social health of the area. Observers of the Market attribute this perception at least partially to its populist origins. The farmers of the Seattle region started the Pike Place Market by selling produce out of the backs of wagons in an effort to eliminate the middlemen, who buy wholesale from producers and sell retail to consumers. On August 17, 1907, about a dozen wagons came with produce for the opening day of the new market, despite the strenuous objections of what some described as "price gouging produce wholesalers." They were met by thousands of eager customers. The next week brought seventy wagons, and again the public bought all of the produce directly from the farmers that produced it. The Market philosophy of "meet the producer" was a terrific success, and over the next three decades the farmers developed a physical infrastructure, allowing them to sell from stalls.

The popularity of the Market continued until World War II, when the internment of Japanese farmers greatly reduced the number of small family truck farms. With the rise of refrigeration and chain supermarkets, as well as the transformations of farmlands into suburbs, the Market went into a period of serious decline. By 1949 there were only fifty-three farmers still selling when ten years earlier there had been over 500. In the 1950s the place degenerated even further so that by the early 1960s, when urban renewal clearance programs were popular, the Market was an obvious area for city planners to redevelop.

Figure 5.6 Pike Place Market in 1912 was still selling out of the back of wagons directly from the farmer to the consumer. (Photo taken from a postcard; and courtesy of the Rudy Bruner Award Archives and University of Washington Press)

The revival of the Market was a grassroots initiative that started in opposition to the city's "1965 Downtown Plan," which called for the demolition of much of the Market area in favor of new construction. The opposition claimed that the Market had significant historical value and that, while it was run-down, it currently supported a resident population of merchant seamen and longshoremen, a substantial number of elderly people on fixed incomes, as well as people without homes. The argument to save the Market was further made by others, including local architect Victor Steinbrueck, who provided sketches celebrating the character of the Market and its residents.[10] He believed the Market represented a significant part of Seattle's history and that the new plan would have removed this character forever.

The voters' initiative defeated the 1965 plan in favor of a 7.5-acre preservation district, in spite of the fact that most of the major business interests, the established political power of the city, and the two major newspapers were firmly in favor of the plan. The basis for a continuing love affair between the Market and the city begun in 1907 was reinforced and continues to this day. Even those who "lost" the initiative are quick to admit that the results of the

Figure 5.7 Victor Steinbrueck's sketches of the Pike Place Market captured some of the character that the Friends of the Market campaigned to protect. (Sketches reproduced from Victor Steinbrueck's Market Sketchbook, published in 1968; courtesy of the University of Washington Press)

process were in Seattle's best interests. The funds eventually acquired to improve the saved Market were the same as those that would have been used to destroy and redevelop it. In the final analysis, there were no losers in the fight.

These two legendary populist actions, the creating and the saving of the Pike Place Market, developed dozens of groups with overlapping jurisdictions which now manage its social ecology and commercial viability. The Friends of the Market, the Pike Place Market Merchant's Association, the Market Foundation, the Public Development Authority, and the Preservation Commission are some examples of such groups. The assembly of such groups is admittedly not an "efficient" management structure, but then, the goal of its activity is not efficiency; it is rather the continued development of the social ecology and self-sustainability of the district.

The Pike Place Market is a community that functions as a distinctive, yet unpretentious, urban place. Its social structure is based largely on the interdependence of many people in the market area: Elderly and indigent residents depend on farmers for some of their surplus food; farmers rely on shoppers to help retain an agricultural way of life; children in the daycare center learn about diversity through exposure to market residents and visitors; and the daycare

relies on volunteers from the Market's senior citizen center. The interdependency between the people who work in, live in, and visit the Market creates a fully functioning social ecosystem.[11]

The rise of the Market Foundation in the 1980s further improved this social interdependence. When President Reagan's administration drastically cut federal spending for social programs after 1981, the Market needed an organization to help maintain its resident population. There was a firm belief that the residents of single-room occupancy dwellings, the elderly, and the children of the new immigrant farmers were as necessary to the health of the Market as the thousands of tourists who visited every day.

Several observers interviewed by the research team credit the Market Foundation's expansive program of activities as one of the ingredients that make the market a "real" place. The Foundation has raised funds to help support a senior center, a child-care center, a food bank, and a health center in the Market community, as well as to help build housing for the elderly and to rehabilitate some existing single-room occupancy housing. In the complex ecology of the Market, the child-care center supports the immigrant farmers selling in the Market while it offers a mission for the senior center; the food bank is stocked, in part, with the less salable but still healthful foods from the farmers; elderly housing overlooks the shopping street, Steinbrueck Park and parking lots, thus establishing a local Crime Watch; and the health center serves the needs of farmers, vendors, elderly, homeless, and children.

The Pike Place Market Public Development Authority (PDA) also contributes to the area's social ecology by ensuring that, in addition to low- and moderate-income housing for the elderly and indigent, some of the property in the district is developed as middle- and high-income condominiums. This addition to the district, along with the tourists, helps establish a kind of modified highest-and-best-use dynamic: One can buy a 5¢ cup of coffee in the coffee shop while across the street coffee is 95¢; single-room occupancy units are right next door to expensive condominiums; and you can buy hardware, fine jewelry, farm produce, fresh salmon, and secondhand clothing on the same block. It is this mix that enables the PDA to establish differential rents for facilities in the Market. A "Robin Hood" rent structure allows a new business time to incubate, and protects the viability of businesses at the low end of the profit margin.

The PDA and the Market Foundation have actively promoted the Pike Place Market as a mixed-race as well as mixed-income and mixed-use area. They have been working hard to promote land banking and family farming, supporting the regular need for fresh produce and providing opportunities for small family farms among the new wave of Asian immigrants that are settling in the northwestern United States. Again we see a symbiotic relationship between the viability of the Market and the social consciousness of its management.

In addition to the PDA and the Market Foundation, the Friends of the Market are very important to the vitality of the place. When the Market needs help, this loosely organized regional constituency is there, and it is both vocal and generous. The Friends initially organized the campaign to save the Market; they were strong supporters of the Market Foundation's fundraising for a new Market floor by giving the citizens of Seattle and visitors to the Market an opportunity to buy a personal piece of it, one tile at a time. The result is an elaborately tiled floor with names of citizens from all over the region inscribed on them. The Friends are always prepared to address any threat to the historical and social character of the Market.

Pike Place is continuing to change with new mixes of farm, fish, and crafts sales, adjustments to the level and type of services provided by the Market Foundation, and structural modifications to its economic base. Through these transformations, the Market is still guided by the courage and empowerment that were part of its origin story. It is a strong symbol of the social health in the region that remakes itself with each new problem encountered addressed; the checks and balances inherent in its inclusive governance continue to contribute to the quality of life for its constituents, who discover and solve new problems and thus reinforce the process of empowerment.[12] The reality of the Market surpasses the sum of factors contributing to its origins and to its maintenance and management because these factors are constantly redefined and renewed as the place evolves.

Place as a Symbol of Social Health

Places are symbols as well as discrete material locations, and some of the most complex characteristics of organizational dynamics revealed in the Bruner Archives address people's symbolic identification with their place. While the concept of such identification is an abstraction, it manifests itself in hundreds of concrete ways in the discrete acts of making and managing places. Pike Place Market, a symbol of the social health of Seattle and the surrounding region, is only one of several projects identified by the RBA Selection Committees that offer a strong symbolic dimension. The San Francisco Redevelopment Authority takes great pride in the mixed-race and mixed-income balance in the St. Francis Square Housing Cooperative, and members of the cooperative are proud to show off several other projects that have used St. Francis Square as a model. The people of the Authority, the residents of St. Francis Square, and the residents of projects modeled after St. Francis Square all tend to view their places as symbols of the emerging social health of the city. The South Bronx community and a long list of donors see the Casa Rita shelter for homeless women and children as an object of pride and social responsibility, and the residents of North Philadelphia see their new Fairmount Health Center as a symbol of hope. One of the first significant steps toward the physical and symbolic revitalization of urban Kansas City was achieved with Quality Hill. Private philanthropic foundations participated in the project because they saw the social value in downtown renewal, and they saw Quality Hill as an indication of the social health to come.

The story of the 1972 Portland Downtown Plan and Program offers another variation on this theme, focused on the revitalization of Portland, Ore. A multistorey parking garage was proposed for the block next to a major downtown department store and the historic Pioneer Square Courthouse. Widespread public resistance to the proposal was part of what propelled interest in downtown planning and helped to establish the urban plaza now known as Pioneer Square. The new downtown establishes Portland as a *public* city with an urban plaza instead of a parking garage, and with other new places for all its citizens, including a riverfront park, a transit mall, newly designed historic districts, a farmer's market, a new cultural and entertainment district, and downtown residential areas that contain a complement of low- to moderate-income housing. The planning process that facilitated the city's rebirth took thousands of hours of citizen committee work. What decisions were made and how they were made demonstrate Portland's commitment to the public domain; the what and how of "city making" establish its value as a continuing agent of social health.

The urban decay that was a part of the Portland landscape prior to implementation of the 1972 plan was a symptom of economic and social "dis-ease." Urban revitalization, if done in pursuit of social as well as economic goals, can be understood to symbolize good health. Like the revitalization of Seattle's Pike Place Market, the rebirth of Portland's downtown over the past eighteen years has had broad popular support. Its citizens own the bricks of the Pioneer Square Courthouse the same way the citizens of Seattle own the Pike Place Market tiles. The Square, like the Market, was born out of controversy and supported by a diverse public constituency. As the city became healthier, it acquired the power of self-fulfilling prophecy: The positive assumption of emerging social health framed the actions that created such health. For the citizens of Portland, the downtown plan implementation now makes the woes of North Portland's crack and gang wars somehow less demeaning; it reminds them that there is hope.

Checks and Balances

Sustaining a symbol of social health, however, requires constant diligence and, every now and then, the symbol must be renewed through decisions that change and nurture the place. Organizing to make such decisions is a second characteristic that appears to significantly influence perceptions of excellence. Over and over again this characteristic is described as a complex web of checks and balances that preserves and further develops the social ecology and physical character of a place. The checks and balances are a way of regulating inclusion and exclusion in place management, usually ensuring that social health and empowerment agendas were fully integrated with economic development and sustainability. In effect, using checks and balances in doing economic development and creating sustainable places becomes a way to facilitate social health and empowerment.

Checks and balances almost always engage a broad constituency in the management of a place; as a result the services and character of the place are not gifts from one group to another but rather the fruits of cooperative labor. The dozens of organizations involved with managing Pike Place, for example, govern everything from the design of pushcarts to the rental structure, from the proportion of vendor stalls set aside for produce to the programming of new housing for the elderly in the Market district. Issues as apparently trivial as a break with tradition of using the Market's historically green paint or of maintaining the unpretentious detailing of the Market are rightfully seen as worthy of long hours of debate on the effect of such design considerations on the character of everyone's Market. Unilateral action is difficult and for good reason. The interdependencies in the Market mean that each action has an impact on all the other elements of the social ecology.

The Portland Downtown Plan and Program is also characterized by a number of different interest groups with related roles in the process, each reviewing the work of the other. The Portland Public Development Authority, the Planning Department, the Citizen's Advisory Committee, and the elaborate association of neighborhoods that routinely receive "alerts" from the Planning Department on proposed actions are all involved in plan implementation at all times. In this fashion the plan remains in the political realm but is not completely vulnerable to the vagaries of change in political leadership. The inherent stability of a broad group of people involved in implementation over the long haul makes the plan one that can survive multiple administrations. While mayors and council members are routinely replaced, the broad base of the plan's constituency remains.

As downtown Portland develops, the dynamic tension over issues such as the "one-for-one" housing replacement policy continually reinforces the advantages of a checks-and-balances system. The city is experiencing great development pressure based on its success over the past decade, and the hard-fought provisions in the plan like the low-income housing replacement guidelines are still debated and enforced in each act of building. There is also pressure on the city's Planning Department from developers to get around the design guideline that calls for buildings to step down to the river edge from the density and height of the city's center. These housing and city form guidelines are not dogma but real, living issues debated, confirmed, and in some cases improved with each act of development in a dynamic downtown. The dialogue opened by the plan guidelines involves the public interests of the citizens and the private interests of developers; the result of the dialogue is that often both interests win. The increasing popularity of Portland as a shopping destination and an office location affirms the values of public amenities, maintenance of physical and social diversity, and a beautiful city. The city is enjoying its economic revival and at the same time avoiding the many deleterious effects of overbuilding and displacing disadvantaged populations.

The numerous cooperatives in the RBA Archives also tell stories of checks and balances. The organizations vary according to the nature of the funding bodies, the relative sophistication of the cooperative members, and the cooperative goals, but the developed structures show strong similarities. The tenants of St. Francis Square, for example, can overturn their elected board's decisions as well as remove entire boards, and they do so when necessary. Any resident manager is subject to the cooperative board and ultimately to the tenants. There are endless committees related to every facet of facility management, and each of the committees, through some type of board, is coordinated with the actions of other committees. Again, there is little opportunity for unilateral action except within very carefully prescribed parameters. Each cooperative we looked at was a smaller version of the interdependent social ecology we found at the Pike Place Market. All were managed with the assumption that more people are smarter than a few and that competence in decision making is at least partially dependent on engaging the broad intelligence of all those affected by decisions.

Seattle's market, Portland's implementation of its downtown

plan, and numerous cooperatives all illustrate that a system of checks and balances is a positive, enabling force in development and need not become what some developers and politicians stereotype as an obstacle to placemaking. Any good checks-and-balances system involves the ability to make decisions while ensuring that no one interest is allowed to dominate the place. The dialogue must remain open to diverse constituencies so that the process of collaboration continually recreates relationships between so-called private and public interests in the city.

Every Problem as an Opportunity

While a complex system of checks and balances can be daunting, it is not inherently conservative. The systems in place demand dialogue and coordination over proposed actions, not the routine application of dogmatic rules or the unilateral actions of individual interest groups. It sometimes takes longer to arrive at decisions, but they are more likely to contribute to, rather than compete with, the evolving social ecology. The problem of one interest group, viewed in relationship to larger constituencies, may become the solution for another group. For example, people from the senior center with time on their hands help out in the Market's child-care center while parents are busy working in the Market. Surplus farm produce from the Market regularly stocks the shelves of the Market Foundation's food bank. In 1987, Pike Place merchants were worried about street youths hanging out across the street from the Market. The nonprofit Market Foundation observed that there was a lack of job opportunities and housing for these young people. Multilateral discussions about the problems led the merchants and the Foundation to seek and receive seed-grant funds to subsidize housing and employment for youths in the Market. The ecology of the Market depends on situations like this, where Market constituencies seek opportunities in all the problems they face.

One approach to seeking opportunities in problems is to include a larger population in the dialogue, bringing the problem of one group to a larger network of related groups. This does not mean that complex interdependencies need be subject to cumbersome bureaucratic procedures. On the contrary, many of the projects in the RBA Archives are extremely complex yet organized in very simple ways. The simplicity of organization is not created by excluding people or organizations with interests in the work; it is often established by inserting a single, flexible voice empowered by all the other voices to coordinate work and to seek the collective

opportunities in individual problems. For example, many citizens as well as professionals and agencies agree that the coordination work of Anthony Pangaro and a small Governor-appointed task force was instrumental to the success of the extremely complex Southwest Corridor Project. It is interesting to note that Pangaro claims he had no formal authority and exercised his influence through coordinating the interests of a very large project constituency with a very simple task-force structure.

Another approach to finding the opportunities in a problem is to accomplish many ends with one action. For example, the residents of Cabrillo Village had to find a source of tiles for the renovation of their homes, and they also needed to diversify their employment in order to reduce their dependence on farm labor. In addition, there was a continuing need for business and leadership training and for employment opportunities for their youth. These problems provided the opportunity to develop a tile factory on site in the Cabrillo Village and for the village to be its own initial market. The skills for creating a business—to make, market, and distribute tiles and to manage people—were all part of a sorely needed educational and practical agenda. The tile factory ultimately accomplished what was needed and went out of business. Much was learned and many tiles were installed, all of which further increased resident pride in their largely self-help housing renovations.

In a similar way, Rita Zimmer of Casa Rita found opportunities in problems. She needed a board of directors for her nonprofit Women in Need organization, she aspired to address housing and social service needs for women and children without homes, and she believed that women did not have sufficient opportunities to participate in the governing boards of all kinds of organizations largely for lack of experience. Her solution was to develop an all-women board of directors which provided in-service training on how to be a board member while it delivered housing and social services through Women in Need.

Seeking opportunities in every problem is part of every story in the Archives, and it often occurs with the help of strong leadership. In some cases the leadership made the project happen. There would be no Casa Rita without Rita Zimmer's leadership in Women in Need; no Fairmount Health Center or Philadelphia Health Services without its director, José Galura; and no Stowe, Vt. bikeway without Anne Lusk. In other cases, several acts of leadership over decades created a climate conducive to excellence. It is difficult, for example, to identify any single individual as responsible for the

Figure 5.8 (facing page) The Southwest Corridor prior to construction. (From the files of Stull and Lee, Inc.)

Figure 5.9 The Southwest Corridor deck over the new transit route provides a linear park through three neighborhoods. (Photo by Ben E. Watkins, reproduced by permission)

success of Pike Place Market; there were dozens of key actors. The development and implementation of the Portland Downtown Plan and the TIL program involved a great many participants. The most successful of these individuals used their leadership abilities to insist that the opportunities in every problem be discovered and widely shared, avoiding quick solutions in favor of those solutions that do more than just remove symptoms of problems.

Finding the opportunity in the problem means never "wasting" a problem. An attitude that problems are both expected and welcomed is an affirmation of the messy process of life, a way to continue building relationships, and to retain a critical perspective on the never-ending placemaking work at hand.

The study of RBA finalists and of the applications in the RBA Archives reveals another kind of affirmation of the world–as–lived. Excellence made in crises, in aspirations for empowerment, and in courageous action comes from a large fabric of interdependent social, political, physical, and ethical circumstances found in places.

Continuing to keep a place excellent is both about building on the origin stories and about remaining open to other possibilities as circumstances change. A symbol of social health derived from a powerful origin story is continually reinvented in place management; checks and balances maintain a critical perspective about the place as it is and as it is always becoming. The process of finding opportunities in problems becomes integral with both the social health and the checks-and-balances dynamics of place. The diversity of origin stories and place management practices has not emerged because people strive to attain some abstract concept of excellence or compliance with a codified rule system for excellence. Rather, these stories arise from the daily struggle to *dwell,* and they are fully situated in the everyday lives of the places and their placemakers.

Reflections: Places of Excellence

The Rudy Bruner Award for Excellence in the Urban Environment can be thought of as a question—an inquiry into the nature of excellence. The program has been structured to get beyond the artifacts of urban design to the processes and values that contribute to excellent urban places. This is not a denigration of the artifacts, but an attempt to situate them in a broader context to achieve a dynamic excellence; one which is both responsive to, and critical of, the human and social circumstances that lead us to build and dwell in cities.

The RBA program is a critique that employs perspectives from planning, economics, architecture, social science, politics, and public administration, each profession serving as a critical lens for the others. The conversation resulting from these different perspectives and evaluative insights is not intended to be conclusive, but it does reveal a strong emerging agreement on some of the basic attributes of urban excellence, many of which we have discussed in this chapter. The respective professions and people who inhabit places are often so bound up in the "common sense" of each individual perspective that they lose sight of the relationships required to live well. The RBA program, by taking a snapshot of the dynamics of excellent places, hopes to reach a better understanding of the processes and values inherent in critical placemaking, one that reasserts the importance of human relationships in placemaking, but without compromising technical, artistic, and critical considerations.

As a critique, the RBA program also offers a way to review the placemaking practices of the First Baptist Church, the Institute, and the Roanoke Neighborhood Partnership. All of these stories have origins grounded in perceptions of crisis conditions. For the First Baptist Church, these conditions included the gradual crisis of an aging congregation no longer able to use their facility effectively, and also their observations that their community was becoming increasingly blighted. At the Institute the crisis was created by technological revolutions, crowding due to growth, and the loss of trust in interunit communications. Anger and the lack of trust between Roanoke's neighborhoods and the city administration reached crisis proportions, helping to frame the actions that resulted in the Roanoke Neighborhood Partnership. The people-in-place in all these stories read the crisis circumstances, organized and empowered themselves, and took courageous placemaking action.

Empowering place constituencies is another characteristic of all these placemaking stories. The church built on a long history of participation and the city of Roanoke initiated one. The Institute made collaboration integral to its process of decision making, thus increasing the power of the staff in the placemaking process. Empowerment in these contexts is about using placemaking as a vehicle to educate, build coalitions, and redistribute power. The same acts of empowerment are used as both a method of inquiry into a place and as a process of decision making about the place. It frames the questions of inclusion and exclusion and decision-making authority.

Both crisis and empowerment in these stories have created the conditions that required courage, the kind that embodies deep personal commitment to placemaking by many people. This courage is central to a reciprocal vulnerability between professionals and the people they would serve, between occupants of a place and the place-becoming. It takes courage to disagree and to believe that such disagreements can strengthen relationships. It also, of course, takes courage to lead or be led over long periods of time. The three projects reported in Chapters 2 through 4 are now between ten and fifteen years old, and many of the key people involved in the origins of these projects are still making significant contributions.

We have already determined that the origins of places also contribute to their continuation as good places, both in the RBA cases and in the stories of personal engagement with the First Baptist Church, the Institute, and the Roanoke neighborhoods. For example, the church's new building was a courageous act of construction in a declining neighborhood; it became a symbol of social health to neighborhood residents, signaling the possibility for renewal. It further affirmed the self-governing and independent nature of the church itself, grounding its everyday experience in the deliberations of its members. The stories of the Office Automation program and Library Move project at the Institute also illustrate how good origins support the social health of a place. The stories have come to symbolize that management genuinely cares about the people they employ. This is not the patronizing care offered by oppressors to oppressed, but rather the continual the caring offered between colleagues in a joint enterprise. It is a kind of caring that values dissent as a contributor to for self-correcting work and as a celebration of social health rather than a denial of difference. The Roanoke Neighborhood Partnership symbolized a new and healthy attitude about the relationship between neighborhood constituencies and the government designed to serve them. It has come to symbolize the best of American democratic ideals at work in the day–to–day management of cities. All of the projects, in other words, have created and maintained places as symbols of social health.

The people who made the First Baptist Church, the Institute, and the Roanoke Neighborhood Partnership work also developed checks and balances, ensuring that continued care be given to the process of changing places. They organized to maintain the empowerment that was part of their origin stories and to deliver on promises. The church members are very active in the civic affairs of their neighborhood, working for the renewal of the entire area. The number of people with housekeeping responsibilities maintaining the church programs and building, and the elaborate committee structure of the congregation, create the checks and balances needed to keep people fully empowered in the story of the church as it evolves. The Institute is now using the stories of its practice as a way to check and balance the central tendency of any bureaucracy to operate in closed or rigidly hierarchical ways. All three projects can compare and contrast the experience of their empowering origins with any given project at hand to establish expectations for self-correcting and empowering work.

Finally, all of the practice stories reveal a creative investment in finding opportunities in every problem. The church project is not just about removing a long flight of stairs to an old sanctuary and satisfying an expanded program of church functions; it is also devoted to a neighborhood ministry and to revitalization of the community. The Institute's Library Move project was not just about moving a library; it was about improving relationships among members of its staff, between Library staff and patrons, and between both patrons and staff and the Facilities Section. The Roanoke Neighborhood Partnership was not just about serving the neighborhoods better, but became a way to establish community, address racism, and enlist the considerable intellectual and physical energies of the neighborhoods in their own development. Each place came to seek ways to accomplish multiple goals with a single project, searching out several opportunities in each presenting problem.

The processes of confirmation, interrogation, and action framing establish the conditions within which placemaking occurs. As projects evolve over time, the characteristics of excellence are further confirmed, interrogated, and changed. Excellence, defined in this way, becomes more accessible and less an exclusive commodity for the select few with special expertise or wealth. No longer is there a question of being able to afford being excellent; there is a recognition that all people have the potential for an excellent life that is grounded in human relationships and cooperative labor in placemaking. The understanding of excellence as it has emerged through the inquiry of the RBA program, and placemaking as it emerges in the context of the First Baptist Church, the Institute, and the Roanoke neighborhoods, reveal the inseparable structures of excellent places and excellent processes.

Intellectual Work as Placemaking Practice

Our placemaking work with the RBA program was a form of academic practice in which we confirmed and interrogated the placemaking of others to learn from their experiences. To designate the practice as academic or intellectual is possibly to invite the misunderstanding that it is located outside of what is commonly understood as professional practice, that it may be thought of as "other than placemaking." We contend, however, that such intellectual work is part of the domain of placemaking; it is essential, not supplemental.[13] We would argue that any time people within a dialogic space engage in confirming and interrogating the specific circumstances of their places and engage in the conduct of critical theory, they are doing disciplined, rigorous, and collaborative intellectual work. When such work asks questions about the larger context or inquiries about a specific idea such as urban excellence, as in the case of the RBA program, this is also placemaking. Ideas make places, especially when collectively constructed, shared, and tested. The intellectual inquiry by the Bruner Foundation is a placemaking practice vested in both theoretical and political standpoints.[14]

The RBA program created the dialogic space in which to explore many acts of placemaking aimed at creating and maintaining excellent urban places (see Appendix for details). The awards program, as a dialogic practice, began with the development and distribution of a call for participation brochure. The application process itself provided the opportunity for many to inquire into their own placemaking work by creating a time and space for a sustained conversation among the people involved in each project about what they had done, what they were currently doing, and why. Hundreds of potential applicants reviewed the criteria for submission and asked themselves and their colleagues questions about their placemaking practice and whether it might be understood as excellent.

The application forms prepared by people from multiple perspectives were sent to the Selection Committees, where they were reviewed and discussed in the first round on the merits of their written package. The review enabled an evaluation of patterns that emerged consistently in many projects, searching among the urban projects for those with special, idiosyncratic, and extraordinary characteristics in order to select a few for further research.

The conversation initiated among the applicants when they submitted their project was further enhanced when the professional advisors visited the selected project sites and interviewed many people. The interviewing process was another space for dialogue in which different perspectives confirmed and interrogated each other and the place. It enabled the various participants to collectively construct new insights and knowledge about their own places and to translate these into a form intelligible and useful to others. As these stories were offered, reconstructed, questioned, confirmed, and tested in each individual place, the activity of placemaking in each location was sustained and enriched. The insights and analysis from the site visits were brought back to the Selection Committees, where they were represented and reconstructed within the framework of the awards jury.

Designing an awards program and analyzing the submissions could be thought of as abstract, academic work. In fact, it is a layered placemaking activity in which circles of dialogic spaces are opened. Within these spaces, places are conceptually and imaginally made and remade.[15] The emerging ideas and beliefs about place, in turn, have the power to reconceptualize other existing places that are also always becoming.

One value of intellectual work is its ability to speak to possibility, expanding options while at the same time informing constituencies about consequences. Whenever people in places and professional placemakers attempt to make better places, there are invariably comparisons between what exists, what has been imagined, what has been experienced, what might be abstractly known, and what might actually occur. The inquiry does not tell one how to act or how to make places; it simply broadens the range of consideration and possibility, establishing the conditions of informed choice. Without such choice and without critical perspectives, placemaking becomes fundamentally oppressive rather than emancipatory.

Many of the stories in the Rudy Bruner Award Archives are about how large, diverse constituencies with a variety of insights found ways to situate their experiences and knowledges in a shared project of placemaking. Situating knowledge requires placemakers to construct a relationship between people-in-place and knowledge from other places, remaking the knowledge and placing it in new contexts. The intellectual work of placemaking uses critical insights about practice, confirming current theoretical, political, and practical assumptions as well as challenging them when they become a part of the forces that deny or subjugate in any specific place. This knowledge gained from intellectual work becomes a part of the dialogic space when shared with other participants of the place. Without this public disclosure and testing in the dialogic space, intellectual work often becomes a basis for exclusion. To *apply or impose knowledge* from other experiences and places into any context denies the particularity of that place and the various knowledges of the people who live or work there. To *situate knowledges* from elsewhere through the process of dialogue is a fundamentally different act because it creates the condition in which groups of people collectively engage in intellectual work and reconstruct knowledge.[16]

It is precisely this distinction between knowledge application and knowledge situating that forms the basis of the Bruner Foundation's efforts in Los Angeles in the wake of the urban violence that erupted after the Rodney King verdict in April 1992. The Bruner Foundation sought a way to share the results of its RBA work on excellent places and processes in order to facilitate a larger dialogue about possibilities in the communities affected by the violence. The national conference "Los Angeles: Working through the Crisis to Quality Urban Living" was another form of intellectual work, that of resituating the insights of several placemaking events reported on in the RBA process into a new context.

The violence in Los Angeles in 1992 was not a new phenomenon in urban America. Dr. Kenneth Clark, in comments to the National Advisory Commission on Civil Disorders (the Kerner Commission) in 1967, described the results of reviewing the work of similar commissions in the past:

> I read that report . . . of the 1919 riot in Chicago and it is as if I were reading the report of the investigating committee on the Harlem riot of '35, the report of the investigating committee of the Harlem riot of '43, the report of the McCone Commission on the Watts riot. I must again in candor say to you members of the Commission—it is a kind of Alice in Wonderland with the same moving picture reshown over and over again, the same analysis, the same recommendations, and the same inaction.[17]

The commission work he cites was done by some of the best minds in the United States on the subject of urban violence. The actions proposed were not "wrong," nor could one fault the intentions of the authors in their desire to help the poor. But the proposals were presented from outside the discourse of the day-to-day construction of places. They formed the basis of action planning but excluded those for whom the planning was intended.[18] None of the programs ever addressed the structural way in which "non-poor" people are implicated in the creation and maintenance of poverty and violence.

The Bruner Foundation was aware of this history of violence in the United States and also very well aware of the limitations of earlier attempts to "fix" the problems of poverty and violence. Yet they felt they could provide a forum in which people who had experienced similar conditions, and had found a way to work with others to address these issues, might assist the people working on the crisis in Los Angeles. Working in cooperation with the Executive Office of the President, several federal agencies, and several local Los Angeles constituencies, the Bruner Foundation organized the conference in November 1992 in Washington, D.C., which was intended to open a dialogue rather than conclude one.[19]

A preconference notebook distributed to conferees described in some detail the stories of other distressed communities that had struggled through crisis conditions and created excellent places as a result. People who lived the struggle to make place in the TIL program, in Cabrillo Village, in the Pike Place Market, and in the Southwest Corridor were invited to the meeting to elaborate on their stories in conversations with those working on the current Los Angeles crisis. Participants from Los Angeles included the resident managers of public housing, local community organizers, local financial and business people, staff from the nonprofit organization Rebuild Los Angeles, as well as federal, state, and local governmental agency personnel on site in Los Angeles with specific responsibilities to deliver service to the distressed areas. Washington, D.C. participants included government representatives from the Departments of Housing and Urban Development, Commerce, and Labor and from the Executive Office of the President, all of which were working on policies relevant to distressed urban environments. Also attending were the chair of the U.S. Civil Rights Commission, representatives of national professional organizations such as the American Institute of Architects, and some nongovernmental organizations with missions related to work in distressed urban communities.

All participants were invited to listen, discuss, and reflect. People from places like Cabrillo Village and New York told their stories to people from Los Angeles and Washington, D.C., and listened in turn. At several points through the one-and-a-half days of work, participants were asked specifically to search for connections to their own problems and situations, writing down their thoughts on specially designed reflection sheets. Plenary sessions were conducted to allow all of the participants to share their thoughts on both the process of investigation and the key issues that surfaced.[20]

The conference resulted in a broad range of considerations and tentative action plans that were proposed and tested among the diverse groups of participants and, later, with their constituencies. The considerations and proposals are too extensive to describe here. However, to demonstrate the possibilities of situating work we will focus on one issue that emerged during the conference: the opportunity to learn from other places, even while realizing that solutions to problems in specific places must be "homegrown"—in other words, collectively constructed in place.

The participants from Los Angeles recognized the power of building bridges to link related conditions, capacities, and constituencies. The existence of communities who had struggled with their own problems and communally found ways to address them offered a sense of possibility. There were similarities in some of the projects that reflected the complexity of the Los Angeles situation in such a way as to offer both organizational and managerial insights. Also, it was empowering to recognize the ways in which communities had transformed what had been constrained categorical programs, like highway construction or urban renewal, into projects that supported broader conceptions of community needs.

The language of *bridging* became a metaphor for being able to use insights from the stories to other settings. Yet many felt that attempts at application were part of the problem; entirely too many people had answers they thought could be applied in Los Angeles and in federal programs. L.A. participants considered the importance of growing their own solutions while they considered the experience of others in different circumstances, affirming the need for good conversations about successful places, but rejecting the idea of a direct application of those experiences in other environments.

For some of the Washington, D.C.–based participants, the discussion on bridging and the entire format of the conference suggested an increased emphasis on technical assistance programs that focused on how to situate experience from other places in Los Angeles without the heavy-handed rhetoric and activity of applications, and without the constraints of categorical programs. It also shifted the emphasis of the discussions on technical assistance from answers to tools and methods of work.

The conference as a placemaking activity built on the intellectual work of the RBA program on urban excellence. Participants had the opportunity to seek new knowledge and new ways of situating knowledge through an exploration of the work of others who had thought much and worked very hard on similar issues with very different contextual circumstances. Each place made, each dialogic space opened for struggling with the possibilities of place, and each act of placemaking offers the hope that excellent places can be made and maintained.

It is sometimes difficult to see intellectual work as profoundly useful and liberating because it can be so abstract and so generalized as to seem irrelevant in the real world of places. But the intellectual work of placemaking need not be removed from the work of people making places; in fact, it has the responsibility to remain faithful to the particularistic circumstances of their lives and places even while seeking patterns that contribute to the understanding of places that people love. The task of opening a dialogic space for confirming and interrogating placemaking acts can occur in many circumstances—for individual acts of placemaking and for many such acts taken together, as in the RBA inquiry into urban excellence. The conversation, when opened to a larger public discourse, is simultaneously responsible to the specific and the general. It is vulnerable to multiple perspectives, to insights from critical theory, and to the possibility of resituating the constructed knowledge to new acts of placemaking. The Rudy Bruner Award's efforts to redefine excellence in the urban environment demonstrate how the intellectual work of placemaking can also be a critical and emancipatory practice.

6

EPILOGUE: A CRITICAL PRACTICE

Placemaking is a fundamental activity; it is the ongoing labor of people that makes, transforms, and cares for places. Placemaking happens in one-time events such as building a new school, designing a new downtown plan, landscaping a park, or saving a market. It is also repetitive, continuous, and, like housework, invisible unless poorly done. Places always need care, attention, time, and energy: The alleys need to be cleaned, the buildings have to be managed and maintained, the garden needs to be weeded, another office must be moved, and so on.

We have argued that the practice of placemaking is not only about the physical making, remaking, and unmaking of the material world. It is about "world making" in a much broader sense because the practice literally has the power to make worlds—families, communities, offices, churches, and so on. Each act of placemaking embodies a vision of who we are and offers a hope of what we want to be as individuals and as groups who share a place in the world. Because of this world-making power, placemaking, if poorly conceived or imposed, can result in the catastrophic or incremental destruction of people and places.[1]

Our seemingly contradictory premise is that the work of professional placemakers potentially appropriates the human activity of placemaking from people-in-place, and that professional placemakers nevertheless have an important contribution to make to this same work. These two perspectives confirm and interrogate our own work as professionals and academics. They reflect our struggle to understand the nature of our practice and to critique it that it may be a more effective and emancipatory form of work.

As part of our inquiry, we continue to problematize the ways in which the boundaries created by professional placemakers to separate and distinguish the various forms of placemaking actually work against the knowledge of place and the work of placemaking by people in places. Professionals have the power to layer, enrich, transform, erase, and destroy the continuous world-making activities of people in their everyday lives.[2] *Emancipatory* and *world-making* are perhaps exaggerated words to describe the activity of building a deck, managing an office, or developing a regional transportation plan. But we intentionally use these words and their power to focus attention on the potential of critical placemaking to construct the world. It is precisely this world-making power that establishes the conditions necessary for genuinely satisfying labor by professionals and people in places.

In this chapter we offer some thoughts on the *location* of the various professionals engaged in placemaking, exploring what it means to be situated in an academic setting or a professional practice office and what implications these locations have for the broader view of placemaking practice we have framed in the book. We seek to understand the ways in which these academic and professional practices are similar and different. Furthermore, we will address the role of knowledge and collaboration in professionalism as a way to emphasize the relationships among the shared, if fragmented, practices, and the work of people-in-place. The intent of this inquiry is not to ignore or erase the differences between practices, but rather to bring them together in particular places and acts of placemaking.

Our aspiration is to situate this broadly conceived critical practice within the daily work of placemaking. The practice we describe is immersed in place and grounded in a complex, contradictory, and layered world. Such a location for practice redefines the social practice of professionalism even while it includes professionals as participants. We recognize that the critical practice of placemaking engenders risks to practitioners, academics, and people-in-place who are situated securely within their currently accepted domains. This risk forms the bases of several queries about our practice.

Some Queries

Placemaking as described in this book raises many questions about the nature of professional and academic practice. When we share our placemaking experiences and reflections with various academic and professional groups, we often hear three kinds of questions. Some groups seem concerned about the implications of combining different professions into the single practice of critical placemaking. How can such differences be conceptualized as "a practice," and what benefits are offered through this reconceptualization? Also, what new constraints appear that might interfere with good professional and/or academic work? Another series of questions raised, mostly by academics, focuses on the theory of knowledge. What happens when the position of knowledge as understood in the domain of science is shifted and dispersed among many practices and people? How can judgments be made about the validity of knowledge without the method of science? A third type of question, usually asked by professional practitioners, focuses on the requirement for collaboration in the critical practice of placemaking. How can it be possible or even desirable to make one's knowledge and experience vulnerable through a collaborative venture? Doesn't such vulnerability make professionals appear even less valuable?

These queries by colleagues and friends have created a rich context in which to reconsider our own placemaking experiences—to confirm and interrogate what, how, and why certain actions and processes have occurred. We have struggled as academic practitioners with questions about practice and professionalism, the theory of knowledge, and the possibilities of collaboration. Here we will offer our developing thoughts on these issues and restate our belief in the power of placemaking.

Shared Practice, Fragmented Professions

All placemakers share in a *practice* of world making: university faculty engaged in research and teaching about placemaking in architecture, planning, philosophy; practitioners engaged in the work of planning and design firms, government agencies, or corporate offices; developers or contractors making a new subdivision; and a family adding a new room to their home. As a shared practice, all engage in transforming the material world through making places and, we will argue, by creating knowledge about places and their development.

In spite of the shared aims and ways of working, the practice of placemaking is fragmented, and some aspects "belong" to different domains and groups of professionals. There is an ongoing attempt to create boundaries that separate and differentiate the work on many levels, revealing a world more concerned with distinction and division than with connection and relationship. Professors and professionals collectively differentiate themselves from "laypeople,"[3] even as professors and practitioners seek to differentiate themselves from each other into separate academic and practice domains.

Within professional practice itself, professionals invest energy in the search for those tasks, liabilities, and responsibilities that are "rightfully" theirs, and those that belong to other domains and so are excluded. All professions and professionals address the issue of who can and who cannot legitimately practice in their field through requirements for admission, codes of ethics, and advanced degrees. Law, medicine, cab driving, academia, the design fields, teaching, hairdressing, and other professions seek to differentiate themselves clearly from those who would practice their profession without proper credentials.

Boundary seeking and boundary protecting are manifestations of a cultural phenomenon that establishes who is legally responsible for various actions. When the boundaries of work are very close, as is the case with architects, engineers, interior designers, landscape architects, facility managers, and planners, there are often legal battles over whose "right" it is to provide a certain service and whose knowledge is most appropriate to the given problem or project.

The aspirations for autonomy and clear boundary conditions serve professional ends and reflect the political and economic situation within which professionalism exists. These aspirations need to be respected, so this discussion is not presented in lieu of professional definitions. However, it is our experience that those same boundaries, offered with the aim of protecting clients and insuring that they receive the best professional service possible, often establish conditions that hinder the complex work of placemaking.

A critical practice of placemaking, because it starts with place and people, is obviously problematic in a culture so preoccupied with making boundaries; yet the world does not divide itself so easily into the professional puzzle. The domain of the practice of placemaking as demonstrated by the stories in this book extends beyond the technical-rational descriptions of facility managers, developers, planners, or designers. Rather, this practice is often situated in many overlapping professional domains and, at times, in the broad gaps in between.

This emphasis on the common practice of placemaking does not deny that there are differences among various placemakers, because specific practices are located in particular "places" within cultures. In this way, the practices of university professors and professionals constitute different cultures even while they share in many ideas and worldviews. These differences are composed of constellations of social practices that have been institutionalized through various formal and informal reward-and-punishment systems. These systems are sustained because they are perceived to be in the best interest of each specific practice and its constituency—whether located in the university or in the domain of the professional practitioners. Even though these distinctions are problematic for many placemaking activities, they are also useful: Each location acts as a lens, a perspective from which to see the world, interpret it, and take action. Each location both facilitates and constrains the work of knowledge construction and action in making places.

Place Knowledge

Any practice, including placemaking, shares aims and methods of work. Practices frame what constitutes knowledge, who can legitimately construct it, and how knowledge is socially and politically inserted and distributed. In this sense, practice is the foundation of knowledge—its creation, interpretation, transformation, and refutation. This assertion re-places knowledge into the world of social practices.

Knowledge as something that is socially and/or politically constructed contradicts the notion that knowledge is objective and separate, located outside the world-as-lived. The belief that it is possible to construct unbiased, objective knowledge within the positivist interpretation of science has dominated thought in western cultures for the last century, and has had a significant impact on the making of places. Implicit in positivism is the removal of knowledge about the place from the place itself and the people who live there, relocating it to the domains of researchers and professionals who "legitimately" construct and apply objective knowledge gathered through the dictates of science. This conceptualization not only takes knowledge generation out of places; it has also been the rationale for separating the university from professional practice in the design, planning, and engineering fields. Professionalism is an outcome of a view that separates the construction of knowledge from its application.

In this framework, the practice of academia is to research, to generate new knowledge, and to pass on knowledge through its educative function. Because knowledge generation is perceived to be superior to its application, the university has been privileged in the knowledge industry. Knowledge not legitimated in this domain, including the knowledge of practitioners, has been excluded from serious discussion. Within the same dualistic framework of basic–versus–applied, the practice of professionals in design and planning is about changing, modifying, and constructing the world. Even though most practitioners are educated in university systems, they often view professors and their knowledge as unrealistic and irrelevant to working in the world.

The boundary that has divided the university as the location for generating knowledge from the professions as the place for rational application of that knowledge has been well critiqued from both within and outside the practices of architecture and the design fields.[4] The work of the university and professional design practices are now understood to be social practices, with ways of working and aims that serve their own interests. One particular aspect of maintaining this theory/application split important to the practice of placemaking is the claim that knowledge generated through basic research and scientific method is distinct from the social, political, and economic uses of that same knowledge. This dualistic conception of knowledge creates the condition for the claim that all knowledge seeking is a "good" in and of itself. In this way, the dichotomy supports the proposition that the university as an institution, and the faculty engaged in basic research, are somehow not responsible for how their work is applied. One might suggest that rather than being not responsible, the researchers and their institutions have been irresponsible.

According to the basic-versus-applied worldview, it is only after knowledge is generated as a discrete artifact that it falls into the political and ethical realms, the domain of the practitioners thereafter responsible for its social uses and abuses. Professional practitioners such as architects, planners, engineers, and facility managers have been viewed as "experts," and the professions have accepted the responsibility for the application of knowledge within their given domains. Planning and design practitioners, engaged in projects such as public housing and urban renewal, "apply" the most current knowledge gained through the dictates of science and theory within their fields. The results of such applications are the topic of numerous critiques on both the adequacy of knowledge and the practice of knowledge application. Professional practitioners have been vulnerable to the university's criticism that they have been misapplying knowledge, and to various publics' complaints that their work has been inappropriate and at times destructive.[5] The university is vulnerable to the criticisms of practitioners and various publics about the inadequacy or lack of relevance of their knowledge to address the complex circumstances of place.

In the same way that the university, using a positivist interpretation of science, had denied the possibility of knowledge construction to professional practitioners, the professions themselves have denied the knowledge of people-in-place. Trusting only their own professional expertise, knowledge, and methods, practitioners in the fields of architecture, planning, and design have given little credence to the knowledge of place dwellers.[6] Not being invited to participate in acts of professional placemaking has never, of course, kept people from making their places. But one consequence of an isolated process of knowledge construction and application within the general domain of science has been that professionals engaged in making places have neither recognized, nor learned from, the struggles and knowledges of people in places.

Moreover, disguised within the language of objective knowledge and technical-rational applications of that knowledge are unstated values, including the assumption that people are passive and dependent on professional assistance, and the modernist belief that environmental changes can eliminate social problems. The evolving critique of knowledge has revealed that the boundary constructed to separate theoretical work from application work not only excluded forms of knowledge and practices, but has been used to maintain class, gender, and racial inequalities.[7] The practice of science, the university, and the professions are not only fallible, but their knowledges and methods are biased and saturated with power.

This critique has made room for a new discourse on the nature of knowledge—what it is, how it is constructed, and who constructs it—and greatly expands our understanding of how knowledges operate. New insights reveal not only the ongoing construction of knowledge, but also the idea that all forms of knowing are legitimate and that everyone is a knower, displacing the fiction of objective knowledge and a single source of truth. Now that the knowledge derived through the employment of science must be taken as a particular truth derived from a special set of methods and practices, the university and its research can no longer be looked on as the sole arbiter of knowledge.[8] The expertise of professional practitioners dependent on applying a singular concept of objective knowledge is also being challenged. Ironically, this challenge to professionalism is happening concurrently with the increased legitimacy given to practitioners who generate multiple kinds of knowledge through their practices. The world within which professors and professionals work at the end of the twentieth century is a very different place from the technical-rational system of beliefs that dominated western countries earlier in this century.

From the standpoint of the postmodern theory of knowledge, we can no longer assume that professors and professionals "know" and others "don't know" in the practice of placemaking.[9] But this presents us with a very complex condition: We cannot act on diffuse knowledge, knowledge that comes from everyone and everywhere. What we need in this new relative world are ways of assessing which kinds of knowledge contribute to our activity and which do not. This new way of thinking not only asks how we decide which knowledges to include or exclude, but also how we use and reconstruct the included knowledges. Is it to be knowledge for power, or knowledges for intimacy?[10] If it is knowledge for power, is it power to control or power to do work?

The postmodern condition of relativity is helping to resituate the practice of placemaking. The social construction of knowledge and place removes them both from the private realm and relocates them in a public and relational practice, a dialogue. People in places and professional placemakers can "legitimately" construct social and place-relevant knowledge to enable and empower communal action. The work of confirmation and interrogation contributes to this activity because it affirms each person's interpretation of the world within his or her own experience, while at the same time questioning that knowledge in relation to the experiences of others and the work at hand. From this conversation emerges situated knowledges, informed action, and insights that contribute to the continual construction of generalized knowledge about how places are made. Errors of judgment will be made, but the continuation of the conversation offers the possibility that the world will, again, be remade.

What, in this new context, is the role for the specialized knowledges of professionals? Affirming the knowledge of people-in-place is not offered as a denigration of or substitution for professional knowledge gained through experience and through academic inquiry. Professionals have much to contribute to the dialogue, but their contribution need not be an imposition of their knowledge over a place. The practice of placemaking, rather, engages the activities of *situating* and *translating* the knowledge of all participants within the dialogic space.[11] Individual and idiosyncratic forms of knowledge and experience, brought to the dialogic space and offered as particular forms of knowing, often require translation in order to be comprehensible in specific placemaking contexts, so that they may then be collectively confirmed and interrogated. The role of facilitation in placemaking, often but not exclusively done by professionals, engages the processes of translating, situating, and problematizing the knowledges brought to the dialogic space surrounding individual interventions, including the knowledges, experiences, and methods of professionals.

Different forms of knowledge, when situated in a particular place with particular people, become a part of the more generalized understanding of placemaking. All of this activity contributes to our communal knowledge about what makes excellent places and about how to open and maintain the dialogic space of placemaking. If we recognize that all knowing represents the truths of particular people, all with limitations, then the work of placemaking within the dialogic space becomes interpreting, inventing, and constructing relationships among kinds of knowledge. An important aspect of this work is its capacity to uncover hidden biases and power assumptions. This is a critical practice: being engaged in the truly human work of describing, making, and maintaining the world and our relationships to it.

Collaboration as Professional Risk

There are real professional risks for practitioners who enter the dialogic space of placemaking and choose to work with the messy conception that many knowledges are legitimate. It is inherent in any truly collaborative process that one has to be willing to risk his or her worldview and knowledge, risk seeing the possibilities of truth in other ways of knowing.[12] This condition in no way diminishes the responsibility of professionals to offer their own beliefs in the collaborative process and to say how they came to hold such beliefs. It simply is not a certainty that such professional beliefs, if conceived outside the dialogue, are necessarily in the best interests of the place and its constituencies. But, we would argue, it *is* in the best interest of the people in their places as well as practitioners to maintain the dialogic space opened during any professional intervention in order to explore continually the possibilities of place and to take action on collectively constructed proposals.

We have repeatedly stressed that the condition of being open and vulnerable, of risking professional and personal knowledge, calls for commitment to a process that continually makes, takes, and remakes places through the practice of dialogue and environmental action. A prerequisite to such commitment is that participants have the choice to participate and, in electing to join, have the ability to influence the process and results.[13] The collaborative attitude engaged in a dialogic space requires vulnerability and the capacity to care not only for the product of the work, but also for the process, the people, and the place. Without such caring and commitment, the rhetoric of collaboration remains hollow and abstract. To "care about" a process, a place, and its people supposes that the strength of affection grows stronger the more each individual develops his or her uniqueness. This form of caring depends on the willingness and ability to engage in openly collaborative dialogues. It involves risks because it requires "the capacity to absorb new and perhaps painful meanings, the willingness to be involved in situations [you] . . . can't securely control."[14] Being "out of control" is, of course, the antithesis of conventional professional aspirations and entails real professional risk. It may also contribute to the making of good places to live and work.[15]

A critical practice of placemaking struggles to address the full range of human experience in place, and it often includes offering traditional professional services when appropriate. But it is important to stress that responsibilities in placemaking extend beyond what is normally understood to be professional action and knowledge into the messy domain of human relationships, represented by words such as *caring, trust,* and perhaps even *love.* Whatever the vulnerabilities, the processes of confirmation, interrogation, and action framing within a dialogic space subject a conversation to the influence of many. Decisions can be revisited again and again as circumstances change, even as concrete action is taken at specific times to change organizations and places. The collaborative space of placemaking creates the possibility that ordinary people can do extraordinary things in rather ordinary ways.[16]

Limits and Possibilities

Calling for collaboration and opening up the nature of knowledge in a practice of placemaking raise many questions. Can competent professionals remain vulnerable and still achieve the consistency of service to the public demanded by their respective professions? Can autonomous persons be vulnerable, open to significant influence, and still accept responsibility for their actions? Can responsible people collaborate with irresponsible people? To understand and operate from diverse positions in collaborative contexts while engaging the world as a professional raises dilemmas that are not easily resolved.

The goal of placemaking activity as we have conceptualized it is the making and remaking of the world and our relationships with it. Sometimes the world in which we must work is composed of difficult, often oppressive, realities. If we accept the precondition that collaboration must be a part of placemaking in support of a project of emancipation or at least democratic action, we must also accept the vulnerability of the collaboration. To do otherwise would be insincere and would defeat the emancipatory potential inherent in a dialogic placemaking practice. Thus we confront the possibility of making ourselves, as professionals, vulnerable to what we occasionally perceive to be self-serving, irresponsible, oppressive, and perhaps even pathological situations and people.[17] Perhaps one of the most perplexing dilemmas in placemaking is defining the *limits of tolerance* when confronted with these difficult realities of collaboration.

This dilemma raises a question of ends and means. If the motive of our "vulnerable stance" is to avoid opposition, complaints, and resistance, then we are in a defensive posture and are being essentially manipulative, not open. Even if we assert a preconceived end, such as professional effectiveness, and do not make this goal vulnerable to the dialogic practice of confirmation and interrogation in the placemaking event, then we may become part of the oppressive and difficult reality we genuinely wish to remake. Defining sincere dialogue and positive human relationships as our goals and critical placemaking as our means has the potential to change oppressive circumstances. If the intention of our practice is positive regard among people-in-place and the collective making of beloved places, then mistakes and errors in judgment will be redefined in a trusting relationship that includes the possibility of forgiveness and healing. Professional effectiveness may be a pleasant by–product. It also may not.

The limits–of–tolerance dilemma is significantly less critical if we resolve the means/end question in favor of openness, trust, and love. If the process by which we make, manage, evaluate, and maintain places over time is rooted in positive regard, then the process itself will be healing. Another way to examine the question of the limits of tolerance is to examine our alternatives. If we do not make ourselves vulnerable to the oppressive and difficult circumstances we wish to change, then we are faced with several extremely complex questions. What is an oppressive and difficult reality? Who decides? How difficult is too difficult for collaboration? If we decide not to collaborate based on an abstract idea of the limits of tolerance, then we will probably contribute to the very conditions we have decided not to collaborate with because our nonengagement will ensure that the condition continues. Our refusal to be vulnerable confirms rather than interrogates the pathology of the situation.

Yet there are circumstances when vulnerability to a distressed reality is both personally and professionally destructive. Collaboration can become collusion. There may be a time when limits are reached and when one must personally and professionally withdraw from the dialogue or more actively resist the actions proposed. If vulnerability fails to create the conditions of honest collaboration and the attempt to communally construct a new understanding of place fails, then the dialogic space collapses and with it the professional placemaking facilitation. This condition confirms that there are limits to the possibility of dialogue. However, just as it is necessary to conceive of the dialogic space in placemaking as tentative and provisional because it relies on the commitment of all participants to keep it open, it is as useful to see the closing of the space as a conditional gesture. To acknowledge the limits of tolerance is not a final act. Friedmann offers some insight into this condition:

> When dialogue fails, the only power that is left is my refusal to cooperate in the project of the other. It is a refusal contingent on the other's compliance with my minimum demands. . . . This "no" to the "yes" of social planning is addressed to my enemy, my brother. It is a nonviolent act. By refusing to participate in his project, I seek to destroy neither him nor the "between" of our dialogue. I hold the gate open, that our dialogue may recommence.[18]

If the limits of tolerance are reached, then we must acknowledge the tension between knowing that there are limits *and* knowing the necessity of unrestrained vulnerabilities. Given this knowledge and no clear guidelines, it may be better to embrace the tension as a dynamic condition of life than to try to resolve it. Furthermore, the choice may not be to stay engaged or withdraw but to find a way to maintain both conditions. Active resistance to intolerable situations can be thought of as nonviolent, and, frankly, tentative acts that hold open the potential of future dialogue. Such choices acknowledge the limits of tolerance situated in current dynamics while also holding open the promise of human competence, reciprocal forgiveness, and future collaboration.

Placemaking is thus a celebration of difference and an affirmation of common intentions. The willingness to engage openly in a collaboratively constructed space about places is a practice based on the belief that people are always engaged in world making. The dialogic space, within which the work of confirmation, interrogation, and action framing occurs, offers the possibility of a resituated professional practice, an affirmation of differences, and a way of taking care of ourselves and our places.

We have faith that people strive to be competent in their placemaking,[19] and it is our experience that professional placemakers can facilitate that activity by creating special places for dialogue about place. Moreover, we believe that placemaking is a fertile site for the practice of democracy. People will engage, indeed are engaged, in a sustained struggle to be the subjects of their own histories and their communities. It is our hope that the practice of placemaking enables dwelling through the making of beloved places.

Appendix

PROGRAM DESCRIPTION: THE RUDY BRUNER AWARD FOR EXCELLENCE IN THE URBAN ENVIRONMENT

Introduction

The Rudy Bruner Award (RBA) for Excellence in the Urban Environment is about assembling stories that reveal critical planning and design practices, the places resulting from such practice, and the values that underpin both practice and results. Relationships among all of the participants in the placemaking process are celebrated and critiqued; the people who helped make the places and those who now manage them are both affirmed and interrogated. Applicants for an RBA are explicitly encouraged to engage all participants in the placemaking process as they reflect on the place they wish to have celebrated through this award. They are encouraged to explore the interdependence of vested interests, and to seek a better understanding of the placemaking dynamics that led them to be proud of the places they have made. The RBA is about the practice of critical reflection on and education pertaining to urban environments.

The awards program was initiated by the Bruner Foundation of New York City in 1985. The first awards were offered in 1987, a second awards cycle followed in 1989, a third was completed in 1991, and the fourth cycle ended in 1993. The structure of each cycle requires applicants to complete a questionnaire and provide essays from different, and at times competing, perspectives on the project to be considered. There have now been over 300 applicants for award. Places submitted for award consideration in the initial years ranged in scale from Portland, Ore.'s Downtown Plan and Program to a small shelter for homeless women in the South Bronx. Places ranged in age from the Pike Place Market with its 1907 origins to the Quality Hill Development in Kansas City in the 1980s.

The RBA program advocates an understanding of placemaking that includes the place, the process of its making and managing, and the values implicit in both place and process. It reveals the limitations of any purely professional vision of excellence, illustrating the process by which multiple and conflicting visions can be successfully reconciled:

> At this moment in American cities, the development process is struggling to find a balance among developers and designers trying to achieve their economic and aesthetic objectives, governments trying to put in place planning and growth policies, and neighborhood groups trying to control the quality of life in their community.[1]

The awards program is unique in several ways. First, in addition to presenting and describing their place, entrants are asked to engage in self-critique and to forecast the future of their projects. Furthermore, the sponsor of the award, the Bruner Foundation, has no specific professional or commercial bias and no formal relationship with either private or government building programs, design-related professions, or building component and material manufacturers. While the Foundation is intensely interested in the forces that work for and against the quality of the urban environment, they have no direct vested interest in any of those forces. All of this establishes the conditions for the Foundation and the team they have assembled to offer constructive criticism and to make public what they learn.

Individuals of the Rudy Bruner Award task force, which framed the awards program, have served as professional advisors to, jurists for, or award winners of over twenty different award programs.[2] The RBA builds on these experiences and owes a debt to all such efforts to recognize excellence. At the same time, part of the process of developing the RBA program involved a critique of existing awards programs. The critique does not suggest that other forms of awards programs are not valuable; on the contrary, they do precisely what the Bruner Foundation cannot do. Many existing awards programs are professional advocacy programs and, to a large extent, very successful ones. Their intention is to celebrate success from a given value perspective. They often focus on the characteristics of the artifact as influenced or determined by a specific profession or interest, and dwell on neither the processes with which such artifacts were made nor those by which they are managed over time. As such, awards programs generally tend not to be invitations for a diversity of players to dialogue but rather, to be assertions of excellence circumscribed within a specific worldview.

The RBA specifically seeks and recognizes the ability of applicants to be self-reflective and self-critical, recording what they learned during the process of project development. In the aggregate, entrants to the Rudy Bruner Award program are contributing to a more general understanding of the significance of the artifacts we build, the processes we employ to build them, and the values that inform both artifact and process.

The RBA application and review process structures dialogues about urban excellence, explicitly creating a space in which to explore the idea of placemaking. The program did not begin with a preconceived notion of what constitutes excellent places, nor did it charge its Selection Committees to apply their own criteria. Applicants for the award are not asked to conform to established criteria but rather are asked to describe the place, processes, and values that most contribute to their perceptions of project success. The RBA Selection Committees evaluate how convincing the description of the project is, in part by employing a research team to evaluate the application against the actual conditions found on the site.

The review process for the RBA is complex, involving three primary stages: (1) screening and evaluation of all applications by an interdisciplinary professional Selection Committee, leading to the designation of five to six finalists; (2) a comprehensive on-site evaluation of all finalists by a research team; and (3) a second meeting of the Selection Committee in which the research team briefs them on the results of its investigations. The makeup of each Selection Committee changes during each cycle of the awards program. In general, it includes a senior architect, a developer or consultant in economic development, a mayor, an environmental design researcher, and a community development specialist usually, but not exclusively, from a nongovernmental organization. Sometimes the Selection Committee includes an urban affairs journalist as well

TABLE A.1
Selection Committee members from the first two cycles of the Rudy Bruner Award.

1986–1987	1988–1989
George Latimer, Mayor City of St. Paul, MN	Joseph P. Riley, Jr., Mayor City of Charleston, SC
Vernon George, Principal Hammer, Siler, George Economic Development Consultants Silver Spring, MD	David Lawrence, Vice President Gerald D. Hines Interests New York, NY, and Houston, TX
Clare Cooper Marcus Professor of Architecture and Landscape Architecture University of California Berkeley, CA	George Hartman, FAIA Hartman-Cox Architects Washington, DC
	Mary L. Decker, Executive Director Chicago Metropolitan Planning Council Chicago, IL
Theodore Liebman, FAIA The Liebman Partnership New York, NY	Neal Peirce Syndicated Columnist and Urban Affairs Author New York, NY
William H. Whyte, Author and Journalist New York, NY	Pamela P. Plum, Past President National League of Cities and Former Mayor City of Portland, ME
Cressworth Landers, Director Community Development Tucson, AZ	Ann Whiston Spirn, Landscape Architect and Author University of Pennsylvania Philadelphia, PA
	Aaron Zaretsky, Executive Director The Market Foundation Pike Place Market Seattle, WA

as someone who has participated in past projects recognized by the RBA.

The transcripts of Selection Committee meetings reveal a rich dialogue on the relationships among different points of view. Such a dialogue is fostered by the diversity of perspectives represented by the Committee membership and by Committee work processes, which helps to assure that no single perspective or committee member will dominate. This dialogic principle has been further reinforced through the use of facilitators drawn from the research team to insure full participation from Selection Committees. One measure of the success of these efforts is that some members of the Selection Committees have radically adjusted their evaluations during the course of discussions. They have attributed their change of mind to learning about other perspectives from their colleagues on the Committee.

One prevailing assumption in the RBA program is important to stress: The excellence of a place is significantly influenced by relationships among the products, the processes, and the values embedded in making and maintaining places. *Products* or artifacts are buildings, public spaces, landscapes, interiors, and so forth that establish the material and spatial condition of a place. Applicants are told that projects of any size are considered as long as they make a contribution to the urban environment, and they are not constrained by scale or time of completion. However, projects should have been in operation long enough to demonstrate success. *Processes* are the practices used to decide on the design of products. The processes to be assessed are those that, in the opinion of the applicants, are the most beneficial to their project. Applicants are advised that the Selection Committee is especially interested in innovations and modifications of traditional processes and in the involvement of new participants. *Values* are the moral and ethical standpoints that define the nature of practice and the degree to which people come to understand places as excellent. The values to be assessed, like the products and processes, are not prescribed by the Bruner Foundation or by the Selection Committees. The program recognizes that values are often implicit in the making of urban places and seeks ways to make them explicit so that others can learn from them.

The Application Process

Organizations that apply for an RBA include a diverse group of community and local advocacy groups; local, state, and federal government organizations; development companies; design and/or planning professionals; and others involved in the process of making urban places, such as institutions or foundations. Each application includes a short project profile listing key project data, a full list of participants, a project abstract, and several short essays pertaining to their view of the project's merits, chronology, key issues, financing, goal structure, and critical commentary.

An important part of the application, regardless of its origin, is inclusion of several specially designed "perspective sheets" which are completed by individuals representing the widest possible range of project constituencies. Such constituencies are as broad as the range of organization types invited to apply. Applicant organizations have provided anywhere from four to twenty-four perspective sheets, depending on their view of the complexity of the project, and on what was necessary to reveal the full range of value positions at work in the place proposed for award. In addition to the perspective sheets, an RBA submission includes additional background material in both text and graphic form illustrating the project, as well as the processes and values by which it was made and is managed.

Each perspective sheet is designed to elicit (1) a specific description of an individual's or organization's role in the project, (2) views of the benefits of the project and how such benefits were achieved, (3) the impact of the project on the social and physical context in which it exists, (4) a reflective review of tough trade-offs that had to be made, and (5) what they would do differently if there were an opportunity to engage the project today. Finally, each perspective sheet records (6) a review of lessons learned during and after project development, and (7) an assessment of what will be required to keep the project successful in the next several years.

The Site Visit Process

In 1987, five projects out of a field of eighty-two qualified applicants were identified for a site visit by the Selection Committee, and in 1989, six were identified for review out of ninety-four applicants. The visit protocol for each short-listed site was developed based on the application, telephone interviews in advance of the visit, and published sources referenced by the applicant and found elsewhere in the professional press or in academic articles and books. During the visit, the research team conducted interviews, made on-site inspections, and collected still more documentation relevant to each short-listed project. For the two rounds that serve as the basis for Chapter 5, the approach to the site-visit interviewing involved two advisors-researchers on-site for three days, interviewing twelve to twenty-five people for a minimum of one hour and often up to three hours. The interviews were managed according to a very informal protocol, which was reviewed with the participants prior to the interview and modified as the interview progressed. The interviews were both individual and small-group, and usually involved a walk through the site with staff from the applying organization as well as other participants in the project. In addition, there was always a tour of the surrounding neighborhood and interviews with some inhabitants in order to assess the influence of the project on the surrounding area.

The interviews were coordinated with but not chosen by the applicant. The people selected as interviewees were identified by the research team based on their review of the application and on discussions with the applicant organization prior to arrival on site. Selection criteria included representation of the full range of perspectives on excellence and an examination of any controversy over the project.

Members of the research team conducted the interviews together and took hundreds of color slides to record their observations; the researchers made sure to be on site during weekdays as well as during one weekend day in order to experience different use patterns. They collected archival reports and documentation of the process of project development and management, and conducted follow-up telephone interviews to address questions that surfaced in their subsequent review of slides, archives, and interview notes. This research further elaborated on the applicant's interpretation of the experience of the place offered for award. The results of this site research was a briefing book, slide presentations for the second round of Selection Committee meetings, and materials used in publications developed for each cycle of the program.

Documentation

The RBA program has produced a full microfilm archive housed at the Lockwood Library at SUNY/Buffalo.[3] There are now close to 4000 perspective sheets from the first four award cycles alone, completed by developers, lawyers, government officials, community groups, planning and design professionals, and users. Each archive entry includes a full description a project, the process by which it was developed, a self-critique of the project, and expectations for its future. The Rudy Bruner Award Archives of 339 projects is a valuable research tool available to all through interlibrary loan programs, the Research Librarians Information Network (RLIN), and the BISON on-line catalog system.

The Foundation is also committed to publishing a book on each cycle of the program. Those interested can gain access to information about the finalists and winners through the following publications:

Urban Excellence (1990) by Philip Langdon with Robert Shibley and Polly Welch

Breakthroughs: Re-creating the American City (1993) by Neal Peirce and Robert Guskind

Connections: Creating Urban Excellence (1992) by Jay Farbstein and Rich Wener

Rebuilding Communities: Re-creating Urban Excellence (1994), also by Farbstein and Wener

Documentation on the November 1992 Washington, D.C., conference, "Los Angeles: Working through the Crisis to Quality Urban Living," includes a two volume set of preconference and postconference notes prepared by the conference director, Robert Shibley, and issued by the Bruner Foundation. In addition, work is under way on a community action planning publication, also by Shibley, on the storytelling methods employed in the Washington conference.

For further information on the current status of Bruner Foundation work on the urban environment or on the continuation of the awards program, contact the Executive Director, The Bruner Foundation, 560 Broadway, New York, NY 10012.

ENDNOTES

CHAPTER 1

1. Heidegger and other phenomenologists frequently use the language of *dwelling* to embody the idea of *people-in-place.* This relational language embeds people in place rather than suggesting a discrete separation between humans and their surroundings. "The way in which you and I am, the manner in which we humans *are* on the earth, is *Baun,* dwelling. To be a human being means to be on the earth as a mortal. It means to dwell. . . . [T]his word *Bauen,* however, *also* means at the same time to cherish and protect, to preserve and care for . . ." (Heidegger 1971, 147). In order to convey the intensity of the relationship, it is sometimes necessary to use words such as *dwelling,* or to use an unfamiliar form such as *people-in-place.*

2. There is available a rich and provocative literature within the fields of architecture, cultural geography, planning, and environment design that focuses on the idea of place. See Heidegger (1971), Norberg-Schulz (1979), Seamon and Mugerauer (1985), Hough (1990), Hiss (1991), Seamon (1993), and Chawla (1994). The journal *Places* is an excellent source of insight into the quality of place and place-people relationships. Much of this literature is situated within the discourse of phenomenology, which attempts to give subject status to place as an actor in dwelling. Our book, although assuming the power of place as an active participant in the world, is focused on placemaking, that is, the activities of people in making places.

3. The modern world has been characterized by a growing professionalization of many tasks that at one time were done by all people, including the activity of making places. Through processes of professionalization, practices seek legitimacy and status by developing criteria for the practice and gateways for excluding others from the practice. Most

of these efforts are rationalized through the claim of public safety and protection. The question of professions and the boundaries constructed to differentiate them will be discussed more fully in the Epilogue.

Illich et al. (1977) offer one of the most cogent critiques of this activity in *Disabling Professions*. The series of essays in this volume reverses the relationship of who is the helper and who is helped, demonstrating that the service professions are actually more dependent on the needs of those being helped than the helped are dependent on the services of those who call themselves helpers. In a service economy, where most people derive their income from professionalized "helping" and the gross national product (GNP) is measured by services rendered, it is critical for the economy to increase the supply of need through an increase in "personal deficiency." In a later volume, Illich (1978) calls this phenomenon the peculiar "poverty of modernity," by which he means that we have become so dependent on the world as we have constructed it that we no longer recognize our freedom and power to act and live creatively and to reclaim for ourselves work that has been sequestered within professional domains.

4. The use of stories or case studies is employed here as a form of reflective practice that starts from the work itself rather than from abstractions about it. It is a textual reading of the practice. We attempt to convey the complexity of placemaking through a narrative that deconstructs each action in its context, and then reconstructs and critiques it. It is our hope that this work will reanimate the practice so that it can be, in turn, critiqued by others.

5. The Caucus Partnership, Consultants on Environmental and Organizational Change, was founded in 1973. Our practice has involved over 200 commissions for public and private clients in four countries and twelve states.

6. In writing about placemaking we occasionally use words in an unfamiliar way to disturb our common concepts. For example, the use of "church-becoming" or "place-becoming" is intended to convey the intensity of the relationship of the actor/action. We are calling attention to the agency of the world and the intermingling of subject and verb. Other forms of language which may be unusual include the use of the slash. So, for example, we use *knowledge/action* and *language/thought* to be clear that we are speaking to a single phenomena which is usually fragmented in the positivist discourse.

7. We use the word *practice* to suggest a way of working in the world, rather than using it as it is usually framed by technical-rational language that refers to practice as the domain for applying knowledge generated elsewhere. Ruddick (1989) argues that mothering is a practice just as is architecture, academia, and science; "practices," she says, "are collective human activities distinguished by the aims that identify them and by the consequent demands made on practitioners committed to those aims" (Ruddick 1989, 13–14). In this sense, those engaged in the research, planning, design, construction, and management of

places can be said to share a practice of placemaking, regardless of the range of activities for which they assume responsibility (design, construction, research, or management), their locations (public service, university, or professional practice), or the names they call themselves (architect, engineer, planner, professor, facility manager). All of these professions and professionals share the aim of making places.

8. Foucault's (1970) archeology of knowledge demonstrates the process by which one form of knowing becomes subjugated or marginalized in favor of others:

> By subjugated knowledges I mean two things: on one hand, I am referring to the historical contents that have been buried and disguised . . . blocks of historical knowledge which were present but disguised within the body of functionalist and systematizing theory and which criticism draws upon and reveals. . . . On the other hand, I believe that by subjugated knowledges one should understand something else, something which in a sense is altogether different, namely a whole set of knowledges that have been disqualified as inadequate to their task or insufficiently elaborated . . . that is through the re-appearance of this knowledge, of these local popular knowledges, these disqualified knowledges, that criticism performs its work (Foucault quoted in Giroux 1988, 99–100).

9. Spatial metaphors, the new language inserted into philosophy by postmodern discourse, appears to be an attempt at reembodiment. It is a way to *re-place* us in our bodies and on the earth. The new words— *deconstruct, construct, space, terrain, territory, collide, crash, slip, commingle, positioned, domain,* and so on—are all about our place, our location in the world. As we use these words and metaphorically construct meanings in our thinking, we act from within ourselves rather than from an Archimedean perspective outside the world.

10. Freire ([1973] 1987; [1970] 1988) has developed the language of confirmation and interrogation through his practice of educating *campesinos* in Latin America. As a process of liberation he both confirms and interrogates their lives to facilitate their own questioning of their existence. This theme will be more fully developed in Chapters 2 and 3.

11. In *Black Looks: Race and Representation,* hooks uses the language of "critical affirmation" to talk of a similar practice that both confirms and interrogates: "Critical affirmation is a concept that embraces both the need to affirm one another and to have a space for critique. Significantly, that critique is not rooted in a negative desire to compete, to wound, to trash" (hooks 1992, 58).

12. John Friedmann (1979) develops an argument for the importance of a special space for dialogue in what he calls radical planning: "We reappropriate the world through dialogue. But the encounter in dialogue is an 'endangered species.' In the interstices of social planning, protected environments must be created for it. The struggle for this space must be initiated at any time" (Friedmann 1979, 152). The intervention of

professional placemaking in the ongoing life of a place is an excellent opportunity for opening such a space in which to collectively remake the world.

13. One of the tasks of postmodern philosophy has been to dismantle the modern construction of *knowledge,* to challenge the notion that knowledge (truth) is one thing derived from only one set of methods (science). Postmodern theorists posit many knowledges and many ways of *coming to know.* The subject of knowledge(s) will be addressed more fully in Chapter 6.

14. Friedmann (1979, 103).

15. "Life is always and already full; it is a total fabric. . . . [I]f anything is added to life that takes time, the web of life is torn and rewoven" (Borgmann 1992, 112). It is an absurdity to assume that there are empty spaces in our lives that need to be filled. Therefore, professional placemakers must always be aware that when they insert a dialogic space into the very filled lives of people for some placemaking activity, it will displace patterns of life and/or open up new ways of living. To take on such a new task means that people must be committed to the activity.

16. In the early 1970s, Rittel and Webber argued against the technical-rational view of planning and suggested that the work of planners lies in the domain of "wicked problems." Problems in planning are "wicked" because there is no definitive formation of any problem confronting planners, there are no rules for when to stop, each problem is unique, and all are symptomatic of—indeed, embedded in—other problems: "Social problems are never solved. At best they are only re-solved—over and over again" (Rittel and Webber 1973, 160). Schon (1983), in his influential book *The Reflective Practitioner,* made the same argument for the practice of architecture (among other professions). Architectural practice is a situation of indeterminacy and instability, and the problems that are addressed in the practice are abstractions extracted from the mess of the world-as-lived.

17. "We can never know what to want, because living only one life, we can neither compare it with our previous lives nor perfect it in our lives to come. . . . There is no means of testing which decision is better because there is no basis for comparison" (Kundera 1984, 8). The making of a place, like the making of a life, happens only once, even as it happens always.

18. To suggest that professional placemakers *translate* recognizes that they are positioned in many locations—as members of the culture, as professionals, as university-trained people, as gendered human beings, and so forth. These various positions mean that the interventionist already participates in diverse discourses and can move between and among them, clarifying and problematizing their own truths, and the perceptions and experiences of people in places. See Lengermann and Niebrugge-Brantley (1990) and Schneekloth (1994b).

19. Vickers (1965) writes of "appreciative systems" as a framework for understanding any situation that uses three questions: What is real?

How is it valued? and What action should be taken? For Vickers, appreciation is the attempt to grasp the dynamic interplay between reality, value, and action.

20. See Habermas (1979; 1984), Geuss (1981), Forester (1985; 1989), and Albrecht and Lim (1986). "[A] critical theory is itself always a part of the object-domain which it describes; critical theories are always in part about themselves" (Geuss 1981, 55). In the practice of placemaking, in which all action is embedded in existing worlds, the ability to understand the nature of knowledge and action as part of this world facilitates the development of a theoretical understanding of the work. We will more fully discuss the issue of knowledge in placemaking in Chapter 6.

21. For example, to conduct critical theory on a game of chess would reveal the following: The empirical analysis would describe the game, the board, the pieces, and the rules—whatever we could observe from the activity of the game and players. The hermeneutic discourse would look at the game of chess somewhat differently. It would explore how the game came to be the way it is, who developed it, and how it is seriously played, that is, how to strategically engage the game. Critical theory would focus on the "gameness" of chess and the context in which it is played. It would reveal how games operate in cultures, why chess has maintained its place as a game of the privileged, and so forth. In other words, it would place chess in its various contexts and uncover the connections and disruptions surrounding the game.

22. All knowledge/action "is grounded in one of these dimensions of social existence, namely in work (instrumental action), in language (communicative action), and in power (self-formative and enlightened action)" (Albrecht and Lim 1986, 122).

23. It is, of course, not only within the domain of professional practice that the conduct of critical theory is embedded in an emancipatory project. The practice of academia, through its primary task of research, is also engaged in value-laden action. See Fraser's (1989) preface "Apologia for Academic Radicals," Schneekloth (1994b), and Chapter 5 for a discussion of the potentially emancipatory power of intellectual work in unmasking debilitating structures through *situated theorizing,* that is, the construction of knowledge and propositions through an engagement in various practices rather than the removal of self required in the construction of knowledge through the methods of science. Fraser (1989) describes the way in which intellectuals, through "expert discourses," bring intellectual work into the public domain to influence and frame action.

24. See Berger and Luckmann (1966) for a pioneering work on the condition and implications for a theory of knowledge that recognizes the social and political construction of "reality."

25. See Shibley and Schneekloth (1988), "Risking Collaboration: Professional Dilemmas in Evaluation and Design," for a more developed argument on this issue. We will also discuss more fully the consequences of not collaborating in Chapter 6.

26. Dewey (1927, 185). The proposition that placemaking can be a significant space for learning about and exercising democracy is developed in Chapter 4.

27. See Perin (1977) and Ritzdorf (1985; 1986) as examples of deconstructive work on how zoning is used as a mechanism for social control through the exclusion of some people and the reification of the single-family home.

28. Forester (1989, 14).

29. Hampden-Turner (1971) critiques social theory and methods within the discourse of science: "We need to question whether a science *about* human beings should be incomprehensible *to* human beings, for it seems unlikely that an incomprehensible social science can help human beings to heal, nurture and enlighten one another" (Hampden-Turner 1971, 8).

30. Freire ([1970] 1988, xi).

31. In a discussion of Twain's *Huckleberry Finn,* Berry (1990) explores the American passion for leaving, for refusing to become a part of a community. The costs of leaving are high because we will never know the responsibility and forgiveness that comes from choosing to be a part of a place and a people. See also Schneekloth (1994a) for development of the idea of frontier and its effect on placemaking.

32. Berry (1990, 83).

33. The bioregional movement is concerned with "staying put," with living in a geographic place as a responsible member of a sustainable and committed community. "While bioregions have certain geographic boundaries, they also have certain mythic and historical modes of self-identification. This identification depends on ourselves as we participate in this process, which only now we begin to understand or appreciate" (Berry 1988, 170). See also Sale (1985), *Dwellers in the Land: The Bioregional Vision,* and the publication *The Planet Drum.*

34. The idea of forgiveness is thoughtfully developed by Huebner (1966) in the context of educational settings. He argues that in the final sense, the act of a teacher is the act of one human being attempting to influence another human being:

> To avoid hubris, the educator must accept the possibility of error—error as he influences and as he has been influenced. Hence forgiveness becomes necessary as a way of freeing one's self and the other from the errors of the past. Forgiveness unties man from the past that he may be free to contribute to new creation. With the power to forgive and to be forgiven, the educator dares to influence and to be influenced in the present (Huebner 1966).

In a similar way, Berry (1990) points to the importance of forgiveness in responsible community making. "Given human nature and human circumstances, our only relief is in this forgiveness, which then restores us to community and its ancient cycle of loss and grief, hope and joy" (Berry 1990, 79).

Note: We use gender-neutral language throughout this book. However, when quoting others we preserve their language which at times uses the male generic. Despite our committment to nonsexist language, we have not inserted [sic] or rewritten their words. We ask you to accept their words as we have done.

CHAPTER 2

1. Another version of this case study is reported in Schneekloth and Shibley (1981), "On Owning a Piece of the Rock," which focuses on an evaluation of the participatory methods used in the conduct of the project.

2. The request from Reverend Wright came to the Extension Service of the Virginia Polytechnic Institute and State University, the public outreach arm of land grant universities. Lynda Schneekloth, then Assistant Professor in the School of Architecture and partner in The Caucus Partnership (then called Consultants on Environmental and Organizational Change), took major responsibility for this project. She was assisted throughout by Michael Appleby from the School of Planning at Virginia Tech and by Robert Shibley, a partner in Caucus. Over the two years there were other faculty who participated (Bonnie Ott, Nancy Kates Canestero, and Ralph Taylor), and many students became involved as part of their studies at the College of Architecture and Urban Studies. During the spring of 1978, Schneekloth conducted a studio on "Participatory Design and Planning." The students who worked on the First Baptist Church Project (Allan Anderson, Michael Haney, Gary Lafferty, Shankar Muthu, Susan Russell, Don Setliff, and Sharon Booker) were instrumental in planning and facilitating the group work, preparing the scores, leading group discussions, and synthesizing information from the walks.

3. The use of the language of voice is particularly relevant in the situation given the oral and aural tradition of the church—in singing, preaching, and storytelling. However, this use should not be construed to imply that the congregation spoke with a single "voice." There were many perspectives about the history of the First Baptist Church and its decision to stay in Gainsboro rather than relocating in the suburbs, and many visions of what the new church should be. As Giroux states: "I have insisted on the notion of voice as a central category in my work because it posits the notion of subjectivity in postmodern terms without giving up the possibility of individual and social agency. The category of voice [is] a referent for both a complex, contradictory, and multilayered notion of subjectivity *and* a view of agency as a practice of self-reflection and social action that is constructed within but not eliminated within such contradictions . . ." (Giroux 1991, 79).

4. The Coordinating Committee members were: Deacon T. C. Banks, Eva E. Boyd, Alease Frazer, Geneva Hale, Shelton T. Reamey, John Reynolds, Walter L. Wheaton, and the Reverend Kenneth Wright.

5. Our practice of problematizing is similar to the work of Paulo Freire as

recorded in *Pedagogy of the Oppressed* ([1970] 1988) and *Education for Critical Consciousness* ([1973] 1987). Freire uses the language of confirmation and interrogation to describe his educational practice in Latin America. As a project of liberation, he both confirms and interrogates with *campesinos* their lives, and in the process of teaching people to read, facilitates their own questioning. The interaction between confirmation and interrogation and the search for underlying reasons and ir/rationality are called "problematizing"—that is, making a problem out of something that had been accepted. This process radically transforms perceptions, and with it, gives power to transform the world because it undermines what he calls "the culture of silence." In Freire's words,

> [m]an's ontological vocation . . . is to be a Subject who acts upon and transforms his world, and in so doing moves toward ever new possibilities of a fuller and richer life individually and collectively. This *world* to which he relates is not a static and closed order, a *given* reality which man must accept and to which he must adjust. . . . It is the material used by man to create history, a task which he performs as he overcomes that which is dehumanizing at any particular time and place and dares to create qualitatively new (Freire [1970] 1988, 12–13).

6. In 1994 the congregation paid off its mortgage for the new church building and is actively pursuing an adaptive reuse strategy for the 1898 building.

7. Group facilitation is a complex activity, one that not many people understand or have developed as a skill. Caucus often includes small-group facilitation training as part of a contractual arrangement that not only assists us with our intervention, but also leaves in the community a cadre of people who are skilled as facilitators. We usually have a three-hour interactive work session that covers generic information on the dynamics of effective group work and the way to record group process on newsprint as a public record. We then review the specific work the group will be doing in the given context.

We cover issues such as what constitutes good group dynamics, what the relationship is between content work and process work, how to recognize and facilitate these different intentions, how to encourage and manage participation, and how to address conflict. We stress the difference between what people normally assume a group leader is, that is, the one who is in charge of both the content and process of a meeting, and the role of the facilitator who is primarily responsible for the process. In this form of group work, it is the structure of the meeting and the group itself that has responsibility for the content. We stress that the role includes the tasks of confirming all inputs and, at the same time, interrogating them in relationship to the task at hand. Unlike many texts on facilitation, we do not insist that facilitators stay out of the content discussion. Rather, we stress that if they wish to offer comments on the content, they can do so by first making explicit that they are stepping out of their role as facilitator. If they feel strongly enough about an issue, they should ask that someone else facilitate for them.

We also do a briefing immediately before any workshop to review the structure of the meeting, to remind people of their role, and to cover any questions. During the meeting, we usually move through the table work as timekeepers and step in if a facilitator is experiencing problems with the group. After a meeting, we have a debriefing session with the facilitators on how the session went, what was learned, how to do it differently, and so on. Depending on the context, we often ask each facilitator to prepare a summary of their table's work, performing the task of translation and expansion of their own newsprint notes.

8. Each of the three questions was allocated about forty-five minutes; ten minutes for brainstorming, twenty-five minutes for discussion, and then ten minutes for ranking their importance. After each of these forty-five minute sessions, there was a "report out" period during which representatives from various tables were asked to share their work with the entire assembly.

9. Data from a 1979 survey conducted by Total Action against Poverty (TAP), a Roanoke community action agency, reported in Booker with Schneekloth (1981).

10. Halprin and Burns developed the scoring technique to use in environmental workshops to frame both inquiry and participation. (Halprin 1969; Halprin and Burns 1974).

11. One of the realities of working with groups in participatory activities is occasional low attendance. This can be very discouraging when many people's time and energy have been spent in preparation for an event. Since it does happen, it is important to think about it and to understand the dynamics. There is a rule of group work worth remembering: In any group, usually about 25% of the people regularly participate and about 5% do most of the work. The rest are interested and involved and will always be there when you need them. Understanding and accepting this condition transforms the perception of what is adequate participation. Also, the actual event itself is only one part of the overall benefit of this type of work. For example, the preparation time in the Close Encounters workshop gave the Coordinating Committee and the consultants a much better understanding of the neighborhood and how it might be addressed in the planning process. Furthermore, the event was not over when everybody went home; the processes of communication and inclusion continued through the weekly talks after Sunday service and the New Building Corner exhibition.

12. *A Pattern Language* (Alexander et al. 1977) is a volume in a series of books that describes a different way of conceptualizing placemaking. It is an attempt to reaniminate what Alexander calls an older way of knowing and interacting with the world. A pattern is a construction that states a relationship between an intention and the material world

required to support that intention. Each pattern states a problem, identifies the context in which this problem exists, gives evidence as to the importance of the problem, and provides a solution. These patterns are purposeful and provocative. It is not the aim of the author of a pattern to dictate the solution, but to provoke thinking about each intention so that the makers of each place can decide to include and/or exclude both the problem and the proposed solution. The other two books of the series are *A Timeless Way of Building* (Alexander 1979) and *The Oregon Experiment* (Alexander 1975). See also Coates and Seamon (1993).

13. There were many different committees involved the planning, design, and construction process: the Coordinating Committee (responsible for the early planning and educative process); the Building Committees (groups of church "experts" involved in working on pattern creation); the Architectural Selection Committee (the group that developed criteria for architectural services, interviewed potential architects, and made recommendations to the trustees); and the Building Committee, which worked with the architect in bringing the new church building out of the ground. This many committees created some confusion about who was actually involved in which activities; it also created some continuity difficulties for the church. On the other hand, it involved more members in positions of responsibility and it encouraged wider participation and commitment to the building process. Reverend Wright and other elders of the church were involved throughout the entire process and served as needed points of continuity.

14. Again we draw on Freire ([1970] 1988) to facilitate our understanding of our own actions. In his educative and political work in Latin America, he uses the idea of a *generative theme* as the focus for decoding situations that limit people and create a sense of hopelessness. The role of the educator is to understand and represent the situations that prevent people from being the makers of their own lives: "Consistent with the liberating purpose of dialogical education, the object of the investigation is not men (as if men were anatomical fragments), but rather the thought-language with which men refer to reality, the levels at which they perceive that reality, and their view of the world, in which their generative themes are found" (Freire [1970] 1988, 86). It is not the limiting situations in and of themselves that constrain people, but the latter's interpretation and perception of the situation. The educator faces a difficult task because as long as the themes and limiting situations belong only to the interventionist, they represent his or her reality, not the reality of the people. The task of the teacher, then, is to find ways to *re-present* the people's universe to them, through them, and with them as they receive it—not as knowledge but as a problem. In his own work, Freire suggests that the generative themes of *domination* and *silence* are required in order to explore the possibility of liberation. In our placemaking work, we find that these same themes appear. They point to the oppressiveness of the current practices of placemaking, which depend on the concept of the expert, as is so articulately described in *Disabling Professions* (Illich et al. 1977).

15. The concept of *participatory consciousness* is useful in understanding the First Baptist Church work. A participatory consciousness suggests that self and nonself are identified at the same time; it is rooted in the idea that subject/object as a dualism does not exist. According to Morris Berman (1984), modern thinking is predicated on a nonparticipatory consciousness that is a "state of mind in which one knows phenomena precisely in the act of distancing oneself from them" (Berman 1984, 27). See also Merchant (1989) for a discussion of participatory consciousness.

16. Lyotard writes of narrative not as a story of the past or the future but of the present:

> [A community that takes] narrative as its key form of competence has no need to remember its past. It finds the raw material for its social bond not only in the meaning of the narratives it recounts, but also in the act of reciting them. The narrative's reference may seem to belong to the past, but in reality it is always contemporaneous with the act of recitation (Lyotard 1988, 22).

CHAPTER 3

1. Even as a *supplement,* the organizational development agenda sets the context for more technical work. Through partial exclusion the supplement actually acquires power in the narrative of our work. It becomes conspicuous by its absence or understatement. Derrida (1988, 136) argues that the context and the text are inseparable, that "there is nothing outside the text," and "there is nothing outside the context." The text/context "implies all the structures called 'real,' 'economic,' 'historical,' 'social-institutional,' in short: all possible referents" (148).

2. Proprietary information and contractual commitments for confidentiality preclude using real names in this account. In this chapter we are referring to the organization as simply the Institute.

3. A working hypothesis in our practice is that any attempt to describe unique organizations as a "type" tends to deny their potential departures from the type. Assigning abstract types to organizations and institutions, like describing people in stereotypical categories, is a form of violence to the richness and potential diversity that is manifest in any organization of individuals. Nevertheless, we acknowledge the importance of *type* as one of several possible places to start the process of socially constructing the description of any specific institution or organization.

4. The dual focus on the technical-rational and the relational is an important theme in much of the poststructuralist literature of the 1970s and 1980s as well as the literature of feminism. Ruddick's (1989) text on *Maternal Thinking* offers an extensive discussion on what she refers to as the practice of care, which requires one to maintain a "double focus": attending to the immediate needs of the child while at the same

time attending to the long-term development of the child. Derrida (1988), in his Afterword to *Limited Inc.,* also describes a double focus to his deconstructionist writing, which is both inscribed within and circumscribed outside of rationalist discourse. He describes himself as one who writes in two "registers" at the same time.

5. See Gold (1973) on the facilitation of repair rather than resisting breakage.

6. Some would argue that the emphasis on confirming existing experiences severely limits the potential for radical transformation, which may be called for in intervention work. Such emphasis may be seen as either nostalgic or, worse yet, manipulative. The double focus of confirmation and interrogation always confirms experience, but not necessarily its adequacy or appropriateness. Through the process of interrogating "confirmed experience" one finds the potential for either radical acts of transformation or incremental adjustment. In this fashion, each intervention accepts the participants where they are and establishes ways for them to build their own critical frameworks for change. Without confirmation one is simply replacing one form of tyranny with another. See Freire ([1970] 1988) for an elaboration on this approach to pedagogical interventions.

   Confirmation per se is also a potentially radical act when it reveals an underlying agreement that each individual was prepared to deny because of an assumption of conflict. Such confirmations become sources of significant liberation and relief when explored in the dialogic space.

7. See Argyris and Schon (1974), *Theory in Practice: Increasing Professional Effectiveness,* for a more in-depth description of the process of recording the *espoused theory* of an organizational unit or individual and contrasting it with their *theory-in-use.* In general, the approach seeks clarity on the way a person or group wishes to behave and then explores with them what behaviors are actually occurring. The difference between the espoused theory and the theory-in-use creates the cognitive dissonance that facilitates change. Often both the espoused theory and actual behaviors are modified during this process of critical inquiry.

8. The Caucus staff who worked on the Office Automation program included Robert Shibley and Lynda Schneekloth, with associates Laura Poltronieri and Ellen Bruce Keable.

9. For a discussion of the use of clients as co-researchers in management consulting, see Hirschhorn's (1988) *The Workplace Within: Psychodynamics of Organizational Life.*

10. The team working on the Library Move project was made up of the Caucus partners Robert Shibley and Lynda Schneekloth, working with Caucus associate Ellen Bruce Keable.

11. This concept of self-correction appears to be uncritical toward what constitutes "good." Within the dialogic space, however, acts of confirmation can and often do become acts of critical interrogation through processes of public disclosure and comparison.

12. For a critique of personal-interest criterion see Meidinger (1987) and our discussion in Chapter 1 regarding how such criterion can be part of

the foundation for continued exclusions of whole populations. While the personal-interest criterion cannot be indiscriminately applied in all cases, neither can it be indiscriminately excluded. No general rule applies except for the need to situate the criteria in the dialogic space of the project, confirming and interrogating its appropriateness.

13. See Shibley and Schneekloth (1988) for a detailed discussion of the dynamics of risking collaboration in favor of gaining commitment to action and the ability to facilitate repair.

14. See especially William Pena's (1987) *Problem Seeking: An Architectural Primer* and Roger Brauer's (1985) *Facilities Planning*. Both of these texts and the institutions that supported them—the American Institute of Architects and the American Management Association, respectively—advocate completing information collection prior to the start of design.

15. The process of interrogating and confirming the situation, especially in questioning a hidden agenda, is the contextual conduct of Habermas's critical theory (1979, 1984; Albrecht and Lim 1986). It is an attempt to understand and publicly reveal the aims and purposes of the players, and the structure in which the decisions are made. It demands the simplicity and sincerity of communicative competence, which Habermas describes as essential to creating the conditions in which dialogue is to become emancipatory.

16. Recent events have led to still further growth of the Institute. Even a planned expansion of the headquarters building will not be large enough to achieve the reintegration hoped for when the Library was preparing to move out. Interviews with both Facilities staff and Library staff in 1993 (five years after the move) reveal that there is no longer any desire on the part of the Library to move back into the headquarters facility. The disadvantages staff predicted would occur turn out to be minor relative to the advantages they are experiencing in their new location.

17. See Schon (1983) for his critique of the assumption that technical is better than nontechnical, or that the technical falls solely within the purview of such "higher" professions as engineering, medicine, or law. He argues that the complexity and ambiguity of the so-called "minor" professions that do not rely on a single codified knowledge base are more able to address the full complexity of situations we encounter in the modern world. Note also that, while he is critical of the technical-rational foundation of the so-called higher professions, he does not deny the need for "reflective practitioners" to also draw on such foundations.

18. The work we are describing is similar to what is called *womenswork* by Tanzer (1992). Tanzer uses the concept *womenswork* to discuss the practice of architecture in modernity, developing the idea that the satisfaction of such work must be *in the process of engagement* rather than in its artifact because the work is formless and lacks closure. This argument about the nature of architectural practice is similar to the discussion of planning by Rittel and Webber (1973), in which they suggest that the work of planners has "no stopping rules."

The professions that engage in the practice of "caring"—interior design, facility management, nursing, teaching, social work, day care, and some varieties of architecture and planning—are still considered to be "women's professions." Although this work has been elevated in the market economy, the professions engaged in housework are undervalued and often underrewarded (Baines 1991). The pattern within the Institute in similar to that in many such organizations: Women comprise the main body of staff workers (except in "manly" areas such as computers, carpentry, electrical and mechanical systems, and so on), and men have most of the management positions.

A problem, however, with using the term *womenswork* is that it embeds the idea of caring exclusively within a gendered sphere, and this has been well critiqued. For example, Tronto (1989) writes, "In suggesting that an ethic of care is gender related, Gilligan (1982) precludes the possibility that care is an ethic created in modern society by the conditions of subordination. If the ethics of care is separated from a concern with gender, a much broader range of options emerged" (Tronto 1989), 646–647). We will use the term *housework* in an effort to address this critique even while we recognize that women still do the bulk of this type of work and, in this sense, it is *womenswork*.

19. An extensive literature on unpaid labor within the domestic sphere has developed in the feminist discourse. See particularly Margolis (1984) for a discussion on housework, and Chodorow (1978) and Ruddick (1989) for a discussion on mothering.

There is also a rich history of literature from management science focused on what Hertzberg (1972) refers to as the *motivation-hygiene theory*. In this work Hertzberg puts forward the theory that the environment is seen as a hygiene factor in the corporate world, not a motivator. As such it forms a background to the more important agendas about the purposes of the institution. It is not surprising that the research supporting this theory is performed largely on men already in the dominant culture of the corporate world. The promulgation of this theory in management training courses and texts over the past twenty years has all the dynamics of a continuing self-fulfilling prophecy.

20. Much of this literature has developed around the debate between Kohlberg's (1981, 1984) states of moral reasoning and the critique of that work by Gilligan (1982), which focuses on its gender bias. Finch and Groves (1983) and Baines et al. (1991) discuss caring as involving both love and labor, usually performed within the network of relationships. Noddings (1984) speaks to the responsibilities of the caregiver and the cared for, trying to untangle what appears to be "natural" and therefore unproblematized relationships. Consider the differences between "caring for" and "caring about," in which the first involves the instrumental and tangible tasks involved in caring and the latter involves expressive and affective dimensions (Dalley 1988, Tronto 1989).

21. The Institute for Business Designers and the Internal Facilities Management Association are very busy "professionalizing." They seek educational certification for those who would call themselves facility

managers, they offer exams testing competence areas, they publish journals, and so forth. It is an irony, perhaps, that practitioners in the very professions they may wish to emulate, such as architecture, interior design, and planning, suffer from the same sense of self-deprecation and low status. They also feel undervalued, finding themselves delivering service without attendant professional recognition, public celebration, and financial reward. See Gutman (1988) and Vonier (1989) for this discussion related to architecture. Efforts to professionalize facility management, elevating its status above the mundane, raise many questions about the meaning and nature of professional housework in the practice of placemaking.

22. See Reverby (1988) for a discussion about the history of nursing and a description of what occurs when nurses are *ordered* to provide emotional care along with physical labor. See also Baines (1991) for a more general discussion.

23. Facilities Section staff performance appraisals, employment criteria, and some dismissals over the past decade have been explicitly based, in part, on the interpersonal competence of staff and their ability to work with others in a way that maintains social relationships. The Facilities staff are required to deliver their professional competence in a socially supportive—one might say "caring"—way.

24. See Gibb (1964) for a discussion of the requirement that trust grow in a climate where there is no recourse to power. He argues persuasively for a condition of reciprocal vulnerability. To defend against insincerity is to reduce one's vulnerability and therefore one's ability to develop a trusting relationship. See also our argument for trust formation in Shibley and Schneekloth (1988).

CHAPTER 4

1. The ideal and language of democracy is contested in our culture and is used to legitimate and criticize many forms of social practice. In this book we use the language of democracy as Dewey describes it, as "a way of life . . . that implies a form of community-in-struggle whose aim is to reconstruct human experience in the realization of such principles as freedom, liberty, and fraternity" (Dewey quoted in Giroux 1988, 86). Democracy recognizes people as *citizens,* not consumers, who struggle as individuals *and* as groups to control their lives and histories. In this sense, a democratic practice is not limited to resolving the problems of formal governance (city, state, and nation), although it is essential to them; it also pervades all forms of social organizations through the processes of inclusion and exclusion in making decisions about resource distribution and the rules of conduct of its members.

2. We would particularly like to thank Margaret Grieve for her willingness to engage with us in critical thinking about this project since we worked together in 1980 to put the Roanoke Neighborhood Partnership in place. Also thanks to Andrée Tremoulet, first neighborhood coordinator of the RNP, for her reading of the manuscript and con-

structive comments, and Stephanie Cicero, current RNP coordinator, for her ongoing reflections on the RNP and her work.

In this chapter, all photographs and quotes without a specific reference are taken from *The Roanoke Neighborhood Partnership Self-Help Manual* (1993) and used courtesy of the Office of Community Planning, City of Roanoke, Va.

3. The role of leadership in democratic governance is complex. The analogy between the teacher-student relationship and the official-citizen relationship has been helpful to us in constructing our practice of placemaking. Giroux develops the concept *emancipatory authority,* which recognizes that teachers and leaders "are bearers of critical knowledge, rules, and values through which they consciously articulate and problematize their relationship to each other, to students, to subject matter, and to the wider community" (Giroux 1988, 90). In this sense, teachers and leaders can guide the possibility of knowing and the subsequent field of action by challenging others to frame their own choices, not to uncritically assume what is. This work as described by Giroux is very similar to Freire's practice, in which he posits leaders to be those who come from another world not as invaders—not to teach or transmit or give anything—"but rather to learn with the people, about the people's world" (Freire [1970] 1988, 181). Note that this practice is characterized as being "with," not "for," and in this sense it is profoundly democratic.

4. See Floyd (1984) for an overview of Roanoke Design '79, and also a commentary by Michael Appleby, who participated in the RNP as an associate of the Caucus Partnership.

5. *Utopia* has become a very unfashionable word in both the dominant instrumental culture and in postmodern philosophy. The word has come to mean a totalitarian, rigid view of how people and the state ought to relate to each other, usually with the individual subsumed by the state. In his critique of public schooling, Giroux writes that

> the bruteness of [a] fundamentally anti-utopian character undercuts any possibility for the development of a potentially progressive and substantive political project. Without a language capable of recovering and reconstructing history, reconstituting subjectivity around an operational notion of human will and agency, and developing a political project based on a discourse of possibility, postmodern philosophy presents itself in opposition to any project designed to foster critique and hope in the service of an ethics and political philosophy linked to the construction of a radical democracy (Giroux 1988, 62).

Like Giroux, we reclaim this very powerful word and use it to express our belief that people are willing to confirm their world, interrogate its meaning and structure, have the courage to hope for a different world in which they are active, and take action to this end. See also Schneekloth (1994b).

6. *Folks* is a word used often in Roanoke. It is perceived to be an affectionate, respectful term that includes all people of the city.

7. Ernest Hutton was project director from Buckhurst, Fish, Hutton & Katz (BFHK), New York; Ron Thomas of D.C. Collaborative was responsible for communications and public relations on the Roanoke project; William G. Conway was economic consultant; and Lynda Schneekloth, Robert Shibley, and Michael Appleby from the Caucus Partnership (formerly Consultants on Environmental and Organizational Change) were responsible for community relations. Margaret Grieve, an independent consultant, lived in Roanoke during the most intensive period of development and managed the day-to-day contact with city staff and neighborhood leaders.

8. At what point does an effort in communication turn into a public relations campaign? When is the privileged position of government in terms of access to the media used to convince people of a "truth" rather than to engage them in dialogue? This is a very complex issue in the late twentieth century, the age of mass media. Forester (1989) addresses the issue of communication responsibilities for planners, building on the work of Habermas:

> Mutual understanding depends on the satisfaction of these four criteria: comprehensibility, sincerity, legitimacy, and accuracy or truth. Without comprehensibility in interaction, we have no meaning but confusion. Without a measure of sincerity, we have manipulation or deceit rather than trust. When a speaker's claims are illegitimately made, we have the abuse rather than the exercise of authority. And when we cannot gauge the truth of what is claimed, we will be unable to tell the difference between reality, propaganda, act, and fantasy (Forester 1989, 144).

We recognized that if the RNP were going to engage the citizens of Roanoke in critical reflection on their neighborhoods and the city, they had to know that they were invited and that the process was open to their influence. This process had to be very public and very clear because in the absence of such communication, rumors often frame public processes. There was a concerted effort to keep as much of the RNP process in the media as possible. For example, as one tool, D.C. Collaborative prepared an evocative slide-tape documentary in which residents spoke about their lives in their own neighborhoods. The development and maintenance of a good relationship with the various media was part of our work in this context. We attempted to maintain comprehensibility, sincerity, legitimacy, and accuracy in all of our communications with the public through the media.

9. The proposal review, designed by Michael Appleby, is a variation on the generic small-group brainstorming process. It is an excellent mechanism to elicit specific comments about a thoughtfully framed proposal. In this group process, participants are asked to respond to three specific questions: What is good about this proposal? What needs

to be modified or changed? What alternatives would you suggest? This process frames the dialogue into both confirmation and interrogation, validating the proposers for their work, and eliciting specific feedback about changes.

10. Andrée Tremoulet was neighborhood coordinator from 1982 until 1986; Ginni Benson coordinated the RNP from 1986 to 1988; and Stephanie Fowler Cicero began her work as coordinator of the RNP in 1989.

11. Personal correspondence from Andrée Tremoulet to Lynda Schneekloth, September 16, 1990.

12. Lewis W. Peery, Chair, Roanoke Neighborhood Partnership Steering Committee, reported in the *Roanoke Neighborhood Partnership Annual Report—1984.*

13. *Roanoke Neighborhood Partnership Annual Report—1984.*

14. *Intermediate institutions* is a term used to describe those many and diverse community institutions forming the framework for much of our lives and that lie between the private life and the public sphere. Within this realm are such institutions as the family, the churches, the Scouts, and civic organizations. Much discussion of individual rights assumes that society involves interactions between a private life and an inaccessible public sphere. The concept of *intermediate institutions* suggests this relationship is mediated by many other levels of contact in which types of interpersonal and contractual arrangements frame the lived, connected web of human relationships. Thus we are not a society of isolated individuals situated among strangers (see Giroux 1988, 56). Furthermore, as Meidinger (1987) suggests, "[d]emocracy is not solely or even perhaps essentially a problem of the state. The ideal and practice of democracy pervade all forms of social organizations. . . . They often do a significant amount of 'governing' by virtue of allocating large quantities of social resources and establishing rules governing the conduct of people who participate in and deal with them" (Meidinger 1987, 20–21). In a relatively small city like Roanoke, the web of intermediate institutions is overlapping, accessible, and powerful in the lives of the citizens who participate in them and offers a forum for the practice of democracy.

15. This idea that power should be distributed rather than gathered in relationship to civic governance is, obviously, a necessary ingredient of democracy. However, as a fundamental belief it is at odds with a conception of city government that assumes one must hold power over others and have control over processes in order to be effective and accomplish one's aims (for example, a new convention center, a baseball field, or a new harbor front). Freire ([1973] 1987) adds to this discussion when he says that those in positions of power (through election, class, race, and/gender) often feel that any distribution of power in the name of the community is a restriction on them; distribution is perceived as something being taken away, as if it were a violation of their individual rights.

16. Reynolds believed governance to be a form of education in which the

knowledge of basic citizen skills should be clearly communicated. Citizens have the right to understand how a city works, who is responsible for what, and how to get things done. It is the responsibility of government to mitigate any confusion about these issues. But more than that, he viewed this process of education and the elimination of misperceptions as a way to communicate what Giroux calls "knowledge about the social forms through which human beings live, become conscious and sustain themselves, particularly with respect to the social and political demands of democratic citizenship" (Giroux 1988, 103). Reynolds' vision of the possibility for a working democracy in Roanoke was the mainstay in the early years of the RNP formation.

17. During the 1980s, many municipal planning departments were transformed from offices that engaged in planning into brokers for economic development, who negotiated between public monies and private investment. Many local departments abandoned traditional public planning activities or hired private consultants to do whatever planning was necessary.

   Even within this restructuring of the practice of planning, there are many ways that planners can and do subvert the privatization of government political functions. John Forester's (1989) research on planning practice explores the following questions:

   > How do planners politically shape attention and communicate? How do they provide or withhold information about project alternatives to affected people? Do planners speak in a way that people can understand, or do they mystify citizens? How do planners encourage people to act, or rather discourage them with a (possibly implicit) "Leave it to us?" What can planners do . . . to counteract unnecessary, deeply ideological formulations of community problems? How can they work or organize to enable citizens' learning, participation, and self-determination? (Forester 1989, 139)

18. Friedmann, a radical planner, writes extensively on this issue of trust in the practice of planning in *The Good Society* (1979). He suggests that in order to have dialogue, there must be trust. But this trust does not necessarily depend on a relationship developed slowly over the long term (although certainly it can), but is rather dependent on an attitude about the world: "We initiate dialogue, not by insisting that others place their trust in us but by placing ourselves in trust with them, by risking ourselves. In this way, reciprocity will be forthcoming, dialogue will be achieved" (Friedmann 1979, 11).

19. The construction of the "private sector" in capitalism is a highly contested arena in many feminist and postmodern discourses. Fraser (1989) describes the bounding of three discursive spheres operating in male-dominated, capitalist societies: the political, the economic, and the domestic. By placing issues and needs within one of these discourses, we set the frame for the location of its discussion; only those issues described as being political are considered open to public discourse. For example, if the question of workplace democracy is rele-

gated to the realm of an economic problem or wife battering as a domestic problem, it will not receive public discussion.

> [D]omestic institutions and official economic systems institutions . . . both enclave certain matters into specialized discursive areas: both thereby shield such matters from generalized contestation and from widely disseminated conflicts of interpretation; and as a result, both entrench as authoritative certain specific interpretations of needs by embedding them in certain specific, but largely unquestioned, chains of in-order-to relations (Fraser 1989, 168).

Critical reflection on these issues is required for competent professional action, but knowing that the "private sector" is a culturally produced domain does not necessarily tell a placemaker what to do in particular situations. The city government in Roanoke worked with the "private sector" on many development issues, and those participating in the private sector in the city had time, resources, and ideas to contribute to the continuing dialogue about placemaking. In light of these aspirations, we struggled with the RNP to find a way for this sector to participate, even though we met with only partial success.

20. See *Roanoke Vision: Comprehensive Development Plan for Roanoke, Virginia, 1985–2005* (1985), prepared by Buckhurst, Fish, Hutton & Katz in association with D.C. Collaborative and Margaret Grieve, available from the City of Roanoke, Office of Community Planning, 215 Church Street SW, Roanoke, Va. 24011.

21. See Dewey (1927, 1938) and Giroux (1988, 1991).

22. Giroux (1988, 100).

23. As quoted in Friedmann (1979, 174).

24. In the summer of 1990, Lynda Schneekloth of the Caucus Partnership and Ron Thomas of D.C. Collaborative (currently Thomas Means, Associates) were contracted to work with the city to reevaluate the role of neighborhoods in city governance in general, and the role of the Roanoke Neighborhood Partnership in particular. We found that the RNP had gone through a difficult period. Many of the players in City Hall changed: Ewert had left, Reynolds had become assistant city manager under Robert Herbert, and John Marlles headed the Office of Community Planning. The city as a whole had changed its focus from neighborhood planning to issues of economic development—in keeping with the rhetoric of the Reagan-Bush years. Coordinator Ginni Benson left in 1988, and the Partnership was without a full-time coordinator for eighteen months.

When Stephanie Cicero assumed responsibility for the RNP in 1989, she worked closely with the Steering Committee to develop and affirm the goals of the Partnership. Through the efforts of Cicero and others, the leaders of the RNP were ready to assume a more proactive role in neighborhood planning. City Manager Robert Herbert restated the city's pride in the RNP process when he said that "Roanoke has been a leader in looking to its citizens for advice on city government issues. We realized a long time ago that they are the real experts on what's best for their neighborhoods." When we did our interviews at the beginning of the 1990s, it was clear that there was still the commitment to having neighborhoods and neighborhood leaders as active partners in responding to the very difficult issues facing the cities in the United States: drugs and crime, children in poverty, disorganized families, literacy problems and so on. It was less clear how to be inclusive in these kinds of problems, which cut across neighborhood borders and lay at the heart of the urban crisis facing the United States. These issues are far more complex than those which were the focus of the original RNP projects. How this partnership continues to change and transform itself and the city of Roanoke bears close watching.

CHAPTER 5

1. The analysis in this chapter, and other commentary on the Rudy Bruner Award in the book, draws on work conducted by Robert Shibley under contract to the Bruner Foundation. The support of the Foundation is acknowledged with appreciation. The interpretations are ours and do not necessarily reflect those of the Foundation's board of trustees or of other collaborators on the development and ongoing management of the RBA.

   The Bruner Foundation was established in 1967 as a philanthropic organization. Before it began its inquiries into the urban environment, it established many other programs. One involved helping to establish a new profession, physician's assistant, during the 1970s. Despite significant opposition, the Foundation fostered the training and acceptance of these skilled medical personnel and thereby expanded health care for millions of Americans in Appalachia, inner cities, and other medically underserved areas. The use of such professionals has since become established throughout the country. A recognition that Holocaust studies had been neglected led to a second program which offered grants for the development of teaching materials for secondary schools. A third example of the Foundation's previous work involved its efforts in the 1980s to help nonprofit organizations evaluate the impact of their activities. The Ruby Bruner Award for Urban Excellence continues this most recent focus through its insistence that applicants to the award assess their experience and make it available to others.

2. For a more detailed description of the structure of the awards program, see the Appendix.

3. The case study material in this chapter is based on the collaborative work of Robert Shibley and Polly Welch conducted during research team site visits for the Bruner Foundation. The final two sections of the chapter are based on more recent collaborations between Shibley and Schneekloth in the development of this book.

   Shibley and Welch served as the RBA program's professional advisors and Selection Committee research team members from 1986 through 1990. Working with the Foundation, this team designed the application for the award, the Selection Committee evaluation process, and conducted the supporting field research. Since that time Shibley and Welch have continued to consult with the Foundation on related projects.

4. "Excellence" is often used to suggest "mastery, control, and/or efficiency." This is not our intended meaning, nor it is the intention of the RBA in citing excellence as a significant contributor to the quality of urban life. Rather, we and the RBA program are using excellence to mean the much messier, more complex situations that speak to the quality of relationships between people and between people and their places.

5. The categories of *origin* and *organization and management* and their attendant characteristics were derived through a review of the 176 cases in the RBA Archives catalogued in the State University of New York at Buffalo Lockwood Library in 1990. The research involved listing categories of dynamics that were presented as influencing either the project origins or ongoing organizational dynamics. These lists were then sorted into clusters of similar concepts and ranked in terms of the relative frequency with which they surfaced. In an effort to single out the most significant characteristics, we identified those that played a major role in over half of the submissions and were also evident in over 75% of the RBA finalists. The result of this analysis was an initial inquiry into the research potential of the Archives; we present it here not as conclusive or exhaustive, but as illustrative of several important characteristics that contribute to the perception of excellence by broadly based project constituencies.

6. Members of the RBA Selection Committees and of the press covering the Quality Hill story observed that the preservation of historic structures and creation of middle- to upper-income housing provided by the project did not address the needs of the homeless individuals illegally squatting on Quality Hill at the time of the fire. The developers described some attempts to relocate the existing residents but, by the time construction had begun, most of the almost 200 homeless residents had apparently just "gone away." See Langdon et al. (1990) for a complete description of the Quality Hill development.

7. See Berman (1988) for a discussion on authorship in contemporary society, and how modernism might be seen as "any attempt by modern men and women to become subjects as well as objects of modernization, to get a grip on the modern world and make themselves at home in it" (Berman 1988, 5).

8. Resistance is also an act of placemaking, usually invoked when dialogue fails or has been suspended. It can serve as a way to reopen the dialogue, or it can occur in a manner that ensures no dialogue will even be considered in the foreseeable future. Many of the stories in the Rudy Bruner Award Archives describe acts of resistance, but most of them were not designed to remove "the other" from the dialogic

space. Rather, resistance stories in the Archives tend to establish the conditions for allowing additional publics to be heard; they are about inclusion rather than exclusion. Freire ([1970] 1988) argues for this form of resistance while he critiques alternate intervention strategies that seek simply to replace one controlling force with another.

9. One aspect of empowerment is certainly a population's ability to iden- tify with the importance given to a place through its architecture, its location, and the investment it represents. Our discussions of em- powerment include the role of the character and quality of constructed buildings and landscapes as ingredients in the making of good places. For additional information on Cabrillo Village see Hatch (1984), who uses the story in part to develop his description of the "scope of social architecture."

10. See Steinbrueck (1968).

11. See Langdon et al., *Urban Excellence* (1990), for details on the Pike Place Market's social ecology.

12. The checks and balances that have been in place at the Pike Place Market specifically related to its economic structure have recently been severely weakened. Changes to the tax laws in the late 1980s caused outside financial investors to seek and acquire more power in the man- agement of the Market. What used to be a good passive tax-shelter investment suddenly had to return a much larger profit. The pressure for short-term gain now works against the current modified highest- and-best-use dynamics of the Market and threatens the rent structure based on ability to pay. It also threatens the delicate balance between crafts and tourist-oriented sales on the one hand, and the "real" pro- duce market presence on the other. It remains to be seen how the financial restructuring may affect the long-term viability and life of Pike Place.

13. Another way to view the idea of *supplement* is to consider the use of the word by Derrida. "What Derrida calls the 'logic of supplementarity' is precisely this strange reversal of values whereby an apparently deriva- tive or secondary term takes on the crucial role in determining an entire structure of assumptions" (Norris 1987, 67). Naming academic or intellectual placemaking as supplemental, then, does not mean we can omit it as extra or not central to the projects of our lives. It is not supplement as unnecessary. Intellectual work in placemaking estab- lishes context and provides opportunities for exploring knowledges, meanings, and human relationships that interpret context and the arti- facts of science and professionalism.

14. "I have tried to keep simultaneously in view the distinct standpoints of the theorist and of the political agent, not to reduce one to the other" (Fraser 1989, 2). Such is the work of placemaking, at once requiring theoretical and practical/political work, each with its own need for rigor and discipline but inextricably interdependent.

15. See the Introduction and Chapter 2 of Franck and Schneekloth (1994) for an expanded discussion of the power of the imaginal and concep- tual in placemaking.

16. See Chapter 6 for a further discussion on the nature of knowledge and its uses and abuses. The history of architectural practice is filled with stores of imposing a particular view of correct knowledge onto others. Charles Moore et al. (1974) describe the concept of taste as one such imposition of superior knowing in their preface to *The Place of Houses*. The preface criticizes the common notion that "good taste" is something architects have, while clients do not, requiring them to pay dearly to get some. The text goes on to critique the concept of taste, and offers architectural knowledge in a manner very accessible to the larger public, situating it clearly into the everyday lives of people in their houses and thus describing "the place of houses."

17. National Advisory Commission on Civil Disorders (the Kerner Commission) Report to Congress in 1968, as reported in Shibley (1992).

18. See Moynihan, *The Maximum Feasible Misunderstanding* (1969), in which he describes the folly of doing *for* the poor during the U.S.'s "war on poverty." Some of the "best and brightest" people who followed John F. Kennedy to office in the 1960s were asked to literally "apply" their knowledge in the Johnson administration's Great Society programs. Moynihan describes disastrous results, not because of what was known, but because of how the knowledge was, or rather was not, situated. Subsequent critiques of Moynihan's text have faulted his characterization of the black family in that it failed to recognize the way women work to hold families and communities together in spite of oppressive conditions. The programs of the war on poverty were certainly not sensitive to the needs or the roles of women. Perhaps if the process of "working with" rather than "doing for" were fully engaged in a war on poverty, such critiques and insights would have been more evident.

19. See Shibley (1992) for a complete description of the conference "Los Angeles: Working through the Crisis to Quality Urban Living." The materials are available through the RBA Archives in the Lockwood Library at SUNY/Buffalo and through the Bruner Foundation in New York City.

A large number of people made the conference possible. Financial support and leadership were provided by the Bruner Foundation, by Janet Carter, its executive director, and by Simeon Bruner, a trustee of the Foundation. The design of the event evolved over several months of collaboration between the Bruner Foundation, its consultants, and staff from the Department of Housing and Urban Development including Paul Fletcher, Sharrone Lipscome, and Roy Priest. Steve Glaude represented the Executive Office of the President. Casey Mann and Leroy Sanchez from the Department of Commerce provided additional oversight. A Bruner Foundation site visit to Los Angeles, with Gwendolyn Clemons, Janet Carter, and Robert Shibley meeting with dozens of people in Los Angeles, helped put the conference in context. Shibley served as the conference director and worked with lead conference coordinators Polly Welch, Joseph McNeely, Gwendolyn Clemons, Janet Carter, and Richard Wener.

20. The agenda for the conference specifically invited participants to "conduct real conversations (rather than performances or posturing) about successful urban revitalization projects involving those who helped make the projects possible and those who are facing similar problems." It further invited them to "develop an alternative to conventional 'expert' forms of investigation into distressed urban communities" (Shibley 1992, 1).

CHAPTER 6

1. The power of individuals or groups to influence others is both extremely limited and enormously transformative. The ability to influence depends, in part, on the vulnerability of the parties within the relationship, and whether this vulnerability is a result of the condition of oppression or is freely given within the space of dialogue. In other words, others can refuse to be influenced; we as professionals can refuse to be influenced. However, the possibility of significant influence in placemaking interventions is real. "[W]e have the power through acts of love or lovelessness literally to create one another. . . . Because we do not understand love as the power to act-each-other-into well-being we also do not understand the depth of our power to thwart life and to maim each other" (Harrison 1985, 11).

2. There is an insightful literature on the role of design and planning professionals in the destruction of neighborhoods and communities; see, for example, Jacobs (1961), Berman (1988), Walters (1988), and Wilson (1991). See also Scarry (1985) for a remarkable discussion on the making and unmaking of the world.

3. Even using the word *laypeople* generates a category of people who "do not know," separating them from the people who "do know." George Bernard Shaw quipped, "Every profession is a conspiracy against the laity."

4. See, for example, Schon (1983), Pérez-Gómez (1983), Harding (1986), and Haraway (1988).

5. Jane Jacob's *The Death and Life of Great American Cities* (1961) was one of the first books to criticize openly the beliefs and practices of the design professions. In this book, Jacobs offers a vision of urban life grounded in the messy, daily practices of the world-as-lived rather than in a modernist's view of an orderly and controlled world. Also, Pruitt Igoe, an award-winning urban renewal project in St. Louis, is used as an example of professional misjudgment in the quest to use architecture to solve social problems. A critical analysis of Pruitt Igoe would suggest that the very intention of public housing as manifest in the United States reveals its class and race structure; that is, "ghettoizing" groups of structurally unemployed and underemployed people only serves to sequester them from the existing power elite. See Walters (1988) for a discussion of the spatial zoning of poverty as a to-

pomorphic response to industrialization and capitalism, and Rusk (1993) for an update on the sequestration of poverty in cities because policies support suburban development.

6. A movement in the 1960s calling for citizen participation in projects gave birth to organizations such as the Environmental Design Research Association (EDRA) in 1968 that sought to bring people back into the design process. The institutionalization of the members of this organization into the university structure, along with the change in national mood in the 1970s and 1980s, shifted the focus away from active participation by people in places to forms of science-based research to be used by designers as "user input." The call for participation, however, continued because federal and state governments mandated citizen-input processes in community development block grant funding and other federal programs. Unfortunately, these processes often eroded into strategies for token participation and citizen appropriation. See, however, the story of the Roanoke Neighborhood Partnership (Chapter 4) and the Rudy Bruner Award stories (Chapter 5), especially Cabrillo Village and the Southwest Corridor Project, for examples of citizen empowerment.

7. The social practices of the university, for example, have maintained class distinctions:

> Throughout much of the world today, universities have replaced religious institutions as the conveyors of social values and prestige. They play a central role in molding cultural and social elites. Institutes of higher learning have become primary purveyors of status (Harrison 1985, 235).

8. Our critique of the social practice of science is not meant to devalue the work of knowledge construction within science, but rather to locate it as a practice. As Haraway puts it:

> So, I think my problem, and "our" problem, is how to have *simultaneously* an account of radical historical contingency for all knowledge claims and knowing subjects, a critical practice for recognizing our own "semiotic technologies" for making meanings, *and* a no-nonsense commitment to faithful accounts of a "real" world, one that can be partially shared and that is friendly to earthwide projects of finite freedom, adequate material abundance, modest meaning in suffering, and limited happiness (Haraway 1988, 579).

9. As early as the 1920s, John Dewey wrote: "A class of experts is inevitably so removed from common interests as to become a class with private interests and private knowledge, which in social matters is not knowledge at all" (Dewey 1927, 207).

10. See Griffin (1992, 295). We can posit a nondualistic relationship between knowledge and intimacy by using the construction of knowl-

edge and place as a way to achieve intimacy while we empower populations to do work.

11. Lengermann and Niebrugge-Brantley (1990) offer an incisive exploration of the role of feminist theory within the discourse of sociology, including a discussion of the practice of translation. They suggest three acts of translation: "(1) the task of enabling subjects to translate their lived experiences into texts which can be shared; (2) the task of translating these texts into the symbol system of sociology; and (3) the task of translating personal, historically specific texts into general statements without losing the individuality of the original accounts" (Lengermann and Niebrugge-Brantley 1990, 327).

12. For an elaboration of the argument on professional risk, see Shibley and Schneekloth, "Risking Collaboration: Professional Dilemmas in Evaluation and Design" (1988).

13. The literature that presents both empirical and rational evidence for the beneficial effects of collaboration also cautions that (1) this mode of operation is not always appropriate, and (2) it would be both foolish and contradictory to *require* anyone, including professionals, to collaborate. See Lickert (1961), Gibb (1964), Thayer (1973), Argyris and Schon (1974), Schon (1983), and Hirschhorn (1988) for the management science discourse on the subject.

14. Sennett (1970, 121). There is an emerging literature on the theory of care within the feminist discourse that attempts to situate caring as a critique of universal ethics outside of domestic and/or religious spheres. A major feminist project has been to challenge the boundaries between the private and public as drawn in the twentieth century and to demonstrate in what ways the personal is political. Within this framework, caring and noncaring are not private acts but public and political activities. See particularly Gilligan (1982), Noddings (1984), Dalley (1988), and Baines et al. (1991).

15. Much of this argument is based on a reading of Xavier Rubert de Ventos, who argues for "interdependence, vulnerability, and dispersion, eccentricity and personal dissolution, availability and receptivity, and the fulfillment not of duty but of desire" (1971, xx). See also Haraway (1988) for a critique of rationality as a stance for working in the world: "Feminist objectivity makes room for surprises and ironies at the heart of knowledge production; we are not in charge of the world. We just live here and try to strike up noninnocent conversations. . ." (Haraway 1988, 594).

16. This concept challenges the "great-person theory of life," the norm in many professionals circles, which suggests that it is only extraordinary people who change things. On the contrary, many significant social movements are the result of many people—ordinary, brave human beings—choosing to take control of their lives. In our own time, witness the civil rights movement, the women's movement, and populist antigovernment uprisings in Latin America such as Las Madres de Los Desaparecidos. In a similar way, beautiful places must have the

attention of many ordinary people to be maintained, lest they fall into disrepair. Again, we assert that this argument does not denigrate the work of individual artisans, craftspeople, or the creative genius. It only locates such talent in the placemaking practice, removing it as a form of tyranny while inviting its discipline.

17. Obviously, the decision to be and remain vulnerable is dependent on one's sense of trust in other people, and on a belief about human nature. Ruddick writes:

> Individuals are not primarily centers of dominating and defensive activity trying to achieve a stable autonomy in threatening hierarchies of strength, although this does describe some individuals and some moments in most lives. They are also and equally centers of care, actively desiring other selves to persist in their own lively being, judging their own well-being in terms of their capacity for a love that "struggles toward definition" (Ruddick 1989, 183).

18. Friedmann (1979, 68–69).

19. Beliefs about human nature are never directly verifiable; they are based in faith. "This is my faith; consider it only a possibility" (Xenophanes, *Fragment 16,* sixth century B.C., from Friedmann 1979, 110).

APPENDIX

1. Bruner Foundation (1987, 1).

2. The task force for the RBA program from 1985 through 1989 included Janet Carter, Ph.D., Executive Director of the Bruner Foundation, and Simeon Bruner, President of the Bruner Foundation. Robert Shibley and Polly Welch served on the task force as the initial professional advisors, developing the awards process, application materials, and Selection Committee approach. They also served as the research team for the first two cycles of the program. Following the second cycle of awards, Jay Farbstein and Rich Wener served as the professional advisors and research team for the program. There have been a number of other advisors to the task force, including Paul Grogen, Ingrid Reed, Margaret Wellington, and Marty Goldensohn.

3. Thanks to Judith Adams, Director, Lockwood Memorial Library, and John Edens, Director of Central Technical Services, SUNY/Buffalo for the development the Rudy Bruner Award Archives catalog. All or part of the Archives can be purchased in microfiche format from the Library.

BIBLIOGRAPHY

Albrecht, J., and G. Lim. 1986. A search for alternative planning theory: Use of critical theory. *Journal of Architecture and Planning Research* 3(2):117–131.

Alexander, C. 1975. *The Oregon Experiment*. New York: Oxford University Press.

————. 1979. *A Timeless Way of Building*. New York: Oxford University Press.

Alexander, C., S. Ishikawa, and M. Silverstein. 1977. *A Pattern Language*. New York: Oxford University Press.

Argyris, C., and D. Schon. 1974. *Theory in Practice: Increasing Professional Effectiveness*. Washington, D.C.: Jossey Bass.

Baines, C. T. 1991. The professions and an ethic of care. In *Women's Caring: Feminist Perspectives on Social Welfare,* eds. C. T. Baines, P. M. Evans, and S. M. Neysmith. Toronto: McClelland & Stewart.

Baines, C. T., P. M. Evans, and S. M. Neysmith, eds. 1991. *Women's Caring: Feminist Perspectives on Social Welfare*. Toronto: McClelland & Stewart.

Berger, P. L., and T. Luckmann. 1966. *The Social Construction of Reality*. New York: Anchor Books.

Berman, Marshall. 1988. *All That Is Solid Melts into Air: The Experience of Modernity*. New York: Penguin Books.

Berman, Morris. 1984. *The Reenchantment of the World*. New York: Bantam Books.

Berry, T. 1988. *The Dream of the Earth*. San Francisco: Sierra Club Books.

Berry, W. 1990. *What Are People For?* San Francisco: North Point Press.

Bion, W. R. 1961. *Experiences in Groups*. New York: Basic Books.

Booker, S., with L. Schneekloth. 1981. *Choices: Alternatives for Housing in the Old Northwest.* Blacksburg, VA: Virginia Polytechnic Institute and State University.

Bookman, A., and S. Morgen, eds. 1988. *Women and the Politics of Empowerment.* Philadelphia, PA: Temple University Press.

Borgmann, A. 1992. *Crossing the Postmodern Divide.* Chicago: University of Chicago Press.

Brauer, R. 1985. *Facilities Planning.* New York: AMACOM.

Bruce, E. M. 1989. Design research practice: A case study in facility management. Master's thesis, University of Wisconsin, Milwaukee.

Bruner Archives. Lockwood Library, State University of New York at Buffalo, Buffalo.

Bruner Foundation. 1987. Call for Participation: The Rudy Bruner Award for Excellence in the Urban Environment. New York: The Bruner Foundation.

Chawla, L. 1994. *In the First Country of Places: Nature, Poetry and Childhood Memory.* Albany, NY: SUNY Press.

Chodorow, N. 1978. *The Reproduction of Mothering.* Berkeley: University of California Press.

Coates, G., and D. Seamon. 1993. Promoting a foundational ecology practically through Christopher Alexander's pattern language: The example of Meadowcreek. In *Dwelling, Seeing, and Designing,* ed. D. Seamon. Albany, NY: SUNY Press.

Cuff, D. 1991. *Architecture: The Story of Practice.* Cambridge, MA: MIT Press.

Dalley, G. 1988. *Ideologies of Caring: Rethinking Community and Collectivism.* New Brunswick, NJ: Rutgers University Press.

Derrida, J. [1974] 1976. *Of Grammatology.* Trans. G. C. Spivak. Baltimore, MD: The John Hopkins University Press.

————. 1988. *Limited Inc.* Trans. S. Weber. Evanston, IL: Northwestern University Press.

Dewey, J. 1927. *The Public and Its Problems.* Chicago: The Swallow Press.

————. 1938. *Experience and Education.* New York: Collier.

Farbstein, J., and R. Wener. 1992. *Connections: Creating Urban Excellence.* New York: The Bruner Foundation.

————. 1994. *Rebuilding Communities: Re-creating Urban Excellence.* New York: The Bruner Foundation.

Finch, J., and D. Groves, eds. 1983. *A Labour of Love: Women, Work and Caring.* London: Routledge & Kegan Paul.

Floyd, C. 1984. Giving form in prime time. In *The Scope of Social Architecture,* ed. C. Hatch. New York: Van Nostrand Reinhold.

Forester, J. 1989. *Planning in the Face of Power.* Berkeley: University of California Press.

Forester, J., ed. 1985. *Critical Theory and Public Life.* Cambridge, MA: MIT Press.

Foucault, M. 1970. *The Order of Things.* New York: Vintage Books.

Franck, J., and L. Schneekloth, ed. 1994. *Ordering Space: Types in Architecture and Design.* New York: Van Nostrand Reinhold.

Fraser, N. 1989. *Unruly Practices: Power, Discourse, and Gender in Contem-*

porary Social Theory. Minneapolis, MN: University of Minnesota Press.

Freire, P. [1973] 1987. *Education for Critical Consciousness.* New York: Continuum.

———. [1970] 1988. *Pedagogy of the Oppressed.* Trans. M. Ramos. New York: Continuum.

Friedmann, J. 1979. *The Good Society.* Cambridge, MA: MIT Press.

Geuss, R. 1981. *The Idea of Critical Theory: Habermas and the Frankfurt School.* New York: Cambridge University Press.

Gibb, J. 1964. Climate for trust formation. In *T-Group Theory and Laboratory Method,* eds. L. P. Bradford, J. R. Gibb, and K. D. Benne. New York: John Wiley & Sons.

Gilligan, C. 1982. *In a Different Voice: Psychological Theory and Women's Development.* Cambridge, MA: Harvard University Press.

Giroux, H. A. 1988. *Schooling and the Struggle for Public Life: Critical Pedagogy in the Modern Age.* Minneapolis, MN: University of Minnesota Press.

———. 1991. Border pedagogy and the politics of modernism/postmodernism. *Journal of Architectural Education* 44(2):69–79.

Gold, R. 1973. Urban violence and contemporary defensive cities. In *Geography and Contemporary Issues,* ed. M. Albaum. New York: John Wiley & Sons.

Griffin, S. 1992. *A Chorus of Stones: The Private Life of War.* New York: Anchor Books/Doubleday.

Gutman, R. 1988. *Architectural Practice: A Critical View.* Princeton, NJ: Princeton Architectural Press.

Habermas, J. 1979. *Communication and the Evolution of Society.* Boston: Beacon Press.

———. 1984. *The Theory of Communicative Action.* Trans. T. McCarthy. Boston: Beacon Press.

Halprin, L. 1969. *The RSVP Cycles: Creative Processes in the Human Environment.* New York: George Braziller.

Halprin, L., and J. Burns. 1974. *Taking Part: A Workshop Approach to Collective Creativity.* Cambridge, MA: MIT Press.

Hampden-Turner, C. 1971. *Radical Man.* Garden City, NY: Anchor Books, Doubleday & Company.

Haraway, D. 1988. Situated knowledges: The science question in feminism and the privilege of partial perspective. *Feminist Studies* 14(3).

Harding, S. 1986. *The Science Question in Feminism.* Ithaca, NY: Cornell University Press.

Harrison, B. W. 1985. *Making the Connections: Essays in Feminist Social Ethics,* ed. C. S. Robb. Boston: Beacon Press.

———. 1991. The fate of the middle "class" in late capitalism. In *God and Capitalism,* eds. J. Thomas and V. Visick. Madison, WI: A-R Editions.

Harvey, J. 1988 *The Abilene Paradox and Other Meditations on Management.* Lexington, MA: Lexington Books.

Hatch, C., ed. 1984. *The Scope of Social Architecture.* New York: Van Nostrand Reinhold.

Heidegger, M. 1971. *Poetry, Language, Thought.* New York: Harper & Row.

Hertzberg, F. 1972. One more time: How do you motivate employees? In *Concepts and Controversy in Organizational Behavior,* ed. W. Nord. Pacific Palisades, CA: Goodyear Publishing Co.

Hirschhorn, L. 1988. *The Workplace Within: Psychodynamics of Organizational Life.* Cambridge, MA: MIT Press.

Hiss, T. 1991. *The Experience of Place.* New York: Random House.

Hochschild, A. R. 1983. *The Managed Heart: Commercialization of Human Feeling.* Berkeley: University of California Press.

hooks, b. 1992. *Black Looks: Race and Representation.* Boston: South End Press.

Hough, M. 1990. *Out of Place: Restoring Identity to the Regional Landscape.* New Haven, CT: Yale University Press.

Huebner, D. 1966. Curricular language and classroom meanings. In *Language and Meaning,* eds, J. B. MacDonald and R. R. Leeper. New York: Association for Supervision and Curriculum Development, Teachers College, Columbia University.

Illich, I. 1978. *Towards a History of Needs.* New York: Pantheon Books.

Illich, I., I. K. Zola, J. McKnight, J. Caplan, and H. Shaiken. 1977. *Disabling Professions.* Boston: Marion Boyars.

Jacobs, J. 1961. *The Death and Life of Great American Cities.* New York: Random House.

Kohlberg, L. 1981. *The Philosophy of Moral Development: Moral Stages and the Idea of Justice.* New York: Harper & Row.

———. 1984. *The Psychology of Moral Development: The Nature and Validity of Moral States.* New York: Harper & Row.

Kundera, M. 1984. *The Unbearable Lightness of Being.* New York: HarperCollins.

Langdon, P., with R. Shibley and P. Welch. 1990. *Urban Excellence.* New York: Van Nostrand Reinhold.

Leavitt, J., and S. Saegert. 1990. *From Abandonment to Hope: Community-Households in Harlem.* New York: Columbia University Press.

Lengermann, P. M., and J. Niebrugge-Brantley. 1990. Feminist sociological theory: The near future prospects. In *Frontiers of Social Theory,* ed. G. Ritzer. New York: Columbia University Press.

Lickert, R. 1961. *New Patterns of Management.* New York: McGraw Hill.

Lund, N. O. 1990. Collage Architecture. Berlin: Ernst & Sohn.

Lyotard, J. F. 1988. *The Postmodern Condition: A Report on Knowledge.* Trans. G. Bennington and B. Massumi. Minneapolis, MN: University of Minnesota Press.

Margolis, M. 1984. *Mothers and Such.* Berkeley: University of California Press.

Meidinger, E. 1987. *Regulatory Culture and Democratic Theory.* Baldy Center for Law and Social Policy Working Paper. Buffalo, NY: Faculty of Law and Jurisprudence, State University of New York at Buffalo.

Merchant, C. 1989. *Ecological Revolutions: Nature, Gender and Science in New England.* Chapel Hill, NC: University of North Carolina Press.

Moore, C., G. Allen, and D. Lyndon. 1974. *The Place of Houses*. New York: Holt, Rinehart & Winston.

Moynihan, D. P. 1969. *The Maximum Feasible Misunderstanding*. New York: Free Press.

Noddings, N. 1984. *Caring: A Feminine Approach to Ethics and Moral Education*. Berkeley: University of California Press.

Norberg-Schulz, C. 1979. *Genius Loci: Towards a Phenomenology of Architecture*. New York: Rizzoli.

Norris, C. 1987. *Derrida*. Cambridge, MA: Harvard University Press.

Peirce, N., and R. Guskind. 1993. *Breakthroughs: Re-Creating American City*. Newark, NJ: Center for Urban Policy Research, Rutgers University.

Pena, W. 1987. *Problem Seeking: An Architectural Primer*. Washington, D.C.: AIA Press.

Pérez-Gómez, A. 1983. *Architecture and the Crisis of Modern Science*. Cambridge, MA: MIT Press.

Perin, C. 1977. *Everything in Its Place*. Princeton, NJ: Princeton University Press.

The Planet Drum. Planet Drum Foundation, Box 31241, San Francisco, Shasta Bioregion, CA 94131.

Rabinow, P., ed. 1984. *The Foucault Reader*. New York: Pantheon Books.

Reverby, S. 1988. *Ordered to Care: The Dilemma of American Nursing 1850–1945*. New York: Cambridge University Press.

Rittel, H., and M. Webber. 1973. Dilemmas in a general theory of planning. *Policy Sciences* 4: 155–169.

Ritzdorf, M. 1985. Zoning barriers to housing innovation *Journal of Planning Education and Research* 4(2):177–184.

———. 1986. Women and the city: Land use and zoning issues. *Journal of Urban Resources* 3(2): 23–27.

Roanoke Neighborhood Partnership Self-Help Manual. 1993. Roanoke, VA: Office of Community Planning, City of Roanoke, VA.

Roanoke Neighborhood Partnership Annual Report—1984. 1984. Roanoke, VA: Office of Community Planning, City of Roanoke.

Roanoke Vision: Comprehensive Development Plan for Roanoke, Virginia 1985–2005. 1985. Roanoke, VA: Office of Community Planning, City of Roanoke.

Ruddick, S. 1989. *Maternal Thinking*. Boston: Beacon Press.

Rupert de Ventos, X. 1971. *Self-Defeated Man: Personal Identity and Beyond*. New York: Harper & Row.

Rusk, D. 1993. *Cities without Suburbs*. Washington, D.C.: Woodrow Wilson Center Press.

Sale, K. 1985. *Dwellers in the Land: The Bioregional Vision*. San Francisco: Sierra Club Books.

Scarry, E. 1985. *The Body in Pain: The Making and Unmaking of the World*. New York: Oxford University Press.

Schneekloth, L. 1987. Advances in practice in environment, behavior and design. In *Advances in Environment, Behavior and Design*, Vol. 1, eds. E. Zube and G. Moore. New York: Plenum Press.

———. 1994a. Notions of the inhabited. In *Ordering Space: Types in Ar-*

chitecture and Design, eds. K. Franck and L. Schneekloth. New York: Van Nostrand Reinhold.

————. 1994b. Partial utopian visions: feminist reflections on the field. In *Women and the Environment,* eds. I. Altman and A. Churchman. New York: Plenum Press.

Schneekloth, L. and R. Shibley. 1981. On owning a piece of the rock: participatory planning and design. In *Design Research Interactions,* eds. A. Osterberg et al. Washington, D.C.; Environmental Design Research Association.

————. 1987. Research/practice: thoughts on an interactive paradigm. In *Proceedings of the American Institute of Architects/Association of Collegiate School of Architecture Annual Research Conference,* ed. R. Shibley. Washington, D.C.: AIA/ACSA.

————. 1990. Dialogic practice. In *Coming of Age,* eds. R. Selby, K. Anthony, J. Choi, and B. Orland. Oklahoma Citiy, OK: Environmental Design Research Association.

Schon, D. A. 1983. *The Reflective Practitioner.* New York: Basic Books.

Seamon, D., ed. 1993. *Dwelling, Seeing, and Designing: Toward a Phenomenological Ecology.* Albany, NY: SUNY Press.

Seamon, D., and R. Mugerauer, eds. 1985. *Dwelling, Place, and Environment: Towards a Phenomenology of Person and World.* New York: Columbia University Press.

Sennett, R. 1970. *The Uses of Disorder.* New York: W. W. Norton & Co.

Shibley, R. 1989. Architectural excellence: framing the debate. In *In Search of Design Excellence,* ed. T. Vonier. Washington, D.C.: American Institute of Architects.

————. 1992. Los Angeles: working through the crisis to quality urban living. New York: Bruner Foundation.

Shibley, R., and E. Bruce. 1989. Excellent architecture: how do we know—and so what? In *In Search of Design Excellence,* ed. T. Vonier. Washington, D.C.: American Institute of Architects.

Shibley, R., and L. Schneekloth. 1988. Risking collaboration: Professional dilemmas in evaluation and design. *Journal of Architectural and Planning Research* 5(4):304–320.

Shibley, R., E. Bruce, and L. Schneekloth. 1987. Thanks for asking! User participation in facilities management. *Proceedings from Facilities Management—The Next Ten Years.* London: Institute for Facilities Management.

Steele, F. 1973. *Physical Settings and Organizational Development.* Reading, MA: Addison-Wesley.

Steinbrueck, V. 1968. *Market Sketchbook.* Seattle, WA and London: University of Washington Press.

Tanzer, K. 1992. Releasing the form to the making: Womenswork is never done. *Pratt Journal on Architecture,* 3:44–56.

Thayer, F. C. 1973. *An End to Hierarchy! An End to Competition: Organizing the Politics and Economics of Survival.* New York: Franklin Watts New Viewpoints.

Tronto, J. 1989. Women and caring: What can feminists learn about morality from caring. In *Gender/Body/Knowledge: Feminist Reconstructions of Being and Knowing,* eds. A. Jaggar and S. Bordo. New Brunswick, NJ: Rutgers University Press.

Venturi, R. 1966. *Complexity and Contradiction in Architecture.* New York: Museum of Modern Art.

Vickers, G. 1965. *The Art of Judgement.* New York: Basic Books.

Vonier, T., ed. 1989. *In Search of Design Excellence.* Washington, D.C.: American Institute of Architects.

Walters, E. V. 1988. *Placeways: A Theory of the Human Environment.* Chapel Hill, NC: University of North Carolina Press.

Wilson, E. 1991. *The Sphinx in the City: Urban Life, the Control of Disorder, and Women.* Berkeley: University of California Press.

INDEX

A page number shown in italic indicates an illustration.

Dialogic space (*Continued*)
as public space, 10, 113, 198,
215–216
Dialogue, 6–8, 10, 15, 16, 23, 61,
111, 139, 185, 186, 198, 231
emancipatory, 225
failure of, 202–203, 234–235
as goal, 23, 135–136,
limits of, 201–203, 229
refusal of, 8
risking, 107, 139, 231
through media, 111, 113, 229
newsprint, 9, 24–25, 28, 59,
86, 115, 118, 220
through pattern language, 46–48
Disabling professions, 2, 213–214
Disabling Professions, 213–214,
222
Discourse:
modern, 195–197, 218, 237–238
empirical, 11, 217
technical-rational, 195, 214–
215, 216, 223–224
scientific-technological, 11,
195
phenomenological, 213
postmodern, xii, 197–199, 213,
216, 217, 223–224, 228,
231–232
critical theory, 10–13
deconstruction, 223–224. *See
also* Deconstruction
Derrida, J., 223–224
feminist, 223–224, 226, 231–
232, 237, 238, 239
relational, 213, 223–224
Disempowerment, 2, 12, 13–15,
213–214. *See also* Em-
powerment; Exclusion
Diversity of perspectives, 2, 7, 47,
113–115, 127, 155, 158,
185, 219
Double focus, 70, 72, 62–63, 223–
224. *See also* Caring; Discourse
in public housekeeping, 104–105
Dwell(ing), 1, 2, 18, 181, 213

Education, *see* Freire, P.; Giroux, H.
for critical consciousness, 219,
228
*Education for Critical Conscious-
ness*, 219
influence and, 218–219

intervention as, *see* Intervention,
as education
liberation through, 56, 219, 222
professionals as educators, 21–
23, 56–57, 126, 159, 196,
222
Emancipation, 12, 60, 159–163,
189–190, 225. *See also* Empowerment; Collaboration;
Democracy, theory of
and critical theory, 12–13, 15,
186, 191–192, 217
"Emancipatory authority," 228
placemaking as, 15–16, 24, 186,
189–190, 191–192, 201–203
Empowerment, 2–3, 111, 114, 129,
158–165, 198, 235, 238. *See
also* Democracy; Dialogic
space; Dialogue; Inclusion
as contributing to excellence,
152, 158–165
through influence, 77, 158, 164–
165, 177–179, 218–219, 237
through inclusion, 9, 14–16, 77,
80, 158, 163, 173, 175–177,
182, 200, 238
public housekeeping as, 108
Environmental change, 10, 14
and organizational dynamics, *see*
Organizational Develop-
ment, organizational dy-
namics
Ethics, xi–xiii, 9, 13–14, 15–16,
18, 195–200, 209, 239
of action, 8–9, 13–18, 99–102,
186, 200
of boundary-making, 14–16
of collaboration, xii, 8–9, 89–92
of communication, 186, 229,
230–231
of inclusion/exclusion, 14–16,
89–92, 224–225
of intervention, xii, 8–9, 63,
186, 200
of knowledge application, xi, 7,
186, 187–189, 195–197
of methodology, 16–17, 96–99
of professional action, 8–9, 13–
18
Ewert, B., 112, 135–136, 232–233
Excellence, 4–5, 149–190
definition, 4–5, 150, 152–153,
181, 184, 206, 234
organization and management,
5, 153, 167–181, 183–184,